Progressive Retreat

FOR MY PARENTS

Progressive Retreat

a sociological study of
Dartington Hall School 1926–1957
and some of its former pupils

MAURICE PUNCH

Senior Lecturer in Sociology
State University of Utrecht

CAMBRIDGE UNIVERSITY PRESS

CAMBRIDGE

LONDON · NEW YORK · MELBOURNE

Published by the Syndics of Cambridge University Press
The Pitt Building, Trumpington Street, Cambridge CB2 1RP
Bentley House, 200 Euston Road, London NW1 2DB
32 East 57th Street, New York, NY 10022, USA
296 Beaconsfield Parade, Middle Park, Melbourne 3206, Australia

First published 1976

Library of Congress Cataloguing in Publication Data
Punch, Maurice.
Progressive Retreat
Originally presented as the author's thesis, University of Essex.
Bibliography: p. 000
Includes index.
1. Dartington Hall, Totnes, Eng. – History. I. Title.
LF795.T66P85   1976   373.423'592   75-41615
ISBN 0 521 21182 4

Text set in 11/12 pt Photon Times, printed by photolithography,
and bound in Great Britain at The Pitman Press, Bath

Contents

NOTE

Quotations from recorded interviews will indicate the sex of the respondent, the period he or she was at Dartington, i.e. nineteen 'thirties' or 'fifties', and that the respondent falls under the Main Sample ('MS') or the Pilot ('P') interviews.

Acknowledgements

The research upon which this book is based was sponsored and financed by the Elmgrant Trust of Dartington. It commenced in 1967 at a time when the Public Schools Commission was breathing down the independent schools' necks (as it turned out, fruitlessly). The field work was carried out in 1968–9 and the writing-up took place largely in 1970–2. The Trustees of Dartington asked that I exercise great care in the use of interview material lest individuals be identifiable, that I refrain from quoting from material in the school's files, and that I restrict my analysis of the school to the period 1926–57. These limitations clearly circumscribed my use of evidence and my analysis and a great deal of rich data has been forfeited to comply with these demands.

This work was originally presented as a doctoral thesis at the University of Essex. From its inception a large number of people have given of their time and energy in helping me to shape the research material into a presentable thesis and into a book suitable for publication. I would therefore like to express my gratitude for the advice, guidance, and cooperation of the following: Geoffrey Hawthorn, Dennis Marsden, Patricia Williams, Spencer Millham, Roger Bullock, Peter Townsend, Paul Thompson, Colin Bell, Ian Lister, Derek Phillips, Patrick and Patricia McCullagh, Penny and Maurice Sheehy, Polly Hunter, Mary Girling, Laura Tricker, Lynne McKay, and my wife, Corry. At Dartington successive drafts of the typescript were commented on by Leonard Elmhirst, Maurice Ash, Bill Elmhirst, Royston Lambert, and Michael Young.

Bunnik 1975   *Maurice Punch*

Introduction on behalf of
Dartington Hall Trustees

The research presented in this report was (as Mr Punch acknowledges on the previous page) sponsored by Dartington itself. We and the other Trustees who are responsible for the school gave him all the help we could. It was, for example, with our backing that he approached ex-pupils. The reason for the endorsement was obvious enough: we hoped that an outsider and a sociologist trying to see the school through the eyes of people who had been at it would have something fresh to say about the past which could influence its future.

Given this endorsement of the research any reader would, unless something were said to the contrary, be liable to draw the implication that the Trustees also endorse the outcome. This introduction is written with the one purpose of making it clear that we do not. Maurice Punch has *in detail* much of interest to say in his report. But in our view his *general* conclusions are not justified by the 'facts' he has collected. It is all a question of evidence.

When, for example, he says in one of these conclusions that 'Males in particular were handicapped for filling conventional occupational roles', or much else equally as sweeping, what is the evidence upon which he relies? The statements of thirty men and thirty women who had been pupils and who figure in his main sample, plus a few others. That might be acceptable *if* the sixty were representative of the two thousand or so pupils who have been at Dartington in the half century since it was founded. But there is, as he admits and then seems to forget, no reason to believe that the sixty can speak for the two thousand. Unlike some other schools, Dartington has not fostered an Old Boys' and Girls' Association and therefore was not able to produce a list of ex-pupils from whom a representative sample could have been drawn at random. It would in any case have needed to be much larger than sixty to enable any conclusions to be properly drawn about girls as distinct from boys; about people who entered the school at different periods in its ever-changing history; and about the people who stayed longer as compared with shorter periods.

There is a second weakness in the evidence which we also fear Maurice Punch has not squarely faced – the part played by this or any school as distinct from a family, or genes for that matter, in forming character. He mentions the family background of his sample, and then fails to discuss the issue of how to distinguish its effect from that of the school. It would be flying in the face of most of the psychological evidence gathered in the last century to believe that the later years, of school, mattered as much as the earlier years, of infancy.

Even were the sample impeccable and the facts about the whole life-histories of people all garnered in, there would remain the almost equally difficult question of the criteria by which one evaluates them. Maurice Punch has in one dimension divided the thirty men according to the extent to which they adapt 'to the societal value system of capitalist enterprise' – whatever that means. Some do and some don't – that is clear enough. But it is far from clear what the ones that do are doing or the ones that don't are not doing. It would surely have been better to have been more systematic about criteria, and also to acknowledge more fully that the kind of lives led by people as adults, important as that may be, are not by any means the only test of a school. One of the cardinal principles of progressive education was enunciated by Christian Schiller, a great educator and member of the first team of HMIs to inspect Dartington, when he said

Children move – because they must. They touch, explore and make, and this is how they learn and grow. No children are alike or ever will be. Children live only for the present, and our job is *to help them fulfil their present stage of growth*. ('Profile of Christian Schiller', *Times Educational Supplement*, 19 September 1975. Our italics.)

Much was made of this by Hu and Lois Child, the heads who succeeded Billy Curry and who on this shared his view, in their book on *The Independent Progressive School* (1962).

And now to our fourth and major point, which is again to do with the conclusions, and above all the most sweeping ones of all in the last chapter. Mr Punch has a perfect right to believe (with or without the evidence) that 'progressive' educators are played-out idealists, and we have as much right to contend otherwise. He began his work in the sixties when social engineering was in the air, and education its handmaiden. Everyone was to be given the social opportunities that formerly had been enjoyed by only a few. Comprehensive schools with sixth forms big enough to assure teaching of subjects across the spectrum of knowledge were the instruments of this movement. Compared to this, the old progressives appeared to have little fresh to say.

Today, the picture has changed. There is a deeper malaise now than then and, at the centre of it, a disillusion with universalistic prescriptions, as with institutional remedies for human problems, with all the depersonalisation of life these bring. The comprehensive school formula is more than touched by this reaction and, wriggle as some of its more sensitive advocates may to humanise it, the old certainty is gone. Events have shown the old progressives were right to hold on. For it is the premise of their original idea, however ill-articulated this may have become, that is now becoming fashionable again: namely, the notion of a person as a person. On a wide front, the reaction in favour of this notion, and of personalistic modes of thought, is pushing back the tide of ideological thought – and, incidentally, causing some self-questioning amongst sociologists, such as was hardly apparent in the sixties. In so far as progressive education has always been part of the personalist philosophical stream, it can feel respectable again.

Yet in itself this is not enough to claim. The see-saw has been see-sawing for too long. It was long ago now that Rousseau gave the intellectual impetus to progressive education through his concept of the development of the child as a child: his rationalisation (if not his discovery) of the condition of childhood. He left the matter, to be sure, in a philosophical tangle, with his bizarre notion of forcing people to be free, such as Marx and others to this day have sought unsuccessfully to unravel. Their endeavours to reconcile the person and the external world (including Society as a paradigm of Nature) in one intellectual frame of reference have been vain but dominant. Likewise, Hume may intellectually have displaced Locke, as the notion of the person as a person has supplanted that of the individual as a particle, however noble, of society: yet the influence of Locke's patristic liberal education ideas – of the young human as a proto-adult, a clean slate to be written upon by received knowledge – probably remains as strong as ever, and certainly so in American educational thought, presumably as a consequence of Locke's influence on the leaders of the Revolution. Simply to be respectable again, in terms of the history of ideas, ought not to satisfy the practitioners of progressive education.

The times we live in, perhaps naturally, are generating changes in our very thought. These changes, it is now possible to see, are as structurally deep as those by which Descartes broke the mould of medieval thought – and perhaps deeper. For they strike at the roots, not only of rationalism, but of idealism as well. This refers to all that is stemming from the great recantation Wittgenstein made in the last period of his life, with his recognition that language does not (cannot) reflect some external reality. (And we are not referring to 'language philosophy'.) This, to some, would seem to put mankind onto shifting sands, so far as all that hitherto has been taken as knowledge is concerned. More to the point, it directs the mind's attention away from knowledge and rather towards meaning: words are not labels, rather 'the meaning of a word is its use in the language'. Many implications follow: not least, concerning Man's relationship to Nature – away, that is, from Cartesian scorn of the natural world, as something to be tamed and made subservient to Man: similarly, concerning materialism and its values, and our now unlimited expectations of exploiting the world: or, concerning alienation and identity and the meaning – that is, the quality – of work and the circumstances in which we do it: or the importance of play, the idea of games – and not just language games – for an understanding of human life – all matters bearing closely upon the present human condition.

How, then, does this affect the question of progressive education? It does so because progressive education, in its several guises, has been concerned, not with knowledge itself, but with the place of knowledge in life. It is a characteristic which progressive educational thinkers seem to hold in common — whether Montessori or Tagore, Dewey or Neill — that they are concerned for the meaning to the child of what he (or she) learns, the context of his living experience, rather than that he should be taught knowledge for its own sake.

We also disagree with the author's thesis that a progressive school belies itself both because it must depend upon some charismatic character to sustain it, and because its children are as conformist (in their progressiveness) as any others. If the former was ever true, perhaps before the idea of schools such as Dartington was widely accepted, it is no longer the case. It was always the children themselves who attracted the Trustees' support for the school. The quality of any outward conformity such children show has always been of their own originating. We would recommend, rather, the reader should take courage from what Maurice Punch (if in contradiction) also says: 'to many people's surprise, the progressive school is a highly self-regulating, law abiding community'. Those who actually know the school (and Mr Punch himself, ironically, did not study the school itself) would agree this is true.

We think too that we have already shown over the past five years of reciprocity with Northcliffe School, Conisbrough, in the West Riding of Yorkshire, a secondary school supported by the LEA, that progressive education is not the fad of a subculture of the middle class, but can also be suitable for adolescent children from an industrial working-class environment. There has never been any doubt that the ideas of progressive schools can apply without distortion to ordinary primary schools. We are now confident of their wider application. Moreover, the scheme has worked, by and large, without de-racinating those children who have been to Dartington from Conisbrough: without, that is, their denying their origins. These are results, then, of real significance because of the presumed incompatibility of progressive and conventional regimes in any one school: the different standards they use, their different values. The Dartington–Conisbrough experience underlines the right to a different kind of educational regime than the only one that is now served up by the state.

We shall therefore continue (if we are allowed) to practise what we consider to be real progressive coeducation, even if some of those practices were established nearly fifty years ago. They remain as inimical to those in orthodox schooling as they then were; the gap has not changed; the Black Papers persist. It is these continuing practices which constitute our nature. We are certainly not in retreat: rightly or wrongly, we believe we are still with the advance.

Maurice Ash
Michael Young

Chapter One
Introduction: The children of the new era

The lack of knowledge that there is about what actually happens in Progressive Education – deeper, the possibility that knowledge, conventionally speaking, is unobtainable about this activity: that it is of the character of faith – is galling to the new educational scientist. (Ash 1969: 13.)

The historical role of the independent, progressive boarding schools has primarily been one of protest. Numbering about twenty and founded between 1889 and 1940 (Stewart 1968), they sought initially to emancipate the child from what they perceived to be the harshness and philistinism of the traditional, 'public' boarding schools; while since the last war, they have contrasted themselves with what they consider to be the bleak academic formalism, the standardisation, and the impersonality of mass state education. In so doing they have questioned educational orthodoxy, have pioneered wide-ranging innovations – in the curriculum and teaching methods, in pupil self-government, in pastoral care and in coeducational provision, and have enjoyed an influence, and a notoriety, out of all proportion to their size. But their quintessential desire was to create a 'free' school – not repressive, not moulding, but liberating – that would, in turn, allow the child to mature into a culture free individual.

As such they represent a rich stream of innovative experience outside of the state system and yet, surprisingly, there exists scant evidence as to whether or not these alternative ventures actually work or, indeed, as to how they might be evaluated. A powerful argument advanced by progressive educators themselves is that only an appraisal of the adult lives of their former pupils can constitute a genuine evaluation of their particular form of education. But this too has rarely been attempted although Bernstein (1967) did endeavour to contact Old Summerhillians. Even studies of former pupils of public schools tend to focus on the narrow areas of occupational achievement and elite status (Bishop and Wilkinson 1967, Wakeford 1969). This work, however, reports a case study of an established, well-known progressive school, Dartington Hall School, and of a follow-up study of some of its former pupils. The research aims were twofold. On the one hand there were structured interviews with former pupils which were designed to examine broadly the kind of adjustments made by individuals to the wider society having imbibed a progressive philosophy at school. While, on the other hand, the author planned to use interview material, documentary evidence, and published

1

sources to formulate a theoretical perspective on the radical progressive school.

Researching the progressive school

The school at Dartington was founded in 1926 and is soon to celebrate its fiftieth anniversary. But mere durability of itself is not necessarily a sensitive barometer for measuring the quality of communal experience and the functioning of Dartington and the fate of its former pupils are here subjected to critical scrutiny. Research, with its sceptical and even debunking tone, tends to document the gaps between ideals and practice and to confront the participants with their failures and ambivalences. In turn, the researched can question the motives, methods, and conclusions of the researcher. The resulting clash can be painful to both sides and one Trustee spoke of a 'dialogue of the deaf'. But it can also be illuminating for the impartial observer seeking knowledge about the intrinsic nature and half-concealed functioning of educational institutions.

For it is important to remember that Dartington commenced with a consciously self-critical ethos together with a strong emphasis on the role of scientific method in setting up its venture. One of its early headmasters called the school a 'research station' and a contemporary educationist wrote:

It is magnificently equipped with every educational appliance that a teacher's enthusiasm can reasonably demand or money buy; and probably most progressive schools regard it as a useful laboratory for the testing of numerous ideas which they themselves have not the means to carry out. (Pekin 1934: 38.)

The children were meticulously tested for intelligence, health records were assiduously kept, and their behaviour was minutely observed and recorded, including at one stage the content of their dreams. Indeed, the buildings themselves were in part constructed to allow the observation of young children for educative purposes.

The founder himself appeared to invite critical enquiry when he warned of the dangers of complacency and self-insulation:

By what means were we to avoid the pitfalls of so many other social experiments – the tendency to become an open-house for cranks, to allow woolly sentiment to oust sovereign reason, to let the control of considerable means protect us from rigorous intellectual self-criticism, or from those underground grievances that would, through fear, never be coaxed into the daylight? ... Lastly, should we become a little insulated, isolated, self-satisfied bunch of folk using our means as an artificial barrier against the buffets of a highly critical, realistic, and competitive outside world? (L. K. Elmhirst 1937: 9.)

But, in practice, it is not always easy to accept the clinical appraisal of an outsider who unfeelingly dissects your dreams. For example, the rich, intimate, and revealing portrait of the American progressive college at Black Mountain (Duberman 1972) was doubtless only possible because the college closed in 1957 and the survivors felt free to unburden themselves regarding its crises, rivalries, and traumas.

Dartington, however, is a going concern and contains several long-serving members of staff who were associated with the period about which I write, while the founder was alive throughout the period of the research. At the same time one can detect a latent hostility to evaluation among some progressives. For example, a Trustee said of the headmaster of Dartington for twenty-five years:

Bill Curry wasn't interested on the whole with what happened to people when they left the school. He didn't seem to be interested in adults at all. He had some sort of defensiveness in his mind about it but perhaps he feared to see what would become of them when he'd finished with them. But he was always unresponsive to the idea of following people up. (Recorded Interview.)

While, at a gathering of educationists sponsored by Dartington, a progressive sympathiser ejaculated:

We shall not change things by doing little bits of research. That is going to get us precisely nowhere at all. We have got to have something just as revolutionary as was A. S. Neill forty years ago. He was a madman – and we have got to have someone who is prepared to be a madman. (Ash 1969: 7.)

It should also be borne in mind here that many progressive schools, while partly enjoying, and even contributing to, their own notoriety have attracted a hostile and damaging press and their marginal and insecure position makes them extremely sensitive to unfavourable publicity. These schools survive by attracting parents who are prepared to pay quite high fees for their children and who have to withdraw their children from the supposed benefits of a conventional education in order to support their own belief in an unorthodox education. The schools fear that a damaging report on Progressive education might make continued existence a real problem for the more economically marginal schools by hindering recruitment. In addition, of course, publication can crystallize some of the ambiguities in the institutional ethos for the participants themselves. In a sense this position gives an unduly flattering power to research studies to mould opinion when we are learning increasingly that research findings rarely resolve value debates about education but rather are used to bolster value positions. Indeed, many current educational debates show that research is always in some respects open to alternative interpretations and to criticism from a really determined opponent. The difference of opinion regarding my findings on Dartington, for example, would doubtless be duplicated following a research report say on Summerhill, or the Liverpool Free School.

Currently, for example, there is a spate of reforms based on 'free' or 'anti-authoritarian' schools in America, England, and Europe which aim at 'freeing' the child from the bonds of a too rigid social and educational structure. The present-day reformers who tend to get the most publicity, such as Holt (1969) and Kozol (1968), are concerned primarily with alternative education for disadvantaged groups who appear trapped by social deprivation and educational inequality. There does exist, however, a long stream of similar responses to perceived deficiencies in state and private educational provision which were sponsored by middle-class liberal intellectuals. The problem for the research-oriented social scientist, however, is how does one go about evaluating these experiences as they are often championed, or reviled, without any evidence as to their functioning. It does appear that there is a body of experience being wasted here and that it is worth posing some exploratory questions as to how one would evaluate this particular style of 'anti-school', whether it be for the rich or the disadvantaged.

For, increasingly, those people grappling with social policy evaluation of all kinds are becoming aware of the fact that the goals of specific programmes are frequently multiple, diffuse, and often conflicting (Marris and Rein 1967). This is compounded in education because there exist very few clear criteria of educational effectiveness (Miles 1964: 658) and because the issues are clouded by politically and ideologically charged values debates – the heated arguments surrounding the effectiveness of both the comprehensive schools in England and the educational innovations of the American Poverty Programme are prime examples (Marsden 1972; Chazan 1973). It is important, then, to appreciate that the model of an evaluation study as a classical controlled experiment may bear little resemblance to reality. Because of the complexity, subtlety, and interrelationships of the variables in the human sciences there is a grave lack of a methodology of evaluation. In addition, there is an increasingly pessimistic view of policy implementation that looks behind the lip-service to rational innovation to the concealed processes hindering successful implementation. Partly due to the effect of these research dilemmas in education – that education is typically slow as an innovative process, because it is rarely possible to see where the pay-off lies and that research findings are inconclusive and open to competing interpretations – some contemporary educational radicals have become more concerned with the diffusion of power and with political or community action (Swirsky 1972).

The early progressive impetus, however, came first from a group of comfortably-off intellectuals in the upper strata of society who demanded a more liberal, more creative, and more spontaneous educational environment for their children and who were prepared to step outside educational orthodoxy to achieve this. The common theme uniting many of these radical ventures was that they wished to escape from formal structures; they pictured the child in an almost Rousseauesque utopia that guaranteed his freedom by de-institutionalising and de-formalising the educative process. To achieve their ends these innovators were prepared to depart radically from traditional educational models by experimenting in the social structure of the school. Yet, at the same time, these radical schools were often suffused with a liberal ideology that determined not to impose its values on their pupils. To have done so would have been to fall prey to the very moulding of character which they reviled as having a pernicious and distorting effect on personality in traditional education. To avoid this charge they abandoned the authoritarian, hierarchical structure of the traditional school and posited a radical alternative to promote the free and unhampered development of the individual child in an environment which contained the minimum of constraints; in short they institutionalised the 'anti-school'.

But what happens, then, people have continually asked, to the former pupils of these nonconforming institutions when they leave and enter the wider society? The problem was stated succinctly by Amabel Williams-Ellis, herself a Dartington parent, in an 'Introduction for Parents' to a 1934 symposium on the early progressive schools:

One of the objections that influence many people who are dissatisfied with the faults of the traditional school is the notion that if their children are sent to a modern school they will, in after life, feel themselves freaks. (Blewitt 1934: 13.)

Similarly, a teacher at a progressive school wrote of the possible problem of adjustment after school:

Children brought up in an atmosphere of beautifully nebulous idealism in a school are likely to be very rudely shocked when they first impinge on outside society. (Pekin 1934: iii.)

In fact, a good deal of the data in this study comes from a number of former pupils of Dartington who have served almost as educational guinea pigs for an experimental education, and who spoke to me of their experiences about when they were at school and since leaving. The interviewees were drawn from two cohorts who left Dartington either between 1935 and 1940 or 1950 to 1954, and who stayed in the senior section of the school for a minimum of three years. These sixty people are termed collectively the 'main sample'. The ten men and ten women of the nineteen-thirties cohort were in their mid or late forties and the twenty men and twenty women of the nineteen-fifties cohort were in their early or mid thirties at the time of interviewing in 1968–9. In addition twenty men and twenty women who left Bryanston and Badminton respectively (both single-sex schools and both less educationally radical than

Dartington) in the early fifties were also interviewed to provide comparative data. A number of initial pilot interviews were also carried out together with interviews with some former members of staff, some Trustees, and some key informants in the old pupils' network. These are all termed collectively 'pilot' interviews. A postal questionnaire was also sent to a number of people abroad.

The sampling was confined to people resident in England, Wales or Scotland. One man wrote from abroad that he had worked as a builder, plumber, lumberjack, trapper, fisherman, ferrymaster, electrician, journalist, farm labourer, Royal Naval courier, summer-resort operator, and book-keeper; this exile wrote:

Before I hand in my knife, fork and spoon I shall return to my old stamping grounds and I shall have a wondrous tale to tell. I have owed so much to Bill Curry, Bertrand Russell, T. E. Shaw, Victor Gordon Wodehouse, St John Philby, and even Adolf Hitler. Bill Curry once asked me up to his house and read me Russell's *Free Man's Worship* and to this very day I can recall passages that flowed in those high precise tones.

Unfortunately it was not possible to interview him! But the example does raise the question of the representativeness of the sample.

In effect our sample is deficient of those former pupils who choose to live abroad and of those who have ceased to remain in contact with the school world. It is conceivable that some respondents may keep in touch with the Dartington subculture because they have been unable to adjust fully to the outside world but then this could prove equally true of some Dartingtonians who do not manifest this lack of adjustment by dependence on the school network. In generalising to the entire Dartington population, and even more to progressive former pupils as a whole, we must do so with extreme caution because of the possible sources of bias in our sample. We must face the possibility in fact that our sample may not be representative of Dartington pupils as a whole.

This difficulty is unlikely to be resolved because of the fact that there is no formal, school-based, old pupil association at Dartington, no systematic records of former pupils, and no comprehensive list of names and addresses from which to draw a random sample. An incomplete list, drawn up in 1960, was supplied by the school and this was supplemented with information from the unofficial former pupil's association, together with advertisements in the national press. Despite strenuous efforts little advance was made on the 1960 list. Until some method is found of contacting all former pupils of Dartington we have to rely on those who have remained in contact with the school; until then our research, despite its deficiences, remains the only systematic follow-up study of former pupils of a progressive school.

Two other qualifications must also be raised now. Firstly, one respondent remarked:

Dartington must be the easiest school in the world to do a follow-up on because of their American style volubility.

Yet that in itself is a danger. Most of the respondents were highly articulate, intelligent people who were rarely lost for words. And for some of them hyperbole was almost a normal way of speech while most immersed themselves with intense ease into the interview situation (one literally stretched himself out with eyes closed as though on a psychiatrist's couch). Secondly, apart from the occasional richness of the language, there was the distinct possibility of selective recall, inaccuracy, and even evasion both because they were asked to recall details of their home and school life, in some cases as long as forty years ago, and because some of the areas touched on were intimate and personal. We must, then, treat many of the quotations cited in this survey with a degree of scepticism.

An additional complication is that progressives tend to reject the very idea that their 'product' can be evaluated – the very notion of a stereotypical progressive being antithetical to their individualistic bent. A. S. Neill, for instance, asserted that most Summerhillians are successful in later life on his criterion of possessing the ability to work joyfully and to live positively, for which academic education is largely irrelevant. By the latter qualification he spiked the guns of those who saw in progressive education merely a recipe for happy idleness. But at the same time progressives maintain that the only way to judge their 'success' is to examine the lives of their former pupils as adults, about which they tend to draw favourable conclusions on flimsy evidence. What, then, do they aim to achieve with their pupils?

Firstly, the contention that there might be any incompatibility between the progressive school and the outside world is firmly rejected. On the contrary, they often assert that their form of education is more normal than the norm and that their pupils should have less trouble in adjusting to 'reality' than people from other types of school. Further, they tend to seek vindication in their former pupils' conventional success while holding a dual standard of accepting 'success' in their own terms; there is even a desire to prove that the latter not only does not incapacitate their alumni for conventional success prospects but also enhances them. This duality is often reflected in the citing of former pupils' later success in higher education.

But because progressive education was different, and because it required its pupils to be different, their adult role was sometimes portrayed as almost a crusade – the progressive graduate was to be a missionary who was to make the world a better place to live in (Child 1962: 67). At the same time aspects of that world were denigrated, including competition, commercial ambitions, and technology.

In the business and professional world there is often a hard and ruthless quality which proves extremely distasteful to those who have grown up in an atmosphere of happiness, justice, and goodwill. (Curry 1947: 120.)

The progressives' cultural, creative, nonconforming ethos complemented intellectual and artistic work more than trade but the personal qualities of the individual were considered more important than his occupational role – better a happy street cleaner than a neurotic scholar. Ideal, however, was a marriage of the two criteria.

In 1896 we gained our first natural science scholarship at Cambridge – but he was also the best darner of stockings in the school and a most promising bookbinder. (Badley 1924: 69.)

If we scan the literature then the adult progressive should be a paragon. For he will be rational, humane, self-confident, adventurous, creative, attractive, an exemplary marriage partner, anti-authoritarian in a wholesome and discriminating way, tolerant, and devoid of prejudice (Child 1962). His traditionally educated neighbour, on the other hand, will be moulded, conditioned, inhibited, repressed, spoon-fed, a scared-to-death conformist, dull, unimaginative, uncreative; in fact, a robot-like, stunted and over specialised pseudo-adult. But, above, all, the progressive adult should be committed and involved, as A. S. Neill (1968: 13) expounded in almost Biblical rhetoric:

If Summerhill has any message at all it is this: Thou shalt not opt out. Fight world sickness, not with drugs like moral teachings and punishments but with natural means – approval, tenderness, tolerance . . . I hesitate to use the word love, for it has become almost a dirty word like so many honest and clean Anglo-Saxon four letter words.

Who are the Progressives?

Thus while John Dewey launched the American progressive movement in cooperation with the public authorities in Chicago, Reddie borrowed £2,000 from a friend to buy an Elizabethan manor house with Gothic additions set in the heart of the Staffordshire countryside. (Skidelsky 1968: 80.)

No cohesive organisation has succeeded in uniting the progressive schools as a body. They tend to be the personal statement of pioneering, strongly individualist headmasters (A. S. Neill, Homer Lane, Cecil Reddie, J. H. Badley, and Bill Curry, for examples) and often these figureheads resent labels and avoid definition. There is no progressive equivalent of the Headmasters' Conference (which confers 'public school' status on its members) and the New Education Fellowship never achieved the cohesion and tactical acumen of the HMC. How then are the progressive schools to be recognised? If we accept the schools' willingness to appear under a progressive banner then fourteen contributed to the 1962 symposium *The Independent Progressive School* (ed. Child). This was less than in the 1934 symposium of Blewitt, and the fall in numbers reflects a contraction due both to the closure of several minor schools and to a general shift to the 'right'. With the exception of Summerhill, most have moved towards a more structured environment, gathering more qualified staff, paying them higher salaries, more clearly defining their roles and the boundaries of their responsibility, playing down the ideas of freedom and considerably increasing the schools' academic stress.

However, an examination of the schools in the now badly dated symposia of Blewitt and of Child reveals an immense diversity – of structure, size, constitution, and ideological stance, – and they range from the radical, coeducational 'Eden' of Summerhill to the single-sex Quaker 'Eton', Leighton Park. Their common factor is that initially they posed an alternative to the traditional public school model – that Arnoldian legacy based on the classics, chapel, sport and prefects (Bamford 1967) – and their radicalism is in direct relationship to their rejection of the values and practices upholding the Public School stereotype.

Above all they resented the regimentation and character building and the apparatus of control associated with it, e.g. the ritual, tradition, uniform, loyalty, orthodox Christianity, fagging, insignia, privileges, hierarchy, and the exercise and submission to authority. They wished to be free of the paraphernalia of elite socialisation and its gentlemanly stereotype. On the criterion then, of distance from the public school model, I have constructed four main sub-types of progressive school.

The Friends' schools

These schools are something of a special case in that they share a common religious background, that of the Society of Friends or Quakers, and that some of their foundations reach well back into the nineteenth century. The Quaker schools are Ackworth (1779), Sidcot (1808), Saffron Walden (1811), Wigton (1815), Bootham (1823), The Mount (1831), Great Ayton (1841), Sibford (1842), and Leighton Park (1890). Two Quaker schools agreed to appear in the 1962 symposium and are included in groups below (Leighton Park and Saffron Walden).

The 'marginal' progressives

Most of these are single-sex schools which tend to see themselves on the left wing of the public school and from which some of them are almost indistinguishable. However, they usually have less emphasis than the traditional school on sport, religion, a narrow curriculum, and hierarchy, and are somewhat more sympathetic to the needs of the individual. This groups consists of Abbotsholme, Bryanston, Leighton Park, Clayesmore, Gordonstoun (all Public Schools), and might include Rendcomb, Dauntseys, Bembridge, and St George's, Harpenden (which is coeducational).

The 'moderate' progressives

These schools tend to retain certain elements of orthodox education (some uniform, prefects, and an emphasis on academic success) yet while placing themselves in the centre stream of the progressive educational tradition. Their radicalism, however, is more educational than social and tends to centre on their coeducation and their emphasis on arts, crafts, and creative activities. This subgroup is formed primarily by Bedales, Frensham Heights, St Christopher's, Badminton (single-sex), the Friends' School, Saffron Walden, King Alfred's (day only), and the Town and Country School. The latter two are situated in Hampstead and presumably the area can support two radical schools because of the high concentration of liberal–artistic families there which made boarding less essential. Bedales and Frensham now appear in *The Public and Preparatory Schools Yearbook* as members of 'The Society of Headmasters of Independent Schools' which must have considerable sixth forms and fairly high academic standards.

The 'radical' progessive schools

These are the subgroup of schools which had set out not so much to reform the public school as to reject it. In doing so they abandoned uniform, compulsory sport, compulsory religious observance, prefects, corporal punishment, single-sex education, and narrow academic goals, as much for social and psychological reasons as for purely educational ones. The diffuseness of their emotional reaction is characterised by Aitkenhead, speaking of the early days of Kilquhanity House:

We did not begin with definitions of education. We were against war, against violence, against corporal punishment, against uniforms, against authoritarianism (and very likely against authority!). In fact largely 'agin the government'. We were for peace, for love, for life, for nature (and nature cure). And of course for freedom – and maybe for community. What a situation! (Child 1962: 76.)

They either rebelled against, or retreated from, traditional education and conventional society whereas the other progressives still centred on educational reform within a largely unchanged society. This 'radical' subgroup consisted of Dartington Hall, Summerhill, Kilquhanity House, Monkton Wyld, and Wennington. Several radical schools which were influential have since closed and these included Telegraph Hill, the Malting House, Burgess Hill, and the Little Commonwealth.

Generally this group of schools were, and remain, relatively small, remote, rural, coeducational schools with a high proportion of boarders. They tend to attempt delegation of power to pupils with schemes of self-government while certain expressive goals, either in the arts or in social areas, dominate instrumental and organisational ends. The expressive aims of radical progressive schools are different from those of the public schools, which espouse ideals of selflessness, service and the religious life (Lambert, Bullock, and Millham 1975). In radical communities the main expressive aim is the development of an individual child's personality at his own rate, free from external pressures and strains. This self-realisation takes place in a tolerant community where adolescent spontaneity and pleasures are held in high esteem, where the children receive the maximum support from adult and peer relationships, and will be liberated from the pressures of competition, parental expectations, and orthodox aspirations. The personal, intellectual, athletic and manual aspects of an individual's development will all receive equal stress. Controls are few and sanctions, which are thought to hinder relationships, are minimised. Some of these schools have been associated with certain esoteric practices such as vegetarianism, theosophy or naturalism, all of which are manifestations of a wider philosophy of child education, such as bringing up the child in an environment which is in tune with natural development. At times they have attracted a somewhat cranky image from certain of these practices, and in the case of some early advocates this reputation was not unjustified. Reddie, for example, had a fixation on soil closets and muesli.

If boys at school are fed upon highly inflammatory food they are apt to lose control of themselves, and to have fits of irritability, leading very often to moral vice, whereas those fed upon a cooler diet of cereals and vegetables run far less risk of these storms of super abundant vitality. (Jusmani 1961: 113.)

While the chief educational theory of Leadbeater, of the New Education Fellowship, seems to have been a vigorous encouragement of masturbation (Skidelsky 1968: 143.)

In the late sixties Millham and Bullock (1973) visited seven progressive schools as part of the research for the Public Schools Commission and reported that together these 'egalitarian' schools sheltered about 1,500 pupils compared to the public schools and their preparatory satellites which house around 100,000 boarders while the independent schools contain some 145,000 boarders. As such the 'radical' progressive sector represents currently a minuscule proportion of all boarding places in this country and remain very much an unorthodox minority.

This was even more true of the inter-war period when Dartington, Summerhill, and Telegraph Hill were considered extraordinarily controversial. At that time they were not merely dispensers of educational innovations but perceived themselves as part of a wider liberal social movement. For instance, the millennial imagery of '*The New Era*' (this was the title of the movement's journal), and of a new type of citizen to populate it, occurs throughout the progressive literature. A. S. Neill of Summerhill was the most consistently radical of the progressive educators and he stated (1968: 102):

There are so few self-regulated babies in the world that any attempt to describe them must be tentative. The observed results so far suggest the beginnings of a new civilization, more profoundly changed in character than any new society promised by any kind of political party.

This millenial view of society, while still echoed by some contemporary progressives, was particularly espoused by the inter-war progressives. To appreciate their frame of reference necessitates a brief glimpse at the social and intellectual climate of that time. In the early nineteen twenties, when several of the radical schools were founded, the liberal intelligentsia were reacting both against the trauma of the First World War with an optimistic pacifism and internationalism and against the undue solemnity of the late Victorian era with a self-conscious, iconoclastic modernism (as typified by Strachey's debunking biographies). By the thirties, however, unemployment, appeasement, fascism, and increasingly factious nationalism led to a period of growing disenchantment and spiritual isolation. Fyvel (1968: 38) has said of the intellectual work in this period that it expressed

The Zeitgeist of those years – the awareness of a disintegrating world, of an English bourgeois society grown hollow and often sordid and unattractive, and of the alienation of the literary intellectuals from that society.

It is perhaps no accident then that a spate of radical progressive schools (almost revolutionary in contrast to the first tree-chopping, soil-closet 'New Schools' such as Abbotsholme) should emerge in this period. They can be seen as in part an answer to the social needs of alienated intellectuals in a modern, industrial society whose position is a highly ambiguous one. They share the same class position as the traditional upper middle class but their status position in terms of life-style may be totally at variance with conventional class expectations. This status incongruency often gives them the role of the social exile or class traitor which may lead to, or be precipitated by, an anti-authoritarian, counter-traditional, bohemian life-style.

Another fundamental ambivalence which afflicts intellectuals is their Janus-like approach to social change. For their dilemma is that they wish to be *avant-garde* in welcoming innovation and modernity as weapons against stultifying convention while, at the same time, wishing to preserve a cherished cultural and natural heritage from the encroachments of industrial society. There is certainly this element in progressive education for at first the movement espoused modernism, science, and innovation in order to breach the defences of the educational establishment whereas later it was somewhat burdened by its own ideology when faced with the failure to continue on an innovative path. There is too a constant railing against technological society in the progressive literature, and the effects of industrialism are often portrayed as having mechanised, dehumanised, and bestialised man. At times it almost appears as if to the early progressives, man had lost his innocence and had to be reborn through the next generation, providing it could be protected from the corrosive influences of a misguided civilization. Further, much of the progressive imagery was elemental and naturalistic, and in its finicky preoccupation with elimination, soil, food fads, eugenics, nature cure, asceticism and purification, symbolised urban, rootless man's quest for absolution and redemption.

The child has a highly complex spiritual personality . . . unless the growing child be born again and again, it cannot enter the kingdom of the spirit. (Lane 1928: 103.)

This was further reinforced by the essentially spiritual nature of the progressive ethic as expounded in the first principle of the New Education Fellowship:

The essential object of all education should be to train the child to desire the supremacy of spirit over matter . . . the new education should therefore always aim at preserving and increasing the spiritual power in the child.

In virtually sanctifying the child ('we shall be made worthy to help in the sacred work', intoned the first edition of *The New Era*), childhood became almost an end in itself with its future secondary. But the future itself was at risk, and an apocalyptical vision was to be the heritage of the progressive child.

The future of the Summerhill idea is of the greatest importance to humanity. New generations must be given the chance to grow in freedom. The bestowal of freedom is the bestowal of love and only love can save the world. (Neill 1968: 92.)

Conclusion

Earlier we pointed to the latent communitarian and millennial elements in the progressive movement. Such analogies are valid and illuminating within their limits, but we should not lose sight of the fact that Dartington was a school. And it is our contention that the experience of a pioneering educational institution such as Dartington can contain lessons for contemporary innovations in education. For Dartington was something of a model progressive school; it possessed the resources to construct a superb educational environment – in physical, cultural, and intellectual terms – that remains one of the most envied in England. Given practically ideal conditions then, in what ways did Progressive Education appear to 'succeed' or not succeed? We can continually bear in mind comparison both with orthodox educational criteria and the progressives' own ideals. But the progressive educational ideology, drawing on sources from Plato and Rousseau to Dewey and Freud, was diffuse, ambiguous, and potentially contradictory. Such an ideology tends to be a self-justifying manifesto, describing almost utopian end states, rather than a blue-print for action specifying the processes of change necessary to arrive at those ends. It never approximated to a readily identifiable doctrine but was more a philosophical flag of convenience that tenuously united a diverse group of practitioners and thinkers (Boyd and Rawson 1965). This diffuseness makes evaluation difficult and certainly militates against quantifiable or definitive conclusions regarding success or failure.

It is perhaps worth stressing that, while there are considerable problems in evaluating conventional educational institutions, this is even more true of certain innovative experiments on the periphery of educational systems. The rigidity of conventional organisations is well documented as well as their resistance to research. What is less appreciated is that the social processes of innovative structures which espouse evaluation and self-criticism may be also subject to structural rigidity and to a fear of, or an ambiguity to, evaluation. For instance, a researcher working in this area will probably find that it is extremely difficult to settle on the aims of the institution, to construct clear criteria for the attainment of goals, to accept written and oral statements at face value, to pinpoint which processes are successful in achieving the diffuse ends, to ascertain which aims are being fulfilled at any one time, to probe critically without offending reputations, and to settle on any precise criteria for evaluating the output of the institution. But perhaps the biggest setback can be the discovery that the innovator regards research as superfluous even where he may publicly espouse its merits. In brief, the conceptual and methodological problems of evaluating the effectiveness of a diffuse educational programme, with wide-ranging and largely immeasurable aims for social reform and the life-long development of the individual, may be compounded by the ambivalence of the participants themselves to the research process.

However, it can be justly argued that it is very difficult for organisations to be continually innovatory, because the enthusiasm and commitment engendered in members at the outset become subsequently a major barrier to change. Many of the things which are now widely accepted in education, such as the importance of the creative arts or a relaxed style of coeducation, required an act of faith and considerable courage when they were initiated fifty years ago. Perhaps it is unwise to expect the progressive school to be eternally relevant. But certainly in the thirties the progressives believed that they were nurturing a new type of person who would help to fashion a nonconformist radical elite of rational, humane, internationally-minded men and women and who would oppose the orthodox, governing elite of the dominant public schools. And, like Eton, the progressives would begin at the top. They attracted the children of the liberal middle class to private boarding schools in Devon, Dorset, Yorkshire, Suffolk and Kircudbright. The free infant, the handmaiden of the New Era, would be granted the freedom to flower naturally in a remote bucolic retreat surrounded by a prying and disapproving peasantry.

This paradox of attempting to institutionalise freedom in a total environment is but one of the many paradoxes in progressive education. For the sociologist's concern with structure and process leads him to treat such aspirations scornfully. Yet people at Dartington simply do not perceive their enterprise as an 'institution' and, when I compared it with other communities, Leonard Elmhirst wrote:

I do not know what you mean by 'communitarian' enterprises. For the first thirty years Dorothy and I resisted any suggestion that we were trying to build, or were building a community. This is why we never enquired, in making any new appointment, what the religion or politics were of the person to be engaged. The question always was – is he, or she, competent to do a proper job?

The research in this area is also handicapped by the somewhat myopic focus of the Sociology of Education which tends to work within a narrow set of criteria. Unfortunately, comparatively little attention has been paid to the internal structure of educational organisations, to processes of innovation at the institutional level, to the internal dynamics of radical schools, to the nature of educational ideologies, to the political context of educational innovation, to the socio-structural position of the school, and so on. This means that our knowledge of alternative educational provision is impoverished by a significant failure to evaluate this rich stream of innovative experience.

This work, then, conceived in 1967 and based on field work in 1968–9, had little other original research to use for guidelines. There was a labyrinth of meandering clichés in the progressive literature but a paucity of evidence. The findings presented here are largely exploratory and descriptive, and the research clearly suffers from the lack of a representative sample. But, whatever its shortcomings, this work does represent the first specifically sociological study of a progressive school and of the fate of its former pupils. Nowadays talk of a 'revolution' in the schools is commonplace, as is rhetoric concerning 'de-schooling' and 'de-structuring' the traditional, authoritarian school which is seen as inefficient and anachronistic (Illich 1971). The vocabulary and the innovations are perhaps not quite so novel as many of the practitioners think. For, in the story of Dartington, with its precocious freedom, we have a socio-historical case study of a revolutionary education. Deeply imbued with an anti-authoritarian and an anti-institutional ideology, Dartington in the nineteen twenties and thirties can be said to have pioneered the 'anti-school'.

Part One
Looking back at the school

Chapter Two

An historical sketch of the school 1926–57

Three educational pioneers

Dartington Hall School provides the central institution for this research. It is of particular interest for three reasons. Firstly, the school was, and remains, part of a much larger communitarian enterprise which provided physical insulation for the school together with involvement in an adult progressive venture; secondly, it possessed the money to implement its ideas on a fairly lavish scale (and, of course, to sponsor research); and, thirdly, in 'Bill' Curry as headmaster it possessed a leading advocate of progressive education whose strongly held views on educational reform were matched by fervent aspirations for a sane, peaceful society.

The founders of the Dartington enterprise were Leonard (1893–1974) and Dorothy Elmhirst (1887–1968). After Cambridge and the Army, Leonard cooperated with Rabrindranath Tagore (a Bengali philosopher, poet and teacher who ran a sanctuary school at Santiniketan) in founding an Institute for Rural Reconstruction called Sriniketan, which is Sanskrit for 'Abode of Grace'. Much of his energies went into a series of educational experiments with young children and he was deeply influenced by Tagore's almost mystical naturalism and his fervent belief in the doctrine of non-interference in the natural unfolding of a child's personality (Elmhirst 1961). Leonard left India for America where he married Dorothy Whitney Straight in 1925.

Together, they considered starting an enterprise of their own. They were agreed that there should be a school for Dorothy's children (her first husband had died in France in 1918), that it should not conform to the traditional English model, that it should be coeducational, and that it should combine the ideas of both Tagore and Dewey. In September 1925 they bought the 820 acres that remained of an estate (since increased to around 4,000 acres) at Dartington, near Totnes in Devonshire (Bonham-Carter 1958). Their wealth and their unconventional assumptions and practices irritated people at both ends of the social spectrum. The first school doctor was not altogether in favour of the Elmhirsts' break with so many rural traditions and once remarked:

If only you and Dorothy could see your way to attend Matins regularly on Sunday and so set a good example to all the farm labourers.

Similarly, the son of an archbishop exclaimed:

Leonard, if only you would hunt. It would put everything right. (Personal communications from L. K. Elmhirst.)

About the same time A. S. Neill was writing somewhat peevishly to Bertrand Russell:

When Elmhirst needs a new wing he writes out a cheque to Heals . . . Heals! and here I am absolutely gravelled to raise cash for a pottery shed. Pioneering is a wash-out, man. (Russell 1968: 187.)

The general purpose of the Dartington estate, which began operations in 1926, was rural rehabilitation by the provision of primary and secondary industries – farming, horticulture, forestry and sawmilling, textiles, cidermaking, and building. Implicit in this large-scale experiment in rural reconstruction was the didactic aim of providing opportunities for a full cultural and social life for all who were employed there. Medieval buildings were restored, Uday Shankar came to perform ritual Hindu dances, and Rabindranath Tagore, Bertrand Russell, A. S. Neill, H. G. Wells, Kingsley Martin, Norman Angell, Noel Brailsford, Julian Huxley, Gerald Heard, Barbara Wootton, and Aldous Huxley gave talks at the Sunday evening meetings. A wealth of talent was patronised by the founders and included Bernard Leach, Michael Chekov, Hans Oppenheim, Robert Masters, Imogen Holst, and the Jooss-Leeder ballet school from Essen. Provincial Totnes, the most ancient royal borough in England, became in the nineteen thirties a haven for artists, foreigners, pacifists, socialists, agnostics and theorists whose unconventional views and behaviour aroused hostility and suspicion from the local populace. One of the research interviewees vividly captured something of these exotic early years in describing the estate he knew as a child:

In a way it was marvellous. Dartington was almost an absurd, grotesque Disneyland. It attracted a lot of hangers-on and you felt that anyone with a weird skill, say a Trotskyite weaver in corduroy breeches with a great shock of hair – would be made welcome. There was a sense of indulgence, of people rising inordinately early, of do-gooders, and of restrained aesthetic opulence but not crass or vulgar. People felt that Dartington was the New Eden from which people would radiate like rays from a rainbow . . . and just to ask at Paddington for a ticket to Totnes was for the porter to look suspiciously at you. It was somehow both absurd and at the same time extremely moving. And one was encouraged to feel part of a generation, of a whole concept that was going to take over the world in some way at some future point, so one felt quite exhilarated. (Recorded Interview.)

Although he did not take up his appointment as headmaster until five years after the school had been opened, Dartington Hall School became largely identified with Bill Curry, and he remained its headmaster for some twenty-five years. Curry was a Northumbrian, born at Jarrow-on-Tyne at the turn of the century, the son of a grocer and the eldest of four children. After the First World War he read Russell's *Principles of Social Reconstruction* (1916) which confirmed his own desire for peace and amplified his views on the relationship between traditional education and a predisposition to brutality and aggression.

Perhaps one idea above all others informed his view of the school; that the sane, rational citizens of the new order should be prepared for it by experiencing a real, sane, rational environment. This involved trusting and respecting the child as a unique individual in order to give it almost adult self-determination. Curry professed a belief in the liberty of the individual child, and he countered arguments that Dartington, like the traditional school, moulded children, by promoting the spirit inherent in Russell's (1916: 102) passage, which Curry never tired of quoting:

Where authority is unavoidable, what is needed is reverence. A man who is to educate really well and is to make the young grow and develop into their full stature, must be filled through and through with reverence ... the man who has reverence will not think it his duty to 'mould' the young ... He can wield the authority of an educator without infringing the principles of liberty.

By the machinery of self-government the children would be brought into the decision-making process and authority would be subsumed by the whole community. And, by reason and discussion, those rules necessary for the maintenance of the community could be framed with the minimum imposition on the liberty of the individual.

The notion of discrete individuals pursuing rationally their own ends was the antithesis of an authoritarian education. The latter was the preserve of partisanship, group-spirit, rivalry, competition, and uncritical loyalty which Curry stigmatised as the seeds of nationalism, fascism and totalitarianism. In contrast, Dartington was to be suffused with liberal principles – no punishment, no uniform, no prefects, no religion, few rules (and those agreed by discussion), no bounds, freedom to choose and attend classes, no sexual segregation, and a real delegation of responsibility by pupil self-government. The ethos, the methods, and the staff exuded (it was not the wish to impose) values that included respect and tolerance of individuality and nonconformity, a faith in reason, discussion, and persuasion, and a denigration of force, patriotism, traditionalism, competition, religion and prejudice.

Above all, Curry revered three main articles of faith in his school. Firstly, that the child was capable of almost adult self-determination and was amenable to rational persuasion. Indeed, he expressed the view that children are more fundamentally rational than adults (summary of speech to estate staff, 1 March 1936, Dartington Hall Records Office – hereafter DHRO). Secondly, the school must accept the problems arising from complete coeducation. And, thirdly, the school, without undue pressure, should enable the child to pursue high academic attainment. The first two stemmed from his general social and educational philosophy of preparing children for an improved life, but the third was largely idiosyncratic.

Curry wanted so badly to prove to the world that a 'crank' school could win a scholarship to Cambridge, at Trinity. If he could get a scholarship to Cambridge it justified his whole thing . . . his whole emphasis all the time was on academic achievement. (Recorded Interview with L. K. Elmhirst.)

Finally, it is imperative to add that the maximisation of liberty for the child, as exemplified by non-interference, was not the negation of adult responsibility and that Curry fully appreciated that the price of liberty was eternal vigilance.

On becoming headmaster in 1931 Curry began to pursue relentlessly his twin concerns – Education and Peace. That he was not solely concerned with education is illustrated by the titles of his two major works, *The School and a Changing Civilisation* (1934) and *Education for Sanity* (1947), while he also wrote the Penguin Special, *The Case for Federal Union* (1939). In the first of these, for instance, he spoke of the struggle of freedom and reason against force and nationalism: the place of the school in this conflict was paramount.

A modern school is one which recognises that the social order must be radically changed if civilisation is to survive at all. (Curry 1934: xii.)

His vision was of a cosmopolitan, cooperative commonwealth. The enemy was nationalism which he castigated as:

A fatal disease of the body politic. It produces high temperatures, running sores, cancerous growths, and outbreaks of homicidal mania. And yet we deliberately inoculate people with it. It is high time we stopped. (Curry 1947: 104.)

Progress depended upon experiment and at Dartington the whole school was an experiment which involved treating children in different and unorthodox ways. The expense involved would be rewarded when sanity, disarmament, and world government were achieved.

Curry was passionately concerned with war, hate, and unreasoning patriotism and fervently believed that a progressive education could produce a new elite of free, rational, democratic, internationalist citizens to populate a sane society. He wrote:

. . . if a better social and economic system is to be devised, we shall need a different type of man and woman to run it. (Blewitt 1934: 56.)

His forerunners were the Greeks, the Enlightenment, Mill, and nineteenth-century Liberalism, and his contemporary reference group was Shaw, Wells and Russell; he shared the Enlightenment's faith in the self-sustaining nature of individuality once given its release from corrupting and fettering institutions. There was too a feeling that, like the nineteenth-century benevolent radicals, he believed that intellectual liberty based upon the use of reason was possible only for an educated elite and could not be extended to the mass of the people. But he desperately wanted Dartington to be the prototype of a new, universal, rational education which could save civilisation from itself. And to implement his radical educational aspirations he turned to a remote, rural estate in Devon.

This peculiarly ambiguous community – international style glass and concrete buildings clashed with neo-baronial fourteenth-century reconstructions and the medieval jousting yard – became something of a secular utopia, a New Harmony on the River Dart (Armytage 1961: 412). This stimulating, and at times exotic, background can hardly have failed to influence the subjects of our research. For the depth of fellow-feeling generated there among the adults was described by a former member of staff:

I think one could truthfully speak of a feeling which, short of a religious community say of monks who really care about their common purpose, or some community of that kind, as much unity of feeling and cooperation in day-to-day life as one could hope to find. (Recorded interview.)

The school 1926–57

Dartington Hall School opened in September 1926 with ten pupils – seven boys and three girls (and three of the children were Dorothy's) – accommodated in the Hall (Punch 1970a). In the early years there was, amid the fervour and enthusiasm, talk of wastefulness, inefficiency, and widespread insecurity, while the proposed unity of the school and estate had proved largely impracticable as few foremen had proved to be natural educators.

The old idea of the estate as an educational hinterland to the school had gone, and from being the centre, the school had sunk to being a poor, and rather disreputable, relation. (Manuscript source DHRO).

One of the staff felt that the school was based on a series of negations, against religion, examinations, discipline, and inhibitions regarding sex, rather than affirming a positive alternative. In particular, he highlighted the insecurity of the staff, both morally and with regard to future employment, concerning the possible consequences of coeducation (Punch 1970a: 29). This fear of the public exposure of sexual relationships among the pupils remained a constant source of concern to Dartington and the other progressives because of the possibility of court action and the closure of the school.

At the same time, Dartington scarcely seemed like a school at all to the children in those early days. There was time to discover and explore and to find out what you were not good at. One hungry little boy, coming from the impoverished diets and cruel punishments of a series of Peakean preparatory schools, fell ravenously upon the food.

Here I was in a Ginger Bread House. There was so much that I never felt hungry for four years. And what food! Apple sauce in great bowls for breakfast, with piles of cornflakes and giant jugs of milk. Roast beef without gristle, set off by crisp Yorkshire Pudding. Bean shoots from China. When once Lady Astor brought Bernard Shaw, as she said to see the children of this strange establishment guzzling away under the table, like dogs, there we were at the tables, eating strawberries and cream, and not just as a special issue to impress the visitors. Strawberries! (Young 1973: 8.)

For the adults too, there was every evening a formal dinner up at the Hall where evening clothes were worn, where the table was resplendent with silverware, shining glass, and finger bowls and where the meal was followed by the circulation of a decanter of port. But this early period was conspicuous by the freedom and excitement of the children.

One day 'Reg' [a member of staff] said, 'This is absolutely bloody. Let's all change places'. So for a whole twenty-four hours we all changed places. The staff became the children and the children became the staff. For a child, looking back now, it was marvellous. It was a life-saver. I mean at ten o'clock at night 'Frank' [a member of staff] would suddenly say, 'Let's all go to Goodrington and have a beach picnic'. And we would all jump in those elderly cars and an old bus, and we would build an enormous bonfire on Goodrington beach and bathe by moonlight. (Recorded interview.)

The Elmhirsts had considerable influence in this heady period (Punch 1975b) while permitting a high degree of staff democracy. But as the Elmhirsts took on more estate responsibilities this arrangement proved impractical and, amidst a ferment of debate, the Elmhirsts decided to seek an outside, objective, expert appraisal which bore fruit in the 'Bonser Report' of 1928. While admiring the school's environment and educational principles, Dr Bonser (an American educationist) came to the conclusion that there were not enough experienced staff to implement the advanced educational theories in vogue at Dartington. His main findings were that much of the teaching was inadequate; the use of the estate departments for educational work had not proved a success; there was a lack of self-discipline among the children; the pupils were being subject to 'emotional analysis' (psychological studies involving the divination of dreams) which was unsuccessful and undesirable; and there was a danger that the children might fall behind in their mental growth. (Manuscript source, DHRO.)

Such astringent views were echoed on a School Reorganisation Committee which recognised that most difficulties arose from the fact that many people were amateurs tackling a professional job, and that there was an urgent need of an executive head or director to pilot an expansion in numbers and to attract a well-qualified staff. That man was Curry.

When Bill Curry arrived from the Oak Lane County Day School in Philadelphia to assume the headship in September 1931, the school numbered fifty-one children, and within three years the numbers had increased threefold. Substantial building had already taken place and further expansion was planned. The effects of the Depression, however, meant that the ambitious plans for a new senior school had to be abandoned and 'Foxhole', conceived as a junior school, continued to be used as senior school while the day-nursery buildings on the estate at Aller Park were converted for use as a junior boarding section.

In March 936, there occurred a collision between the buoyant school and the commercial representatives of Dartington Hall Limited; the latter considered the business enterprises were being jeopardised by the unsavoury reputation of the former. Curry, recently estanged from his wife, met his critics in a lecture and discussion lasting over three hours. It was a clash between the altruism and ideology of one half of the enterprise (particularly as represented by Curry and the school) and the hard-headed realists of the other half, at a time of financial insecurity. Curry had to defend both his educational ideals and his personal life – he was not a communist, the school did not encourage sexual intercourse, nor was it biased politically, and so on. And he argued that teachers should be judged on their efficiency as teachers, not on their personal life. His opponents pointed out that the school was losing money and seemed contemptuous of outside opinion (Curry, for instance, was accused of laughing at the Mayor of Torquay when he asked to see the School Chapel!) and that this contravened the aims of the estate generally; namely, to be both profitable and to be of general application. A letter on the subject ended on an ominous note, 'It is a matter for the Trustees to decide whether or not the two [School and Company] should continue as they are, side by side but not together'. (Manuscript source, DHRO.)

In retrospect, however, Dartington in the thirties seemed to function as a progressive school was meant to, with an eager and devoted staff, with excellent facilities, and with the headmaster in his prime. A clientele was being built up and the rapid expansion was beginning to promise to pay-off as the numbers had increased fourfold in eight years, making the school potentially economically viable. Speaking of the self-government, Curry noted that 'the supremacy of reason seems to be acknowledged'.

But if reason pervaded Dartington it fell on stony ground in contemporary Europe. Later, Curry (1958: 186) wrote, 'The war years are best forgotten. Our growth and development had not been merely arrested but reversed'. In the summer of 1940, with invasion imminent, sixty-four children were taken away in a single term. Some of the staff volunteered for active service, some registered as conscientious objectors, others were conscripted or directed into war work, while several teachers of German nationality were interned. Thought was given to moving the school to North America as a campus school, but a university sponsor could not be found. But by 1941, with invasion less of a threat and with some children sent to board to avoid bombing, the numbers were consolidated at between 120 and 130 pupils and they never fell below that figure again. The need for stringent economy gave rise to the practice of Useful Work, whereby the children took over chores previously done by domestics, which became permanent (and compulsory).

In 1941 Curry reviewed his first ten years at Dartington in a report to the Trustees. It is a fascinating document because Curry gives a devastatingly clear critique of Dartington's weaknesses, at a time when his own aspirations were in smithereens, but, ultimately, he could not admit defeat or failure. Briefly, his conclusions were as follows. There had never been a year where the staff were in a hundred per cent agreement with each other or with him, while the school attracted a proportion of staff who were in a state of neurotic revolt which did not become apparent until after they were appointed. Some children were sent to Dartington only after they had failed in conventional schools and the parents had only turned to progressive education when all else had failed. Indeed, a majority of the parents did not appear to have an intelligent grasp of what progressive education meant and, for a fair proportion, it seemed merely to be the most up-to-date method of spoiling their children. He regretted, therefore, not having one hundred per cent of the children on scholarships, which would enable him to select children irrespective of the parents' ability to pay the fees. A deep dilemma arose from the children who should never have been admitted but who, once at the school, might be damaged by being sent away again. Perhaps, for this reason, some of the problem children had been kept too long and this had affected others in the school. Theft remained a nagging problem. He detailed the difficulties of having teaching groups organised for each subject. Even with a small school and an 'almost fantastically extravagant staff–pupil ratio' the timetable complexities were enormous. They had been forced to retrogess to divisions into 'forms'. He insisted that the school should continue to prepare children for School Certificate. Not to do so would be to lose the best pupils and to leave only the stupid, with no hope of passing, and the rich who could confidently look forward to a life of idleness. One could hardly be satisfied, he argued, with a school containing only those two categories. He felt that the coeducation was on the right lines but that the real test would be the lives the pupils lived as adults – would most of the children marry, would they have happy marriages, and what sort of parents would they make?

Finally, Curry expressed a disbelief in early boarding as many of the younger children were only sent because they were unhappy at home. Indeed, he argued that the ideal society would not have boarding schools. There was something unreal and unnatural about them which created psychological tensions. Success at Dartington could only be achieved on a scale which would rule out boarding for most pupils and thus the indispensable conditions of success negated the possibility of the school serving as a model. Yet he remained an unrepentant believer in scientific rational humanism and averred that liberty was worth what it cost. (Manuscript Source, DHRO.)

In 1944 a reorganisation was planned to incorporate a 'Middle' school with the Senior School (13–18) at Foxhole, the Middle School (10–13) at Aller Park, and the Junior School (6–10) and Nursery (3–6) at the house known as the 'Old Postern'. Ironically, the war had solved many financial problems both for the school and the estate, and there was a surplus in several of the war years. Curry rejected the implications of the Fleming Report of 1944, which called for voluntary integration between the state and independent sectors, because he said local demand did not justify it, and because the staff were not adequate to the curriculum changes involved in implementing the Commission's proposals. A small reunion of former pupils took place in 1944; and most agreed that the school had become less experimental. 'The ideas behind the school had remained static and had been overtaken by the currently accepted ideas of a dynamic society'. (Manuscript source, DHRO.)

The initial period of recovery and retrenchment after the war was estimated by Curry to be one of his most difficult periods.

Many of the newcomers among the pupils had graver problems than we had suspected, and some had a curious spirit of hostility and rebellion, and an unwillingness to come to terms with the school, which we had never encountered before. Some of the newcomers among the staff had very little idea of what it was all about, and I myself and many of the older staff were very tired. (Bonham-Carter 1958: 190.)

The realities of the post-war situation affected the school's morale, inflation and rising costs brought financial problems, some difficult children had been recruited, and Curry was, by now, a tired man, physically and mentally, and also a sick one.

After the war he was a very tired man. Looking back I'm inclined to think that he felt a defeated man already. The agony of the war and keeping the school together had been too much for him. He was personally agonised by the things that happened in the world and in those few years he'd aged remarkably. (Recorded interview with former member of staff.)

He was found to be suffering from diabetes, and in 1949 was given a well-earned leave of absence, when he went abroad for three months to recuperate.

But, gradually, enrolment increased – 178 in March 1946, 185 in September 1946 (the largest since 1939), 200 in February 1947 (then the largest in the school's history), and, finally, 218 in July 1951. But there was a deficit of £3,000 in 1946 and this rose even higher in the following year when the Trustees helped out the school with a gift of £4,500. The fees for boarders were raised by £35 p.a. (placing them in the region of £200 p.a.) but they had to be raised yet again in 1948. The 1944 Education Act had threatened enforced inspection of all independent schools and the Trustees prevailed upon Curry to consider inspection for 'approval' (as opposed to complete 'recognition'). Curry had opposed inspection since as far back as 1938, but, in the event, a sympathetic team of four of His Majesty's Inspectors visited Dartington in 1949. Briefly, they reported that the teaching was in part inspired, in part inadequate; that there were too many passengers on the staff because of war-time appointments; that, in two areas where they had expected excellence, Art and Physical Education, the standards were, in fact, low; but that the Headmaster was at the height of his powers (Report of HMI, Dartington School, 1949). Yet Curry had remained uncomprising on those practices, such as nude bathing and shared bathrooms, which separated Dartington from most other schools.

From about this time, however, relationships with the Trustees began to decline and Curry gradually became isolated and aggrieved. Ostensibly the main cause was finance – Aller Park had become a financial nightmare, parents seemed less inclined to favour early boarding, the staff were almost exploited, and the real value of the endowment had declined alarmingly. He rejected state aid as he was out of sympathy with planned egalitarianism; indeed, he feared he was becoming a reactionary. Scholarships were reduced, fees were increased, and economies in the preparation of food introduced. In 1954, a French woman asked if her children could visit Dartington for a few weeks to experience this 'école paradis'.

But by 1956 Curry was ill and disillusioned, had lost faith in himself and the school, and felt unable to carry on. He wrote: 'A world which appears to be so obstinately disinterested in its own survival is one in which the long-term hopes for our sort of education are hard to sustain' (Bonham-Carter 1958: 189). There had been a declining enrolment among young children while parents preferred their sons to have a more rigorous education in order to prepare them for the realities of a competitive world. In fact, Curry considered that some parents perceived a Dartington education to be admirable in Utopia but simply did not guarantee what their sons needed. He considered the financial problems to be almost insoluble and that this partly explained his state of chronic anxiety and fatigue (Manuscript Source, DHRO). He resigned, ostensibly for reasons of ill-health, at the end of the Spring Term 1957. Curry had been the guiding mind behind the school for a quarter of a century and he left it with the reputation of being one of the most experimental, and one of the best known, coeducational schools in England (Tibble 1967; Punch 1970b). He died in a road accident in 1962.

Chapter Three
The parents

Our parents are a minority of a minority. They must be sufficiently well-off to afford boarding school fees; in addition, they must have thought seriously about education instead of accepting whatever is customary in their class and neighbourhood, have had sufficient independence of mind to come to unorthodox conclusions, and sufficient faith and courage to put them into practice, notwithstanding the almost inevitable barrage of criticism from their friends and relations. Such a group is likely to be both intelligent and cultivated and since intelligence, broadly speaking, is inherited, our children have been much above the average, both in general intelligence and in professional expectations. (W. B. Curry in Bonham-Carter 1958: 218.)

Fundamental to an understanding of the Progressive School – and, of course, the Progressive Child – is an appreciation of the social milieu from which it recruits. In other words, what seem to be the common factors, if any, among the backgrounds and values of that tiny minority who are commited deeply enough to the progressive educational philosophy to select a school such as Dartington, Summerhill or Bedales for their children? One would expect a home congruent with such schools to be free-thinking and non-conforming and the parents to be members of the creative, liberated intelligentsia: we would anticipate one or both parents to be in journalism, the arts, entertainment, or academia rather than, say, the Armed Forces, Commerce, or the more staid professions such as the Church or the Law.

Indeed, Dartington in the nineteen thirties could boast the following among its parents – Bertrand and Dora Russell, Aldous Huxley, Miles Malleson the actor, Ernest Raymond the novelist, Clough Williams-Ellis the architect, Stephen King-Hall the broadcaster and journalist, Victor Gollancz the publisher, Ernest Freud – the son of Sigmund and father of Clement, Robert Flaherty the film director, and Richard Church the writer; in the post-war period it could mention J. D. Bernal, scientist and Nobel Prize winner, Sean O'Casey, Geoffrey Grigson, F. R. Leavis, Ben Nicolson and Barbara Hepworth, and Richard Crossman. Indeed, one respondent from the nineteen thirties period described the Dartington of his day as the 'village school of the Bloomsbury intellectual set'.

In addition if one traces the respondents' lineage back to the grandparents, then some respondents revealed glimpses of extraordinary forebearers – erractic, bizarre, and determined. One founded the Royal Ocean Racing Yacht Club, another built 'most of the railways in South Africa', one grandfather

29

who was a special constable was imprisoned for refusing to arrest suffragettes, another of working-class origin and a printer by trade taught himself Italian in order to read Dante, while one grandmother was involved in the suffragette movement.

She had very determined ideas about the non-authoritarian education her children should have and sent three children to 'Brambledown' [a moderate coed. progressive school]. But then grandfather put his foot down and said 'I'm not having any more of my children turned into radicals' and sent the fourth to a public school. He turned out to be more radical than the others and that's my father. (Fifties Woman MS.)

A great-grandfather started with a small printing press under his bed and proceeded to build up a national daily newspaper; a grandfather tried to set up an anarchist community in Scandinavia but was thwarted by his house-proud wife; another made a fortune selling barbed-wire in the Great War; one was a Rabbi; one grandfather left school at twelve to work in the mines and his son became a university professor; we find another grandfather who left for South Africa with £20, joined with Cecil Rhodes, and built up a farm; yet another built 'Her Majesty's Theatre'; and, finally, one was a humanitarian politician who helped to expose the atrocities of the Belgians in the Congo and who was imprisoned on a technicality for pro-German sympathies in the First World War.

Education and politics were often mentioned with several grandparents having been in the teaching profession; one was a Liberal MP, another a founder member of the Fabians, a grandmother was a militant suffragette, while several were radical socialists. Finally there were the 'non-conformers' and breakers of tradition.

My grandfather was irreligious in the sense that he'd rush around eating pork and that sort of thing, whereas my grandmother could still read Hebrew and kept all the orthodox Jewish festivals. (Fifties Man MS.)

The example, *par excellence*, of the rebel was the grandfather in the Army, who sired an uncertain number of children by a variety of women.

He was an extraordinary character. My father was illegitimate because the old general was a moral delinquent who performed the extraordinary feat of having two sisters pregnant at the same time – the product of one of these is my father, the other one is my aunt, who if you think about it are both cousins and also brother and sister because they had the same father but their mothers are sisters. (Thirties Man MS.)

Their children, i.e. our respondents' parents, often have, then, a classical nonconforming background; other parents revolted against their ultra-traditional backgrounds; others, as we have seen, were in creative occupations; while some were simply conventional upper middle class people but with somewhat difficult children. England in the twenties and thirties presented these people with either the authoritarian traditional boarding school or the state grammar school. For people who valued individuality, creativity, and nonconformity the educational outlook must have seemed bleak. In fact, the social and political climate of that time was such as to drive intellectuals to radical education for nourishment: Fyvel (1968: 41), for instance, mentions two elements which served to increase radicalism generally among intellectuals of the nineteen thirties:

The general reaction to the Tory's coalition government acceptance of mass unemployment at home and appeasement of monstrous dictators abroad was a violent swing to the left.

We must continually bear in mind this climate when examining the balance sheet of advantages and disadvantages transmitted to our respondents as children by their parental backgrounds. Curry, for instance, spoke of the 'one parent in a hundred thousand' who saw the experiment as a genuine advance and was prepared to pay for his belief (Ash 1969: 198).

Occupations

Not surprisingly, both because of the cost of private education and because independent boarding tends to be an upper middle class preserve in England, the great majority of the sample's parents were contained within Social Classes I and II of the Registrar General's Classification of Occupations. Some 93 per cent of our Dartington fathers (i.e. fifty-six out of sixty) came within these two groups of whom 27 per cent are in Social Class I and the remainder, 67 per cent, in Social Class II. The three fathers not in either of these two groups were a sales representative (Non-manual III), a footman (Non-manual IV), and technically the sole 'manual' worker among the sample, a tailor (Manual III). One father who did 'nothing' was not classified. Stewart (1968: 322–3) produced figures on the parental backgrounds of a range of respondents from progressive and Quaker schools covering nearly thirty years (he achieved only a 56 per cent response rate) and concluded:

The fathers of 81 per cent of the children at these progressive schools fall into social classes I and II as compared with 19 per cent of 'the economically active and retired males in England and Wales in 1961'.

This proportion is almost directly comparable to that of public school parents (Kalton 1966: 35–6) and Millham and Bullock (1973: 7) reinforce this point:

Naturally the parents and governing bodies of radical progressive schools are from sections of the upper middle class, whose attitudes to education and child-rearing are more liberal than those of parents and staff in public schools. Many such parents

TABLE 1. *Classification of fathers' occupations by Roe's and Registrar General's categories.* (Darington figures above; control group figures below in square brackets; percentages in round brackets.)

Social Class	I Service	II Business	III Organisation	IV Technology	V Outdoor	VI Science	VII General culture	VIII Arts and entertainment	Totals (social class)
I	2 [2]		5 [2]	2 [3]		2 [5]	5		16 (27%) [12] (30%)
II	4 [2]	2	13 [12]		9 [3]		4 [8]	8 [1]	40 (67%) [26] (65%)
III (Non-manual)		1	[1]						1 (2%) [1] (2.5%)
III (Manual)				1					1 (2%)
IV	1								1 (2%)
V									
Totals Roe categories	7 (12%) [4] (12.5%)	3 (5%) [0]	18 (30%) [15] (37.5%)	3 (5%) [3] (7.5%)	9 (15%) [3] (7.5%)	2 (3%) [5] (12.5%)	9 (15%) [8] (20%)	8 (13%) [1] (2.5%)	59* [39]†

* One unclassifiable.   † One respondent an orphan.

work in communications industries, in the arts or in academic circles, but apart from fewer clergy and commissioned officers the parental background of progressive school children scarcely differs from that of pupils of a leading public school.

However, the Registrar General's Classification does not really tell us a great deal about the differences within each class and so a classification based upon Roe (1956) will be adopted (Table 1). This gives eight horizontal categories differentiating the nature of the occupation. If we examine the table the father's occupations can be seen to cluster around four main functions – Service (12 per cent), Organisation (30 per cent) – the largest single category, Outdoor (15 per cent), and, combining VII and VIII, Culture. plus Arts–Entertainment (28 per cent). In short, the fathers tend to be in the following occupational sectors – managerial, cultural–creative, agricultural, and service–welfare. The agricultural–outdoor bent one would expect from the bias of the Dartington estate, the school farm, and the school's emphasis on the practical and on nature. Indeed, ten fathers (and one step-father) were actively engaged in the Dartington enterprise in some capacity – two Trustees, three teachers, and five employees. In addition, four wives of this subgroup also worked on the estate as well as two mothers whose husbands were not connected with Dartington.

A quarter of all the fathers, 25 per cent or fifteen out of sixty, either possessed their own businesses or were involved as partners in a family or other business. Three fathers had been high-ranking officers in the Armed Forces (an Admiral, a naval Commander, and a Wing-Commander) while one other father was a military chaplain; but of these, three left the Forces for alternative occupations. Indeed, among the fathers as a whole there were nearly a quarter who had had, or continued to have, one or more occupations – in some cases with quite radical changes in mid-career. There was, too a small minority with an element of relative instability in their career patterns. In effect, the Dartington fathers had their conventional occupations to a greater extent than we might have expected, such as managers, accountants, company secretaries, a financial controller, and an estate manager. Stewart (1968: 332) also notes that, among his respondents' fathers, the dominance of the 'organisational' group (at 41 per cent by far the largest category) is sur-prisingly heavy. There was, however, a significant minority in cultural–creative roles such as novelist, actor–dramatist, anthropologist–sculptor, broadcaster, musician, painter, and so on.

With regard to the mothers, roughly two-thirds worked before marriage; some were simply described as 'mothers' or 'housewives' after marriage when the majority did not pursue a formal occupation. The arts, culture, and enter-tainment had claimed 17 per cent of the mothers, 15 per cent had been teachers (nine mothers were teachers or lecturers and one was at Dartington for a time), 8 per cent had been in secretarial occupations, and there was a wide range of miscellaneous occupations including an architect, a chiropodist, a tax inspector, a milliner, a dental receptionist, a psychiatric social worker, a veterinary assistant, a dress designer, and one ran a holiday camp.

Educational background

The educational experience of the sample's parents was predominantly in orthodox education – usually single-sex, often private, and with a fair proportion of fathers having been to a public school (38 per cent). Dartington mothers were less likely to have attended a public school but correspondingly more went to 'other independent' schools. Roughly the same proportions of fathers and mothers had been state educated (37 per cent and 35 per cent respectively) and this generally meant grammar school although a small proportion of parents has been only to a senior elementary school. Just less than a third of the fathers were graduates compared to 12 per cent of the mothers, of whom 10 per cent had been to a College of Education. Of contemporary public school parents Lambert *et al.* (1971a: Chap. 4) noted:

In most public and the leading progressive and independent schools, a majority of parents were themselves educated at independent schools and a substantial majority of the fathers (80 per cent) had been boarders themselves, mainly at public schools. Indeed, a quarter of the fathers of boys now at public schools were boarders at the same school as their sons.

Combining the fathers and mothers we find that 17 out of 120 of the Dartington parents (or roughly 14 per cent) had been educated abroad, usually in the United States or Northern Europe. This is but one indicator of the cosmopolitan clientele that Dartington attracted and which is doubtless underrepresented in my sample because of residence abroad. Thus Curry reported in 1955 (Manuscript Source, DHRO) that childrens' national backgrounds included 'Jewish, Austrian, Holland, Germany, India, Sweden, Denmark, Norway, Spain, Persia, and the USA'. Two fathers and three mothers were progressively educated; of these, two were a married couple, both Bedalians (there was also a Bedalian married couple among the pilot interviews), two other mothers were also from Bedales, while one father had been to the German Coeducational New School at Wickersdorff. But, generally, our respondents' parents have mostly experienced orthodox education and this is only to be expected as progressive schools would have been virtually unheard of in their childhood.

There was, too, a minority of Dartington parents who found their experience of conventional education distressing (also, several members of the

Dartington Trustees had had unhappy experiences at traditional schools in-
cluding Leonard Elmhirst and his son Bill Elmhirst, Michael Young, and
Maurice Ash). At least a third were unhappy to some extent at their schools.
For example, one father went to 'Mount Pleasant' (an historic public school).

He loathed it. He was probably the same sort of lad I was, petrified of everything, and
with a hopeless stammer – even worse than my stammer. I imagine it was hell, he
spoke very badly of it. (Fifties Man MS.)

Another respondent remarked:

My father had very little education. He was ill a lot, and he hated school, hated
teachers. He was probably victimised by teachers and that had a lot to do with us
going to Dartington. (Fifties Woman MS.)

Finally, there were several parents who were themselves deeply involved in
education, some as teachers or lecturers, some taught their own children for
periods, and some even ran their own schools. This commitment to education,
coupled with unhappy experiences at orthodox schools, may well have disposed them to think critically when choosing a school for their own children.

Marital status

One respondent wrote that Dartington had provided her with a refuge from
two unhappy homes – her father's and her mother's. And, continually, the
'broken home' cropped up in the evidence with stories of divorce or separation, remarriage, death of a parent, geographical separation, and, especially
with the fifties cohort, the disruptive effect of the war on family life. It seemed
to become almost the norm at Dartington to come from a disturbed
background.

My parents had had quite a long stretch of living apart, and my father came down to
visit me and we went for a walk. After about half an hour he said, 'I should like to tell
you that I'm remarried and we've got a child'. My first feeling was 'ah, now I'm quite
definitely in the Dartington swim'. (Thirties Woman P.)

In fact, at the time of interviewing, exactly one-third (or twenty) of the Dartington sample had parents who were separated or divorced. In six cases the
home was disrupted by either the death of one parent or marital break-up
before the respondent commenced at Dartington, while in a further twelve
cases this occurred while the child was actually at the school.

Generally, this was the parents' first marriage (for 88 per cent of them in
fact) except for four fathers and five mothers with previous marriages; sixteen
fathers remarried as did eleven mothers. But the figures are not the whole
story; e.g. one mother was divorced but has since separated from her second

husband; one father had married three times; one couple both remarried to other people but now the mother is divorced again; another couple separated for a number of years but are now reunited; one respondent's parents had both left their previous partners, had lived together, but were now parted; and one respondent's mother had died when she was a young child and her father remarried, only to separate later. In an extreme case one man replied to a question on his mother:

My mother? Which of five? My father had five effective marriages. Three were legal and the others were long term mistresses or quasi-marriages. (Thirties Man MS.)

Frequently the child was caught up in the emotional turmoil surrounding the marital disharmony — the conflicting loyalties, the bickering, the difficulties of adjusting to a step-parent, the problems of assimilating step-children, and the physical upheaval of a split home. Some respondents gave poignant and harrowing accounts of the strains of deeply divided homes which seemed to remain fresh in their minds as they recalled them, as in this extreme case:

My mother's first marriage was to 'Fletcher' and my half-brother and half-sister are his children; she didn't marry my real father but he was cited in the divorce. I was born into the 'Fletcher's' marriage but I was illegitimate. That is, I was born inside the wrong wedlock though I was registered as 'Fletcher's' child. I never knew my real father as a resident parent, never had a home in that sense, and, much later, my mother married someone else, my step-father. He didn't have any occupation, he'd do anything or nothing, a gentleman of leisure, a pub-crawler. My mother and my real father quarrelled bitterly and I have indelible memories of childhood with appalling shouting rows, pulling us in either direction while we were present. As for my step-father, my mother was the dominant personality and supported him in every way. They had terrible fights too, every night of his life he went to the pub and came home drunk and he would start a drunken argument. (Thirties Woman P.)

Curry once wrote about a difficult boy who had a family that was deeply religious on the father's side and free-thinking on the mother's: it was, he felt, but one of the 'numerous incompatibilities that caused his parents to separate'. And, in quite a few cases, there occurred splits between partners who seemed poles apart, either in values or background, e.g. one father was from a theatrical background whereas the mother's father had been a colonial official; another couple diverged widely on how to treat their daughter — the mother was permissive, and the father aggressive and even violent; one father was a left-wing radical whereas the respondent's first step-mother was right wing (he remarried again to a woman of more radical leanings); one mother was an extremely sociable Conservative married to an unsociable Labour supporter; and another was from a public school, Forces, and business background while the mother detested his commercial ambitions; one respondent considered her father highly cultivated and literary but her mother a 'philistine'; and, finally, another father considered himself a writer, rather than a businessman which was his formal occupation, and left his wife to marry an artist.

From what we have been allowed to glimpse by our respondents the home background of a sizeable minority appear to contain deep, and sometimes irreconcilable, incompatibilities. The implications of this for the children are profound. Respondents spoke of lack of affection, of difficulties of communicating with one or other parent, of traumatic separations, of parents competing for their allegiance, of bewilderment at contradictory expectations, of parent-substitutes, and of tension, bitterness and the familiar emotional problems attendant upon 'broken' homes. Such a background has crucial consequences for why boarding was chosen, for the extent of emotional disturbance among the pupils, and for the pupils' adaptations to Dartington. However, the evidence on this section should not be taken to imply that the majority of children at any one time were from 'broken' homes though they may have constituted an influential and possibly self-conscious minority.

Socialisation

The subject of socialisation contains many complex ramifications and boasts an extensive literature (Klein 1965: Vol. 2). Here we only have space to skate over a few crude indicators of whether or not the Dartington parents conformed to a 'permissive' stereotype in socialisation techniques. Some 68 per cent of respondents, for instance, considered that their home backgrounds were 'permissive'. Furthermore, 32 per cent believed that their parents deliberately set out to avoid sanctions, and 35 per cent held that their parents espoused a belief in positive freedom as a socialising technique – which would be 'congruent' with the philosophy at Dartington.

Unfortunately, upper middle class socialisation is perhaps the least studied area although numerous memoirs, but thereby inherently unrepresentative (Ariès 1962: 216), could be cited for comparative purposes. These of course are generally of traditional practices in child-rearing whereas progressives we would expect to have counter-traditional attitudes. Thus some 38 per cent of respondents held that their parents did not believe in corporal punishment and a similar proportion of parents were said to have used rational persuasion as a method of control. Physical violence was rare and sanctions mentioned were either normative or else deprivation in some sense. All this suggests a tendency to a permissive, normative, rational, intra-punitive approach.

But what does characterise the evidence is the ambivalent position of our sample, half in and half out of the traditional upper middle class. Nannies and governesses, for instance, figured prominently in several interviews while in a very few cases a conventional working-class approach prevailed. Apart from the heterogeneity of the sample the evidence suggests that, while many of our parents might be united in their values on child-rearing, their individual approaches are such as to deny often the connotations of permissiveness. Coercive sanctions might be defined as ethically inappropriate and yet normatively effective. For example, some parents were said to have used biting sarcasm as a control.

There weren't any rules to keep, but sarcasm I think really if we misbehaved. In that sort of way they were very free and easy. The sort of thing my father would attack me on was to suddenly say I was a middle-class prig. (Fifties Woman MS.)

In other cases the parents' methods of control were variable, unpredictable, or contradictory, and sometimes father and mother used diametrically opposite sanctions. One respondent recalls of an extreme case, which does illustrate the possible gap between precept and practice:

Their sanctions were very variable and sometimes very cruel. For instance, I suppose we had been swearing once, we had a string of slightly dirty, off-beat kind of words, and they. put soap in our mouths, tied us to a chair in the garden, and took a photograph of us. But there were two standards in our family because my step-father swore like mad; he used to say crazy things like 'there's no such thing as rude'. It was a sort of point of pride that they never smacked us, but they would tie us to a chair and photograph us, you know, well blimey! (Thirties Woman MS.)

There are, too, three other strains in child-rearing which must be mentioned – a certain encouragement to precociousness, a fostering of early social independence, and a tendency to over-indulge. Frankly, some children were spoilt (or worse, alternately spoilt and neglected). A certain nonconformity – of dress, language, and behaviour – did lead with some to the condoning of expressions and acts which might be considered audacious or even outrageous in polite society.

I told my family, when they asked me why I wanted to leave the convent 'because the nuns are so damn silly!' This remark was greeted with delighted laughter. (Fifties Woman Postal Quest.)

Self-awareness was also encouraged together with a consciousness of being different.

I was probably a showpiece when I was in America because they were probably rather intrigued by this rather pretty English boy, well articulated in grammar . . . and a showpiece later on when I was at Dartington, perhaps being shown off to one's parents friends as an example of someone who was at Dartington. (Thirties Man MS.)

Some environments were indulgent and children emerged from these apparently extremely self-willed.

I was a spoilt brat, lying on the floor kicking and screaming if I didn't get my own way when when I was small, tantrummy type of thing. My father I didn't see an awful lot of and probably they spoiled me a bit when they did see me. I remember having terrible hysterics. Once in Harrods when I was about twelve, I remember absolute bedlam for hours on end. I thought the end of the world had come. (Fifties Man MS.)

For our purposes it is sufficient to note that our parents' child rearing practices range from upper middle class traditional to working-class traditional but with a majority that might be characterised as 'counter-traditional permissives'. While the idiosyncracies of some families tended to mitigate their permissiveness the notion of free development espoused by many parents was highly congruent with Dartington practice.

Parental values

Generally our respondents' parents were not church-goers, considered themselves left-wing, voted Labour without being particularly active politically, and were not deeply involved in clubs or other social organisations. But, again, we must emphasise that within the general picture there was considerable variety: for instance, probably few people would believe that Dartington in the thirties had two parents who were later arrested for suspected Fascist sympathies. At the other extreme a pilot respondent's mother has organised advertisements in a national newspaper calling for an end to the Vietnam war (and was arrested for demonstrating ouside the Soviet Embassy) while another pilot respondent recalled the feeling of shame when, as a child, she would remain seated with her mother at the theatre while the audience stood for the national anthem. Mothers have driven ambulances during the war, have helped with 'meals-on-wheels', have organised the local family planning association, have licked envelopes for the Communist Party, and have assisted refugees from the Spanish Civil War. Fathers have stood for local and parliamentary seats (usually unsuccessfully), one fought in Spain, another performed famine-relief work in Russia in the twenties, another wrote novels with a strong social message (one novel being a strong plea for the abolition of capital punishment), and others were active in the pacifist 'No Conscription League' during the First World War (one father displayed proudly a photograph of himself in Dartmoor where he had been sent for conscientious objection). The activists are, of course, a minority but there is a radical, humanitarian, crusading, cause-seeking thread running through the evidence.

In addition, many Dartington parents were, by occupation or temperament, actively creative and sought to encourage and stimulate their children intellectually and culturally. There were lots of vivid accounts of parents taking their children to the opera, to concerts, museums, the theatre, historic buildings, of musically or dramatically inclined parents, of impressive record collections, of reading aloud the classic novels, and of involvement in cultural societies. One man, for instance, recalled the highly cultivated atmosphere of his home:

I mean during the war the Amadeus Quartet formed, they formed almost in our house really, and you heard them playing their quartets every evening: and if ever there was an art show or something in the locality we all rushed to see it. Sometimes my father would come along with some Latin poem which he'd laboriously translated so that we could hear it. 'What, grow up without knowing Catullus!' he used to say. And then mother would sometimes read Goethe aloud to us. (Fifties Man MS.)

Finally, we would like to call attention once more to the ambivalences in some parental attitudes. One sixth of the Dartington parents were Conservative in the thirties but there were also a handful of radical parents who became over time disillusioned with the left and turned to conservatism.

My father was very Labour when I was born. He'd been out on the dole a lot in the slump. But now he's right-wing Tory and gets on the phone to us every now and then and rants about Labour and devaluation. (Fifties Woman MS.)

My father used to be left-wing and he was a communist at one point when everybody was, early nineteen twenties it must have been. Now I would say in ripe old age he's almost conservative. (Fifties Woman MS.)

There were also indications of certain tolerance limits to their radical stance with some parents retaining class biasses of which they were probably unconscious. Some, for instance, were highly critical of the narrowness, the parochialism, the prejudice, and the hypocrisy which they perceived in much of conventional middle-class existence and yet had their own blind-spots.

Mother obviously still has very strong caste feelings herself. I mean it always struck me as if it wasn't quite logical to preach socialism and that we were all equal, and then she would complain because one had a friend that wasn't quite out of the top-drawer. (Thirties Woman MS.)

Personalities

In reading the interviews and during investigations in the archives a striking feature of some parents' personalities attracted attention. The evidence on this is not representative as the amount of data from each parent in the school files differed widely but it does seem to reinforce the picture of a certain personality type or types that might be attracted to radical education. Firstly, there were dominant or possessive mothers. It is noticeable, for instance, that much of the school's correspondence is from and to mothers; furthermore our fifties cohort grew up during the war when evacuation and military service doubtless strengthened dependence on the mother.

I followed mummy around, I never saw my father. She was obviously looking for the right school for us, and she was always there in the background, she didn't just dump us and leave us. I think she she helped in schools and when we went to Dartington she built a house nearby. (Woman P.)

Also in many broken marriages the mother probably retains possession of the child. But one heard of dominating mothers who were almost excessively interested in their children: Dora Russell (Russell 1968: 96) for instance, adopted an extreme feminist position.

If she had children she would consider them entirely her own and would not be disposed to recognise the father's rights.

Some seemed to want to bring up their children with no interference, and sometimes that included the husband. There were cases too of the weak, ineffectual, submissive or even absentee father. One illustration sums up the evidence on this section:

You will no doubt have observed that when I refer to my parents I tend to talk about my mother. My father is a very quiet, retiring sort of person, who is very gentle and slow in his movements, and my mother is rather neurotic and has rather strong views about things and is inclined to behave in a dominant, bossy sort of way. (Fifties Woman MS.)

Secondly, and perhaps linked to the former personality trait, we can observe, almost paradoxically, the elements of an authoritarian disposition.

She was a very early Freudian and apparently took me to see Anna Freud. There were very definite things on how I wasn't to have toilet training . . . In fact mother had very very fixed ideas on what a free education should be. (Man Fifties P.)

There occurred a perfectionist streak which transmitted itself to the children — some set impossibly high standards for their children; one father sacked fourteen nannies whom he spied on continually; and another father demanded (much to his daughter's embarrassment) that his children should always take an asbestos rope fire escape with them when visiting friends. One respondent in his early thirties has never had a key to his home and still knocks on the door for this mother to let him in. With others the adherence to progressive educational values appears to have been rigid and dogmatic and suggests the authoritarian radical.

Thirdly, there was a core of parents with 'rebellious' traits; a tutor wrote of one girl that her father had been a rebel from his youth and that this had helped to make her so intellectually precocious.

Several parents exhibited bohemian symptoms, often in reaction to a traditional upbringing which they rejected. One father used to chase cows on horseback ('this is in Surrey by the way, not Texas'), another lived off rabbits, started a novel, and fought in Spain, while another rejected his religious background and became a conscientious objector. His daughter said of the latter:

All my father's family were clergymen and my father had a very violent reaction against them in the most bitter sort of way and this conscientious objection of his really came from all that. (Fifties Woman MS.)

Fourthly, there was a noticeable strain of parents, and especially mothers, with thwarted ambitions or a talent left unfulfilled.

My mother worked on the stage, you know musical comedy, 'Beggar's Opera', understudied at Glyndebourne, that sort of thing. But her career was wrecked by marriage. She tried to train seriously later on with her voice but she had terrible nerves. There was tremendous potential which she never used. (Thirties Man MS.)

Two main areas of non-fulfilment cropped up in particular – education and the arts. There were several tales of impoverished backgrounds hindering academic attainment and of parents seeking recompense academically through their children.

I think I was my mother's favourite because I was having the academic success she regarded as having relinquished by not having gone to university and so she identified with me wholly, and I think my sister suffered quite a lot from this. (Fifties Woman MS.)

But the strongest impression is of mothers with their aspirations to the stage, music, or the pen left unfulfilled, baulked or deflected by marriage.

Fifthly, and finally, some parents expressed an unwillingess for handling the child role, perhaps because of professional commitments or emotional preoccupations. Weinberg (1967: 174) uses Parson's example of the American middle class family's inability to handle the illness role as a parallel with the upper middle class English family's difficulty in coping with the 'child-role'. McConnell, of Eton, (1967: 170) hints broadly that the upper middle class child is perhaps best left to the boarding school where he can be catered for by specialists:

In very few cases do parents have the temperament, the knowledge and experience or the time to be ideal mothers and fathers. It is better for a boy to spend the school term in a house dedicated to meeting his needs than in a home where emotion may warp judgements, inexperience of the young may lead to mistakes, while pressure of business and social commitments may lead to neglect.

An example of unwillingness to cater for the child role was given by a Dartington respondent:

My mother I think was rather gay and she was always rushing off here and there. But she has said, quite frankly, that she simply isn't interested in small children and I can't really remember her as a small child at all. I was looked after entirely by this nurse except for one hour every evening, between five and six, when I was with my father. (Fifties Woman MS.)

One thinks here particularly of the conflict between domesticity and the demands, strains, and tensions of intellectual and creative work: in such professions there often occur elements that may militate against conventional parenthood, e.g. travel, long or variable hours of work, deep commitment to work, the need for a high degree of concentration, the necessity for peace and quiet, and, at times, a demanding social life. This was perfectly exemplified by one parent who wrote to the school, that if forced at pistol point to choose between work and family, the choice would have to be work 'because she would die without it'. The very achievements of certain parents could constitute a handicap for children and a tutor wrote of one extremely diffident boy that he feared he could never emulate his father's brilliance.

The congruent home

In many of the sample's family backgrounds there were numerous examples of nonconformity and counter-traditionalism in relation to the prevalent values of England in the twenties and thirties. This sub-group of parents would approximate closely to an ideal type progressive parent — say radical, permissive, and free-thinking — and we would anticipate that they would provide a home background highly 'congruent' with the values of a progressive school. One respondent, for instance, described the close fit between his home and the school:

There was no element of discordancy in it for me. For instance, the school filled up steadily with Jewish refugees while I was there and my earliest political memory was knitting woollen squares for Basques. And all this was absolutely in keeping with my parents' views. So in an intellectual sense the school was the same as my family background. (Thirties Man MS.)

Another recalled how the children of NW3 made their presence felt in a humorous manner:

Then Jason used to get up at supper and shout 'three cheers for the Hampstead Association!' and they'd give three cheers quickly before everyone else could drown them with shouting. (Fifties Woman MS.)

Using three indicators — socialisation, political preference, and church attendance — as predictors of whether or not the home was congruent we found that just less than half, i.e. twenty-six or 43 per cent of homes, were ideally congruent with progressive ideals. Conversely, the remaining thirty-four, or 57 per cent of homes, had one or more indicators that the parents had some measure of 'incongruency' with progressivism, e.g. the father voted Conservative or the mother was a regular church-goer. In other words, our sample's parents were by no means all ideal typical progressive parents.

Indeed, if we look at comparative evidence from interviews carried out with samples of former pupils from two other schools – Badminton and Bryanston – then we can see clearly that both these moderately progressive institutions attracted parents who fitted more closely the conventional, upper middle class stereotype. For example, many of the fathers had been to single-sex, public, boarding schools and were occupationally more likely to be in the 'Organisational' category than the Dartington fathers, e.g. banker, underwriter, shipping agent, and prison supervisor. Bryanston, for instance, would provide such a parent with a fairly humane and cultivated environment, with individual academic guidance, for his son, yet still basically within the public school and establishment fold. Generally the 'control' children had more settled educational records than our Dartington sample and reported far less disturbance in their backgrounds. Later we can compare the Badmintonians and Bryanstonians as adults with the evidence from the main sample.

Three points suggest themselves from our evidence. Firstly, that the somewhat neurotic intellectuals who figure prominently in the popular mythology of the progressive parent comprised probably only a minority of the parents who patronised Dartington – though doubtless a highly visible and articulate minority. Secondly, the 'incongruent' parent may well have chosen a progressive school because it provided some special services not considered part of orthodox or traditional education's aim, e.g. an emphasis on cultural–creative pursuits, individual academic attention without undue pressure, or a propensity for dealing with the difficult child. But, thirdly, while the 'Problem Child' and the 'Problem Parent' (A. S. Neill wrote two books with exactly these titles) tend to attract attention, there are fairly relatively conventional parents who patronise the progressive schools. Their children are likely to find it easier to fit into polite bourgeois society than those rampantly progressive children who display the symbolic stigmata of a radical education and a 'liberated' home background.

Chapter Four

The children

Bertrand Russell gave me the following advice on running a progressive school. 'Unless you can't avoid it, have no parents. They're a damn nuisance!' (Recorded Interview with L. K. Elmhirst.)

Why Dartington?

What reasons did the respondents themselves spontaneously give for their parents' selection of a progressive school? Some 37 per cent believed that their parents had chosen Dartington primarily because of their commitment to the progressive educational philosophy. Other reasons included its outdoor aspects; the child's health; that the parents knew Curry, the Elmhirsts, or members of staff; the parents lived locally or worked for the Dartington estate; evacuation during the war to the countryside or parents living abroad; that it was the best school of a series visited by the parents; and that a relative or sibling was already at Dartington or another progressive school. In only three cases, all of boy's parents, was coeducation mentioned as a possible factor.

But perhaps the three most interesting findings are, firstly, that 50 per cent mentioned their own educational difficulties at previous schools as a contributory factor to their parents' choice. Secondly, almost half the parents were divided on Dartington, with mothers as main proponents in ratio 4:3 to fathers. Early on Amabel Williams-Ellis (Blewitt 1934: iv) had expressed this dilemma:

A very common situation at present is that the child's mother favours a modern and the father – particularly if the child is a boy – a traditional education.

Lambert (1971a: Chap. IV) documents the more crucial role played today by mothers as opposed to fathers in the selection of a progressive school. One female respondent remarked:

I did once ask Daddy whether he would have sent us to Dartington if we had been boys and he said no. He thinks we ought to have gone to Shrewsbury and I asked why. He said that the boys didn't play enough games at Dartington and their hair was too long. (Fifties Women MS.)

And thirdly, only 12 per cent mentioned a 'broken' home. However, the latter may well have been an important latent reason for choosing boarding (though

45

not necessarily progressive boarding). Lambert *et al.* (1971a: Chap. IV) make the point that a case of social need at a prep. or public school would probably have boarded anyway (and many prep. schools have orphaned, deprived, or damaged middle class children) where a comparable pupil at a progressive or state school may not have boarded except for social need.

We estimate that 70 per cent of our sample had some measure of disturbance in their background either before or during their period at Dartington. Frequently this arose from a 'broken home' − divorce or separation of parents, geographical separation, evacuation, death of a parent, parent interned, or a serious illness in the family. There were, too, stories of difficult emotional relationships with parents; of parents suffering severe emotional or social upheaval because of marital, occupational, or social problems; and of symptoms of maladjustment arising in respondents because of these. One respondent, for example, gave a picture of an upper class home, where material privilege was matched by emotional deprivation and where the parents' views on radical education accorded with their personal needs, which is worth quoting at length.

I was boarded at the age of three where I was universally hated and I lived for the holidays − I sometimes have almost total recall about it when I'm under LSD − so as bleak and forlorn as any child's could be short of beating. I wasn't physically punished, everyone was nice, everybody smiled and the environment was an ice-box emotionally speaking. A succession of nannies and boarding schools. I remember temper tantrums, being shut in my room, and breaking up my toys but probably most of the telling-offs would have been done by one of the governesses. In fact, I remember trying to get at my parents because they were so ungettable at and one time I could get them was early in the morning so I used to wake them at five in the morning and that used to get them angry. But that was the only spark I ever got − the only time they were ever there! . . . Their ideas on education were a mixture of belief − my parents were friends of the Russells and believed this was the right thing, the message of the twentieth century − and also it was quite useful to get rid of me when my parents didn't get on particularly well. They were later divorced. Their views on the social importance of education probably fitted very conveniently with what their personal needs were. They were very good and honourable parents within their own very stark limitations − mother was a depressive and father was extremely self-centered and left us and became engaged with several mistresses. They meant me well in a specious sort of way. But mother was too depressive to live with people and father was off with various popsies. (Thirties Man MS.)

Let us examine some other examples. One girl's parents disappeared in the concentration camps of Eastern Europe and she herself spent several years in hiding; another girl's mother was an alcoholic, a morphine addict, promiscuous 'to the point of nymphomania', and died in a mental hospital; one boy's mother escaped from Singapore but his father was captured and interned by the Japanese; one father who worked abroad was thrown out of the country after being threatened with execution during a revolution; one mother tried to commit suicide after a broken mariage and the near death of a baby son; and another mother remarried to a schizophrenic who then lost his job. Some of these are extreme examples of gross disruption in the family background accentuated by war but there were also one or two cases of 'complete' homes which were emotional ice-boxes.

Drawing upon evidence in the interviews and the school files we have crudely graded the perceived effects on respondents in terms of symptoms of maladjustment: 13 per cent appear to have had symptoms of maladjustment to a considerable extent, 43 per cent to a lesser degree, but a further 13 per cent (i.e. six men and two women) exhibited behaviour difficulties of varying kinds at previous schools which did not amount to maladjustment. Curry always tried to see both parents and the child before accepting them in order to appraise their suitability. He complained continually that some parents concealed the child's complete history until after acceptance and that it would take several days of interviews and observation to have a realistic impression of the child and his or her relationship with the parents. (Headmaster's Reports, DHRO.) In Ash (1969: 33) Dr Winnicott, a child psychiatrist, admitted that he and his colleagues lied in order to get difficult children into schools. Several contributors to Child (1962: 126–8) disclaimed that the progressive school was suited to take any but a small proportion of difficult children and there appeared to be a desire to erase the image of progressive schools as schools for the disturbed.

The idea that 'this kind of school is very good for "problem" children, but not for normal ones (like my Giles, or Sarah)' would, if generally maintained be utterly destructive of the whole project. Because of its essential normalcy . . . the school can perform its social duty and help along a very few of the halt and lame.

Obviously there were devotees of progressive education among the respondents' parents – the readers of Neill, Curry, and Russell – but our evidence suggests that there were powerful 'negative' reasons for parents choosing Dartington. Reinforcement of this view can also be inferred from the question as to what were their parents' expectations of the school; 65 per cent, by far the largest proportion, mentioned 'personal happiness and/or adjustment'. Instrumental ends, such as academic work, career, skills, and so on, did not figure so predominantly as personal, 'expressive' ends. This could imply that the concern over 'happiness/adjustment' arose because of previous unhappiness; in addition it does seem almost to place the burden for the child's well-being on the shoulders of the school. Ideally, the home and the school should be in tandem to ensure the child's happiness but this was not always the case, while the parents' expectations of the school were noticeably diffuse.

The incipient conflict that can arise between the home and the boarding school emerges in parents' correspondence to the school. Indeed, some of the early progressive schools almost sought to replace the family and some extremely early boarding was encouraged as a result. Dora Russell expressed this (Blewitt 1934: 29):

We believe that it is of the utmost importance to the child to be able, as early as possible, to function as an individual in a group of individuals of his own age, and that a wider atmosphere than that of the family is needed by the child in our closely knit society where cooperation and mutual help should replace the old competition of family against family and group against group.

Unfortunately I cannot quote from the vast number of letters in the archives (it is almost as if Curry preferred writing to parents rather than seeing them) but there are indications that parents' initial congruency with progressive values could weaken as the child grew older and instrumental considerations began to obtrude. Lambert (Ash 1969: 225) claims that public schools 'regard parents as a nuisance, clients to be treated diplomatically, but escorted off the premises as soon as possible'. At times mutual recrimination can arise between the parents and progressive schools as the latter often usurps some of the functions of the family while the latter almost uses the parents as scapegoats. A. S. Neill, for example (Russell 1968: 182) claimed:

My pupils are the products of ignorant and savage parents.

Differences of opinion arose particularly over academic progress. One father expressed doubts over the ability of a progressive education to achieve the high academic standards he desired in his child. He felt that the desire for knowledge was not natural and that children were grateful for some compulsion to help them learn. Unless the children received training in the art of focussing their knowledge, they would be handicapped in any society, be it socialist or capitalist. Two respondents also expressed their parents' concern over their academic achievements:

The last few years Daddy began nagging us, saying 'you must pass your exams'. I only passed Art. Father was furious because he spent so much on our education and my sister hadn't done very well either. And we turned on him and said 'Well, you shouldn't have sent us to a place like Dartington if you expected us to work hard'. (Fifties Woman MS.)

Well I was very late learning to read and very bad at writing and shocking at spelling and I don't believe I learnt to read until I was about ten and my parents were of course worried by that stage. They've said since that had they been able to get me in anywhere else they would have taken me away from Dartington. (Fifties Man MS.)

Previous schools

If the evidence on this section could be considered truly authentic then it would serve as a searing indictment of traditional education. For almost 80 per cent of our respondents were unhappy in some degree at the schools attended before Dartington – 29 per cent very unhappy (men outnumbering women 2:1 in this category), 40 per cent were somewhat unhappy, and 10 per cent were mildly unhappy. We are, of course, conjuring up memories of between twenty and forty years ago and that data is fraught with the danger of bias; particularly as the traditional school was somewhat derided at Dartington and this may have caused some children to conjure up retrospective criticisms. But, even if we approach these accounts with caution, there is no doubting their heartfelt tone.

Our respondents were relatively early starters at school – a third of the sample had attended some form of school before the age of four. If we take the statutory school starting age of five as a convenient criterion then 50 per cent of the respondents were already at school. With regard to boarding, 22 per cent of our main sample went away to boarding school before the age of seven or 48 per cent before the age of ten. Generally respondents had been first to a small nursery or kindergarten. On average, respondents had been to three schools before Dartington but with 23 per cent having attended a greater number. For instance, one woman claimed to have been to fourteen schools, though this was more than matched by a pilot interviewee who had been to seventeen, while one man experienced a succession of schools.

Yes. And my mother was determined I should go to a paying school and then she used not to like the schools we went to and we moved again. And so we flitted in and out of schools with quite monotonous regularity. I didn't like changing schools and I used to make a hell of a fuss every time I changed schools and take a long time to settle down. But I used to be terribly good at being ill in the winter, usually from about October to March, and so my education, apart from all these schools, was interrupted by a tremendous amount of illness. I had pneumonia, ear trouble, chicken pox and so on. Sometimes I was away from school for a good deal of the winter. And then my family are terribly fussy about food and I hated school lunches. I used to hate Tuesdays and Thursdays which were special days for school lunches and I used to frequently rebel about this and not want to go. (Fifties Man MS.)

If we include all previous formal schools then most of the main sample have been exclusively privately educated – none were exclusively state educated who had been to more than one school before Dartington. Most had had some experience of coeducation – 55 per cent had been to both mixed and single-sex schools, 33 per cent to coeducational schools only, and 12 per cent to single-sex schools only. Some 43 per cent had been to day schools only. Although the whole range of progressive schools was mentioned – Summerhill, Bedales,

Telegraph Hill, Hurtwood, Burgess Hill, Fortis Green, Lane End, the Malting House, St George's Harpenden, King Alfred's, the Town and Country School, and the Park School (Buffalo, USA) – only three respondents were educated solely at progressive schools. Of these one attended a Montessori nursery, Telegraph Hill, King Alfred's, and Dartington; and another went to Telegraph Hill, Summerhill, and Dartington. In addition there were eight children who were educated entirely at Dartington.

Some of the children seem to have embarked on an odyssey through conventional education which they could not adapt to or which their parents continually found wanting. Either due to personality problems or a permissive home they found the traditional school difficult to tolerate and they experienced something of a profound culture shock on entering its portals. In what areas did problems arise?

One of the main bugbears seemed to be the imposition of traditional authority on the individual to which many of our respondents were not acquainted and the harshness of which seemed difficult for them to stomach. Thus 27 per cent mentioned problems of discipline or authority, 19 per cent disliked the 'regimentation', and 13 per cent objected to corporal punishment. Compulsory sport, friction with staff, religious instruction, formal examinations, and undue academic pressure were other stumbling blocks. Bullying, teasing, discomfort, homesickness, lack of friends, and psychosomatic symptoms were also mentioned. One boy lost weight during term time at his prep. school.

When aged eight, nearly nine, I went to a boarding school, where I suffered greatly. The corporal punishment wasn't all that much worry to me, but the very restrictive regimented atmosphere was extremely troublesome. I lived on a farm in the holidays where I could enjoy tremendous freedom and I hated the restrictive rather callous atmosphere of this traditional place. It was very rough, there was a Latin master there (this is highly slanderous, I think the poor man is still alive) but he was a notable bully who used to work himself into a rage. I've seen him knock a boy head over heels backwards and hit his head on account of an impediment in the boy's speech. This was the extreme but I didn't get on at all well actually. I was very much in my shell and it was a result of all this that I was sent to Dartington, by my mother's efforts, at the age of twelve. I mean I used to lose weight during term and I obviously felt it a bit more keenly than the others. (Thirties Man MS.)

Several interviews were prime examples of the self-fulfilling prophecy whereby severe treatment only serves to magnify the symptom it is meant to eradicate.

In these last two schools were very traditional disciplinarians, with lots of caning and strapping and beating, and I think temperamentally I'm a coward, I'm frightened of physical punishment. They would beat you for academic errors and I got more and more frightened of school work. It got so I was frightened to make a stab at things and when I came back to England I'd got a pretty awful anti-school thing. (Fifties Man MS.)

Another boy, and it was the boys who seemed to suffer most, accidently shot a boy in the foot on the rifle range and was thereafter persistently victimised by the staff. The strength of one case of injustice still ranked nearly forty years afterwards (and despite the tolerance with which Dartington was meant to imbue him!).

My feelings about physical violence at the school were very marked.

[Interviewer: Bullying?]

Not so much bullying but I can remember being severely beaten by the headmaster in the most sadistic manner, cold bloodedly. And in a way I've never forgiven him even to this day. I think I'd knock his teeth in if I got a chance today. It was just about as opposite the other end of the pole as Dartington. And this was because I didn't turn up for cricket or something, some bloody stupid thing like that.

[Interviewer: Was it a formal beating?]

Oh yes, bloody pants down in the headmaster's office. (Thirties Man MS.)

These reactions may well be symptoms of the insecurity, anxiety, and aggressiveness that can accompany maladjustment. Equally, there is a patent incompatibility between the permissive, child-centred home of the liberal intelligentsia – where the child is habituated to individual attention, nonconforming behaviour, and to questioning the accepted – and the authoritarian, hierarchical, group-oriented traditional school. Thus in twenty-one out of thirty-seven cases of unhappiness the previous school concerned was ultra-traditional and often a single-sex boarding establishment in the public school mould. One boy, for example, survived but one term at an allegedly barbaric institution where he witnessed some savage bullying which reduced two boys to the status of being almost 'sub-human'.

I expected it to be (a) reasonable but (b) unpleasant. I got there and discovered it wasn't just unpleasant; it was absolutely insane and totally unreasonable. I tried to make friends but it was impossible because they were all maniacs. None of the laws of human society that I'd grown accustomed to applied ... The person I was ceased to exist. To put it bluntly I was shattered and a complete mess and it took me ten years to sort it out ... Later I went to 'MacIver Academy' [traditional boys public school emphasising self-discipline] which I disapproved of morally. I thought the ethos was (a) very strong and (b) bullshit from top to toe. One hundred per cent bullshit. In fact it taught me to lie quite well; I realised you should lie all the time. I'm proud I never had a single cold bath there and you were supposed to have one every day and fill it in on your plan. I learned to be dishonest and if I hadn't left 'MacIver' for Dartington I might have ended up well armoured for the rat-race. (Fifties Man MS.)

In another case, the respondent captured the ambivalence of the bohemian

intellectual who disapproves of traditional boarding but can see little alternative to it for his children.

They did not visit very often. Nor were their visists particularly agreeable when they
had done so, because they sought to impose their own ideas – I'm talking now about
'Bushgrove Prep.' [bleak traditional prep. school] – as to what a school should be like
and 'Bushgrove' wasn't at all what they thought a school should be like. But they
weren't going to do anything particular about it. Therefore, their reaction was to
rather behave as if they were visiting a different school than the one they were visiting,
and visiting a different boy than the one they had as their son. A rather procrustean attitude coming perhaps in rather unconventional clothes and wondering why things
were so ponderous and why one perhaps was a bit nervous, not realising that they
were off to London or America and leaving one behind to the gloom of the corridors
of 'Bushgrove'. (Thirties Man MS.)

But then four respondents were highly discontented at their previous
progressive school. One boy at 'Dunwood' (a small radical progressive
school) found himself at the bottom of a savage pecking order and retired to
the security and comfort of his bed.

But the school was grossly incompetent in terms of management and the place was
cold and uncomfortable. Nobody would curtail anyone else so there was an absolutely unremitted hierarchy and if you were at the bottom of the pecking order, as I was,
you got pecked chum, and pecked bloody hard. I was bullied bloody often and I had a
horrible time. For two years I took myself to bed at four-thirty every evening after tea
because it was the nicest place to be. It was safer and more comfortable in bed than
anywhere else. (Thirties Man MS.)

A girl spent many weekends at 'Brambledown' [a large coeducational
progressive school] weeding the garden as a punishment; another girl
experienced the 'dirt and chaos' of war-time 'Dunwood' where she suffered
from malnutrition and where her unkempt hair became matted and had to be
cropped off. The traditional school undoubtedly exacerbates the symptoms of
maladjustment which many of our respondents exhibited but it is also evident
that these could also manifest themselves in a progressive environment.

Probably some twenty-three respondents (i.e. 38 per cent of the sample)
were withdrawn or were asked to leave their school prior to Dartington and
this inability of theirs to survive in their previous schools (or of their parents to
accept fully their ethos and regime) must be a highly significant factor in selecting Dartington. These histories of interrupted education, bullying, beatings,
competitive games, physical discomfort, learning difficulties, and of
emotional and psychosomatic disorders will have an important bearing on
respondents' adaptations to Dartington. In a way it was a cruel irony that the
children of the new era often suffered from enuresis, eczema, asthma, tics,
speech defects, nightmares, temper tantrums, sleep-walking, food fads, and

other disorders. Finally, there was one respondent who proved remarkably resilient:

I went to a Dickensian prep. school in the West Indies. It was barbaric with lots of flogging. (Man Fifties P.)

He also said that he enjoyed it.

Assimilation to Dartington

Most respondents (58 per cent) commenced at Dartington before the age of eleven, normally between eight and twelve, but with a few latecomers (two started at fifteen) and 17 per cent starting before the age of six (three at age two and four at age three). Nowadays, the average age for starting at progressive schools is eleven (Lambert *et al.* 1971: Chap. IV). They arrived from diverse backgrounds – some from broken homes, some from abroad, some from day schools, and some from public schools. Dartington was at pains to select families which would identify with the progressive values and ideally there should have been no discordance between the home and the school. Yet, some 35 per cent of our sample said that they had experienced some difficulty in adjusting to Dartington – 12 per cent considerable difficulty, and 23 per cent some lesser difficulty. Problems arose in relation to their previous schools and home background, some to the strangeness of this novel environment, and others to the boarding situation 'per se'.

The atmosphere that these children were moving into was intimate, neo-familial, warm, welcoming, but relatively unstructured compared to most schools. One girl contrasted it favourably with her previous progressive school, 'Brambledown':

I loved it right from the start. One felt it was a sensible school – one was sort of treated as a human being. I liked everything about it and for all the three years I was there I loved it. Well, I think perhaps I was slightly special as my mother had recently died and there was nobody at home. And Dartington became my home and I used to look forward in the holidays to going back to school. I think I was terribly lucky that I was at Dartington. It was such a super, marvellous place. And, on my God, after 'Brambledown' not to be regimented and not to have bells ringing all the time. (Thirties Woman.)

Furthermore we can contrast the reactions of two contemporaries. One arrived at Dartington from an artistic home and accepted it as to the manner born.

I can't remember questioning what went on in Dartington. All I have is a memory of accepting it. It seemed to me quite natural in fact. I can't remember arriving at Dartington and suddenly having a new-found freedom, having been let out of an old time school, but then my home life wasn't all that different to Dartington in any case. My parents didn't lead a conventional restricted life and they weren't conventional or restricted people so a lot of the attitudes and opinion expressed at Dartington must have been quite natural right from the word go. My parents were progressive left-wing in attitude. (Thirties Man MS.)

Whereas another boy, arriving from a harsh prep. school and a divided home, expressed his wonderment at the openness of the children.

[Interviewer: What was your first impression on arriving at Dartington?]

My first impression was when I met the school on the train at Paddington, about the extraordinary open friendliness of the children. The way they came to meet me, so that this reserve and suspicion and hidden self-centredness that was characteristic of the prep. school was absent, and I felt the extraordinary openness and friendliness of the children and their self-confidence. There was the incredible difference in atmosphere of the school train, one of people being shipped off to the concentration camps and one of the children going off on a holiday. And, when I got there, there was an incredibly different atmosphere, everything was strange, rather beautiful, and they were fairly free with the money, the food was extra-ordinarily good, they couldn't possibly have afforded to keep it up. It was very exciting. It was like going to Paradise after the place I had been at. (Thirties Man MS.)

Some children experienced a release from previous tensions and often psychosomatic symptoms disappeared in the benign and healthy environment. This release was symbolised by the expressions which people used to describe it – e.g. 'Dartington was my salvation', 'it was like passing through the Iron Curtain', 'it was Mecca', 'I thought it was wonderful, like paradise', 'here I was in Ginger Bread House', and so on. For some boys in particular the permissive tone coming straight after say an authoritarian, single-sex institution, proved too inviting and it was more or less accepted that they would let off steam for a term or two.

[Interviewer. How did you take to Dartington on arrival?]

Oh I went berserk. I was a hoodlum for the first term. I was pretty amazed, the first thing I think I saw was a pet hut being set on fire and burnt down with people standing rocking it, and I was pretty saddened by this, I think I was appalled and amazed at first. And then, later that term, I took part in some nasty bits of vandalism. But after that first term I think I simmered down a bit and started doing some work and really quite enjoying school for about the first time. As far as I was concerned it was the real sort of beginning of the cure I think to my anti-school attitude. (Fifties Man MS.)

Progressives have often insisted as far as possible on early boarding and on selecting homes compatible with its values. Their arch rival, the public school, reduces the potentially disruptive influence of new intakes by relying on the long and thorough anticipatory socialisation to its values both in the upper middle class home and in the preparatory schools. Kalton (1966: 27) for example, cites evidence that 88 per cent of entrants to independent HMC boarding schools have at some time attended an independent preparatory school. The progressive school can rarely, if ever, anticipate such unanimity and consequently it is threatened to a greater extent by the cyclical necessity to resocialise new entrants to its unorthodoxy. At Dartington, for example, out of sixty respondents only seven had attended a progressive school immediately prior to Dartington (although an additional seven were educated solely at Dartington). In other words 77 per cent of our main sample arrived at Dartington from an orthodox educational background.

To test some of the assumptions on assimilation to progressive education we looked more closely at those who found some difficulty in adjusting to Dartington (35 per cent of the sample) compared to those who claimed that they had no problems of assimilation. Ease of assimilation did not appear to be related to a significant degree to whether the home was 'congruent' or 'incongruent'; if anything a slightly higher proportion of those from congruent homes mentioned difficulties as those from incongruent homes. Equally it appeared that a greater proportion of early arrivals (ten years of age or under ten being the median age for arrival) had problems in adjusting than those who came late. In effect both these findings seem to cast doubt on the advantages of early arrival from a congruent home.

But some respondents differed from others in a significant respect which may have overridden the two factors already mentioned; namely, some of the children were maladjusted and the problems they described may well be symptoms of their basic disturbance rather than evidence of assimilation of the nonconforming Dartington subculture. For instance, of the twenty-six respondents from 'congruent' homes sixteen had symptoms of maladjustment and this would help to explain the anomaly that a congruent home did not appear to be an advantage with regard to assimilation. Indeed, generally those pupils with evidence of maladjustment found it more difficult to adjust to Dartington that those without maladjustment and it is arguable that their problems would have manifested themselves in almost any environment.

The Junior and Middle Schools

The average age of the sample starting at Dartington was 9.5 years which meant that most of them began their career in one of the three boarding houses at Aller Park on the estate. Each of these was designed for about fifteen children, all of whom had their own room, and there was two resident, female house-staff – a housemother and a cook. Generally the child's pre-adolescent years at Dartington were characterised by games, play, pets, gangs, exploring the environment, very little academic pressure, and maternal housemothers.

The concept associated with this period in the Dartingtonian's career was that of the 'fallow period'. Primarily the pre-Foxhole (the Senior School) years were ones of shedding the old persona, perhaps inhibited by a number of years at a traditional school, and socialising to the new progressive culture for those whose background had not provided it. The Junior or Middle School, then, served largely as an assimilating institution for Foxhole so that release of tension, growth of self-confidence and sociability, and familiarity with freedom were given precedence over academic work. For such reasons parents were encouraged to send their children as early as possible and direct entry to Foxhole while not unknown, was frowned upon.

There was usually a pet-shed and the keeping of pets was an important latent source of affectivity; once some children looked after a motherless lamb from the farm and one girl cared for some goats but normally the pets were hamsters, rabbits, guinea pigs, and mice. Before the war there were a number of horses and a riding instructress at the school while, both before and after the war, one or two children kept their own ponies or horses.

For much of the time life at Dartington during these initiatory years appears to have been idyllic. There was a strong emphasis on outdoor activities, sleeping in tents during the summer, and playing in the woods. Other pursuits included swimming, riding bicycles, model-making, constructing trolleys, cricket, football, and building tunnels in the woods. And in some respects the junior and intermediate years of education appear to be its most attractive – it tends to have a freshness, a spontaneity, and an unpretentiousness that can contrast with the senior years.

At the same time it is clear that academic work could suffer in favour of other activities and that this could make for a certain lack of groundwork in the basic subjects.

I was constantly in the workshops, very much. Or running about all over the countryside – there were lots of woods, and the timetable wasn't full, so we built huts in the woods – and it was rather difficult to get back to classes. (Fifties Man MS.)

In retrospect, the Junior or Middle Schools appear very much as an interlude, a playground for working off repressions and inhibitions and growing accustomed to freedom, before the more cerebral atmosphere of the Senior School.

You were told that the Junior School was where you worked off steam and that you took academic education seriously when you got to Foxhole. (Thirties Man MS.)

Chapter Five

Social control

I wonder if Bill [Curry] would have been honest enough with himself to become a headmaster for maladjusted children because that in effect was what Dartington was. And the better boarding schools for maladjusted children were as near Dartington as they could get. (Thirties Woman MS.)

Disturbed and difficult children

Before turning to the question of social control and authority in the progressive school, it is necessary to consider the nature of the maladjustment among the children at Dartington because this has important consequences for the amount of disturbed behaviour in the school, its effects on other children, and for the attitudes towards treating it. We have seen that just over half our respondents (56 per cent, or thirty-four out of sixty) had some elements of disturbance in their background which had led to symptoms of maladjustment in varying degrees. Unfortunately it is impossible to assess accurately the proportion of disturbed or difficult children at Dartington in any one period because there is no systematic evidence available.

But there is no doubt that Dartington, and the progressive school in general, attracted not only the 'normal' child but also the gifted, the eccentric, the temperamental, and the disturbed. One father, for instance, forthrightly paraded the talents of his son in a letter to Curry and insisted that in no way was he a problem child; the only difficulty, he added, was that the boy was a musical genius. Yet being gifted may constitute one form of maladjustment; for this child had an IQ of 169 and yet was reported to be obstinate, clumsy, and was unable to use a knife and fork efficiently at the age of eleven. Indeed, from the tutors' individual reports on children it is clear that nervous and habit disorders were common among some pupils, as were learning difficulties. Curry (1947: 190) himself recorded difficulties with the immediate post-war generation of children.

The children from overseas taken back after war were somehow emotionally deprived, in a sense stunted, and many of them difficult.

From the files it appears that behaviour disorders occurred in a small minority of cases and psychotic behaviour in one or two extreme cases. Organic disorders were very rare but not unknown. There appears to have been slightly

57

more cases of behaviour disorder in the thirties and mid-forties than in the early fifties when more cases of psychotic behaviour appear in the reports. In an extreme case two boys were sent to another progressive school, but this was largely designed to remove them from unfortunate home circumstances. However, Curry did mention bullying which seemed to reflect a streak of almost sadistic cruelty in the family and an interest in pornography that amounted to that of the adult connoisseur. In another extreme case an eight-year-old boy was involved in a stabbing incident that could have been serious; Cyril Burt and Susan Isaacs were consulted and the latter wrote that analysis was evidently required.

There were too the eccentrics who posed no real threat to the community – one boy collected flies to eat, another played Oriental music for hours on end on a wind-up gramophone, one threatened to fly, another rode around the estate on a Shetland pony brandishing an air pistol, while yet another crotcheted 'an extraordinary garment, almost like chain-mail, with a pair of eye-holes and nothing else, which he used to wear when he was bicycling'. The interesting point is that so many of the eccentric and the disturbed were boys. Finally, we must touch briefly on the attitude of the other pupils and the staff to the difficult children.

There can be no doubt that, because of its lenient regime, its psychological orientation, its permissive academic methods, its physical freedoms, and its sympathetic treatment of the individual child, Dartington served as a benign, therapeutic environment which, in most cases, reduced manifest disturbance in the child. One heard too of enuresis, weight loss, eczema, and respiratory complaints improving after arrival. Furthermore, it was undeniable that the children generally displayed a great tolerance towards the deviants; or, it might be truer to say, they accepted bizarre, idiosyncratic behaviour as almost normal.

Everyone was very, very tolerant. People could be extremely eccentric and go around breaking all the windows and you didn't think 'how awful'. You wouldn't be appalled by it, you'd be slightly amused and think, 'oh, he'll have to pay for that', not 'what terrible behaviour!' They could become very popular actually but in a slightly joking way and turn themselves slightly into fools, sort of play the part a bit and become quite popular. (Fifties Woman MS.)

Except in a few instances, the bullying and teasing which such vulnerable children might have attracted in the traditional school was notably absent. One man explained why this was so:

There was a bumptious, prickly, aggressive little boy who used to provoke you until you wanted to hit him. He used to goad older boys like me and I often felt like giving him a thick ear. But Bill would always have generated this view that bullying was very much disapproved of so that you were not in fact morally free to hit a smaller child. (Thirties Man MS.)

Another man expressed the feeling of collective indignation when one small boy, who among other things had been shot at with an air-gun, had been mistreated:

I organised a sort of vigilante thing after 'Jasper' was bullied. I was so angry, and we tried to get 'Clive' and some others who had pulled him upstairs, and hung him over the stairs by his heels. We tried to chase them but they were hidden, luckily for them, by some girls. I mean we were in a very violent mood. I'd got the bigger boys to chase them. (Fifties Man P.)

Curry, for example, tried to induce tolerance by discussing the problem of the bully and what he called 'the murderee' or professional victim.

People were fairly benign to these difficult people. Curry would talk to us and we would read his books and we realised that the bully was obviously not a happy person. But it's not always easy to make kids understand if something of theirs is stolen. (Fifties Woman MS.)

He also believed in the therapeutic value of not interfering unduly.

There was one boy who had a terrible temper and he used to throw himself downstairs and lash at his cupboard and so on. He used to get these terrible tantrum things. I always remember rushing to Curry, 'he'll kill himself!, he'll kill himself!'. You know, really worried. He would say 'For goodness sake, let the boy alone. He will be all right'. He was obviously a rather unusual person but we tended to accept them. (Fifties Woman MS.)

Additionally, the progressive schools tends to recognise the young person's right to a specifically adolescent role, aspects of which such as noise, aggression, mood change and emotional sexual life, seem to conflict continually with the control processes of more orthodox schools. A certain amount of rough and tumble, that would have caused alarm elsewhere, was simply accepted at Dartington and Curry (Bonham-Carter 1958: 172) hinted that the provision of furniture, for example, should take this into account:

Dorothy Elmhirst took a keen personal interest in the choice of such thing as carpets, curtains, furniture and crockery, and her own unerring taste ensured that the initial equipment was most beautifully selected. In each house there was a common room which we furnished very agreeably as a sitting-room. Attached to this common room was a kitchenette for which was chosen a set of delightful Swedish crockery, a different colour for each house . . . [the blue cups] lasted, I fear, a very short time. The furniture in the common room too, lasted but a short time. I do not mean that it was deliberately damaged, but just that children are rough and careless. Here, also, replacements were on a cheaper and more utilitarian scale.

But that symptoms of maladjustment, real or imitative, posed considerable problems for the maintenance of social order will become clear below. For the dilemma that this minority of children poses for the progressive school is that they both need a progressive school and, at the same time, are most likely to break it up (Ash 1969: 169).

Responsibility, authority, and sanctions

At Dartington a group of boys broke seventy windows on one occasion by throwing potatoes through them. If Waller (1965: 10) has described the orthodox school as being in a state of perilous equilibrium, how more true is this of the progressive school? In fact, to many people's surprise, the progressive school is a highly self-regulating, law abiding community with tranquillity more in evidence than dissension. It engenders a good deal of respect for individual liberty which is tempered by classical utilitarianism in respect of reconciling the individual to the community. Dora Russell (Blewitt 1934: 29) wrote of Telegraph Hill:

Our first principle in the school is that one should leave one's neighbour alone to follow out his interests, provided that he does not interfere with the similar liberty for others. At the same time, we stress the necessity of everyone rendering some service to keep society going, and discourage greed and exploitation by individuals or groups.

One respondent claimed to see Mill written large in Curry's practice:

Curry believed in J. S. Mill. Everything came back to Mill in the end, everything was all right so long as it didn't interfere with your neighbour. We had this complete code of self-affecting action. Anything we did, like sleeping with a girl, was not irresponsible or immoral in any way, so long as it didn't hurt their feelings. But it was not done to attack or bully someone in a lower group for instance. (Fifties Man P.)

At the same time it is a vulnerable institution whose reasonableness and continuity can be suddenly threatened. One element that Dartington seemed ill-prepared to cope with was physical aggression. Its norms were so posited on rationality that it appeared to have little response when force threatened reason.

I do remember the really terrible upset if people really challenged the system. I took over getting people to leave breakfast to go and do Useful Work. Occasionally some hard cases would just refuse, like 'Guy', and also they were much stronger than me. I mean 'Guy' beat me twice in fights and I couldn't force him to go. He would just totally refuse and this really upset me. (Fifties Man P.)

And it was the physically strong, natural leader in early adolescence that Dartington seemed to find difficult to counter. One tutor wrote of a 'young Napoleon among children' while another wrote of a young gang leader that his lawlessness and bravado was curiously mixed with a feeling of authority and that he behaved like a young dictator taking a crowd along with him.

A similar role was played by a respondent who recalled his childhood deviance with relish:

| Interviewer: Did you get into much trouble at Dartington? |

Yes, a fair amount. I was such a rebel, right from the beginning. I used to organise, going out at night, night raids, raiding orchards, raiding the larder. At Aller Park it was much the same, again a complete rebellion against all the staff. 'Fran' [member of staff], I organised the whole school against her, I led a gang all the way through in fact. At Foxhole it was roof climbing. Once we changed the lock on the staff common room (I was in charge of the metal work shop and we were always making things like keys and guns) and locked all the staff in! We got to the stage at Foxhole of being pretty sophisticated criminals, quite frankly. They tried all sorts of things with the larder but it was the challenge of getting in there. We used to take the putty out of the window and replace it with plasticine so we could just take it out each time. They put bars in so we cut the bars and replaced them afterwards. (Fifties Man MS.)

In one case a powerful, energetic boy became one of the worst mischiefs the school encountered. His answer on the question about discipline covered more than six, typed foolscap pages.

I began stealing in forty-two and certainly for two years I would steal anything that came my way. Money, food – this was the great thing because of rationing and one was always hungry. I remember very clearly a coup we carried out on a kitchen. It was while this girl was singing 'Boom' in the French cabaret and meanwhile the rest of us had already got the windows to the kitchen in Foxhole open and made a master key into the main pantry there and we shifted, I think about several hundred cigarettes, a lot of chocolate bars, a great quantity of Horlicks. Cheese? No cheese was on another occasion, a lot of bottled gooseberries, no, loganberries. I also stole outside the school. We used to go into Woolworths with gas capes, things like a bicycle cape, and this conveniently covered the counter while your hands were filling your pockets underneath. Also one used to break into things like the apple store just across from Foxhole and this was a great source of amusement because they used to put more and more barbed wire up to try and stop us getting in and we found more and more ways of getting in. But it was all in a rather sort of James Bondish way, it was the hell of getting into the thing, not so much what you stole. I mean a few apples. (Thirties Man P.)

There are two relevant points to consider here. One is that the children were habituated to a greater respect for the person than for property and that stealing or window-breaking, certainly on the estate, while obviously not condoned was certainly not considered as heinous as 'crimes' committed outside.

One thing about Dartington is that you could be delinquent without the probability of going through the law courts or approved schools. For example, I went up to the barn one day with some other boys, stole a hundredweight of potatoes and threw them through some glass windows and pinched some corrugated iron off some roofs and used it for a raft on the Dart. (Fifties Man P.)

Secondly, what constituted an underlife in the ordinary boarding school was perfectly admissible at Dartington (one girl said the staff helped bake a cake for her midnight feast) and in a sense this robbed the children of illegitimate paths to adventure. Some difficult children got themselves into a demoralising cycle by dropping classes, or being put outside, and getting so far behind it was not worth going back; time hung heavily on their hands (one boy allegedly asked for a rest from having a rest!) and if they were able to incite a crowd they might turn to destruction as a release for their energies.

On the other hand, there were children who exercised a responsible influence over the rest of the community; one boy with organising ability (he arranged Useful Work and built a fresh-water pipeline for the swimming pool) had come late to the school from a public school.

I know one of the staff said, 'Well, there's no head boy here, but my goodness, I'll bet "Alistair" is more of a head boy than any other school has got!'. (Fifties Man MS.)

There were, in fact, a host of positions open to people for the exercise of responsibility, initiative, and control but these tended to be accumulated by a small number of boys and girls. For instance, one respondent declared:

I was captain of the football team, a 'responsible person' for swimming, on Agenda Committee, Dining Room Committee, Store Supply Officer, teacher of Latin to 'C' group and one individual pupil for a term, Sailing Club Committee, 'competent' sailor, and Library Committee. (Fifties Man P.)

Another respondent, a girl, was on seven committees at once. Clearly, some children enjoyed exercising responsibility.

I think there were certain characters that made a bit of a fetish of being responsible, in fact they almost kind of revelled in it. Some of the guys who ran the Cabinet were rather inclined to think that they were policemen and looked upon themselves as getting a grip of things. (Fifties Man MS.)

Usually these elected positions were filled by the socially mature, admired, boys and girls near the top of the school. What is interesting is that when the staff selected 'responsible people' for swimming they chose socially prestigious people, irrespective of their ability to swim. One respondent described his search for this socially admired responsibility:

Another great status symbol rather strangely was responsible people for the swimming pool. First it was chosen by the Cabinet but then it was chosen by the sports teachers. I was appointed a responsible person in group C [first year in Foxhole] which was again unheard of because of my age and I was very pleased with myself. But I was then struck off the next year because I was too young which I was very bitter about as I had already been appointed one in C group. It had nothing to do with swimming ability, it was entirely your social standing. I wanted to be considered responsible and I think most people did. It was useful in that you could take up to seven people into the pool but it was a question of prestige. (Fifties Man P.)

There were, too, a certain number of sanctions available to the staff in the maintenance of order. Eating breakfast alone in an old army hut was used in the early days of the school.

What is now the White Hart dining room for the students was at that time a ruin, and in that was put a very old army hut, and because 'Rosalie' always made me late I spent many breakfasts in the hut, or rather waiting in the ruins looking into Leonard's study and booing him. Most people didn't care but I minded, I was terribly conscious of time and of being late. This was the legacy of the village school I'd been to before which was so regimented. (Thirties Woman P.)

Being turned out of the class for disruptive behaviour was also employed with some effect.

I think the way they did punish us, or did punish me, was to turn me out of a class because then I became terribly upset. Mind you, I was inclined to make a noise and talk and interrupt the others, I could learn very quickly and some of the others didn't have the capacity, but I remember being kicked out of my favourite subject and being terribly upset and I had to stay out for a fortnight. (Thirties Woman MS.)

Other sanctions included going to bed early for infringement of the bedtime regulations; forfeiting 'breakage money' for damages; having to repair broken windows; having to work, say sawing logs, to recompense an injured party; or, in the last resort, being asked to leave.

Finally, we must make room for three important elements in the maintenance of order. Firstly, there was an extremely diffuse concept of behaviour that was 'anti-social' which by being largely undefined seemed to be all the more pervasive (rather like the Repton School rules which contain the following, 'any breach of common-sense or good discipline is an offence'. Wakeford 1969: 97). Secondly, and this really is most revealing, there was no prohibition about informing and this is most unusual in that 'ratting' is a cardinal crime in nearly every total institution, and boarding schools in particular (Punch 1966: 114–18).

There was quite a lot of destruction but we had this breakages system of a small money deposit from each pupil. So it paid to keep your nose clean and report everybody you saw breaking things up. (Thirties Woman P.)

The ordinary school has a system where you don't sneak, no sneaking and that sort of thing well if somebody was cutting up rough or starting any bullying, we would warn the person 'look this isn't very good and you're going to be reported'. They might say 'fuck you go and report us'. Well they'd be reported and then probably the upshot of it was they wouldn't be allowed to attend class for a week or something like that. (Thirties Man MS.)

Thirdly, and most crucially, the children developed a strong identification with the school which made them determined not to act to its detriment.

People would think it would be very wrong to get the school a bad name. If one was going to have affairs then you should be certain that you didn't become pregnant or you conducted yourself in a way that didn't give the school a bad name. I think that was really the only overriding thing I would say. Personally I definitely don't look back on it as a happy period but in spite of that I remember very clearly having this feeling that we were a minority who were open to criticism the whole time. All one's family apart from one's parents were horrified that one was there at all and you felt well you'd just got to close the ranks and I would never have admitted to anybody outside that I wasn't happy, would never have dreamt of it. I think it was simply, apart from Neill's school, that we were just about as way out as you could be in those days and we were what we reckoned was a very select band of less than a hundred people or whatever the school was then – when I first went there we were only twenty-eight – so one really felt one was an absolutely amazing minority that everyone, well the eyes of the world were on us so we imagined. (Thirties Woman MS.)

Again this identification with the school has its public school parallel in the Malvern School rules (Wakeford 1969: 97).

The good name of the school depends on the good behaviour of each individual boy. Any conduct which may harm its reputation is a breach of the school rules.

It appears explicitly as a technique of control in a passage by A. S. Neill (1968: 64) where he describes a boy and girl arriving in late adolescence at Summerhill where they fall in love:

'I don't know what you two are doing', I said, 'and morally I don't care, for it isn't a moral question at all. But economically I do care. If you, Kate, have a kid, my school will be ruined'. I went on to expand upon this theme. 'You see', I said, 'you have just come to Summerhill. To you it means freedom to do what you like. Naturally, you have no special feeling for the school. If you had been here from the age of seven, I'd never had to mention the matter. You would have such a strong attachment to the school that you would think of the consequences to Summerhill'.

Curry and self-government

Initially Curry described Dartington as philosophic anarchy tempered by benevolent despotism; but with 'participation' a key word from the school's inception and with its small size conducive to group decision-making, a democratic structure evolved of an elected 'Council'. This went through several constitutional mutations – there was a 'Council', then a 'Cabinet', and, finally, a 'Moot' with an 'Agenda Committee' – each one usually preceded by a breakdown in the existing machinery. The importance of self-government in the progressive school can hardly be exaggerated. A. S. Neill

(1968: 59) states that a school without self-government cannot be called a progressive school. However, some schools hedge over the nature of their self-government and J. H. Badley (1955: 188–9) has said of the Bedales School Parliament that he was in the chair, decided what questions to deal with, and held the final decision. He admits that 'parliament' is something of a misnomer as it was not meant to alter by a majority vote the 'fundamental principles' of the school. He stated:

I did not believe that freedom and self-government was possible in a community in which the majority are immature and inexperienced.

Formally, it serves two main functions – to incorporate the children into the running of the institution, rather than making them the passive recipients of authoritarian edicts, and to prepare them for citizenship in a democracy as adults. Informally, it was the organic and constitutional linchpin between the individual and the community – it was an opportunity to socialise to norms of rational debate; it welded group cohesiveness; it imposed sanctions; it applied pressures to conform; it was a tension-release mechanism for grievances; it enabled the staff to sample and gauge pupil opinion; it offered positions of authority to children; and it symbolised the grant of real power to the pupils. But its prime purpose must be to legitimise authority by the pupil's complicity in formalising those rubrics without which the interaction between individuals devolves into anarchy. This is particularly germane in a school, however progressive, because the staff must wield final authority in some matters. Hence Curry retained a final veto on the somewhat elastic concepts of 'health' and 'safety'.

Curry worked through the self-government and through meetings of the whole school to educate the children for freedom and, despite attempts to delimit his power and despite his deliberate self-effacement, there can be no doubt of his profound influence. His personality was widely interpreted by respondents – some replies bordered on the hagiographic, many were adulatory, others were sceptical, and a few were condemnatory – but none remained immune from him. The aura of mystique which surrounded him was undeniably charismatic.

I'm not a very useful barometer pro or anti Curry because I owe him so much in an emotional and practical way. Funnily enough, he wasn't a great teacher, but he had great personal magnetism. As a tortured child, he gave me the impression of being deeply sincerely interested in me and my problems. I felt he was totally concerned with my problems. (Fifties Woman P.)

Oh, I latched on to Curry. Curry was my Dad really I think. It was an atmosphere which pervaded when he was around, of extreme tolerance and reason; and it didn't matter how trivial something was, you knew you could go to him for whatever reason and you would always get a reasoned, plain sort of answer. And you would accept it because everybody had such respect for him. He had this atmosphere, I don't know whether it was developed on his part at all, whether he did things in a certain way consciously but you just went along with it. It was marvellous. It was so civilised. I don't think you could live in a more civilised sort of atmosphere. (Fifties Woman MS.)

Clearly this mystique worked for some people rather than others and one respondent recalled practically no contact with Curry at all during his schooldays:

Curry amazed me because he had so little to do with us. If he wrote anything about us he certainly didn't do it from first-hand experience. He simply didn't have anything to do with us at all. I think he spent a lot of time with some students sorting them out but if you were a sort of fairly goodie-goodie you just never had anything to do with him at all. Apart from saying hello if I saw him, which was very rarely, I don't think I ever went into his room and had an interview with him the whole of the time I was there. (Fifties Man MS.)

But generally Curry tried to influence the children by his fundamental reasonableness and claimed to avoid moral pressure. In his speech to the estate in 1936 (Manuscript source: DHRO) he stated the following:

It is wrong to expect children to conform to standards of behaviour which they cannot understand. For instance, it is now generally believed among psychologists that children have no social sentiments until they are nearing adolescence. To impose such standards merely produces hypocrites. Discipline takes no account of the enormous harm caused by the feeling of guilt. The results of this are generally anxiety, unhappiness, and further misbehaviour. This is especially true of the form of discipline known as moral indignation.

This ideal, of reasonableness, was further amplified by a respondent:

Bill made a point that rules were ridiculous. There was his standard public speech about going to a school where the children are not allowed to run down the corridor and so he says to a child, 'why aren't you allowed to run down the corridor?' And the kid says, 'I don't know'. And this to him was typical, to have a school rule where people didn't know why it was a rule. That was the height of ludicrousness. It was a point of pride to him that there wasn't going to be a rule in his school which wasn't perfectly obvious to everybody concerned why that rule existed. (Thirties Man MS.)

And yet there were undoubted underlying tensions beneath the cool mark of reason which he liked to convey. For example, an incident occurred in the late thirties when perhaps the deteriorating international situation was depressing him.

He was virtually a dictator in the Council. As I say he'd listen to reasonable grievances and if they were reasonably formulated he would probably humour us by acting on them in cases which were marginal. He was certainly effective because he was so extraordinarily articulate for those who liked people who are extraordinarily articulate. To an impassioned girl bursting in, I remember 'Sammy MacNamara' bursting in with some grievance, unreasonably expressed, and he shouted at her, 'You don't know what you're talking about, you're unrepresentative, you're a caucus, you're Hitler!' Well, this was ludicrous, Sammy being a twelve year old girl but he suddenly saw in her the incarnation of all the unreasonable, terrible forces engulfing Europe. You can imagine a lot of girls in adolescence don't really want to have a cold, reasoning, excessively articulate man quietly with his hands on his lap. He was odd looking, an egg-head, he was the original egg-head. But he suddenly saw the cool waters of reason being stirred by tumult and infamy, and I'm not exaggerting this, it's exactly as it happened. He went red in the face and so on and 'Sammy' fled from the room. (Thirties Man MS.)

In the last resort, he was prepared to use his personal authority to prevent any legislation being passed which he considered antithetical to the real interests of the children or the essential values of the school. In fact, the sort of legislative problems the self-government would consider seem to have varied little over the years judging by the Minutes, with bedtimes, pocket-money, noise, hitch-hiking, complaints about food, complaints of untidiness from domestic staff, and specific problems of discipline cropping up continually. The former two, in particular, seem to have led to perennial battles at school meetings which were generally far more prone to the swings of public opinion than the Council. One boy, for instance, persuaded the school not to take a holiday for the 1937 Coronation.

'Dennis' convinced everybody that they didn't want a holiday for the Coronation and persuaded the whole school, and they all voted against the holiday. Then, of course, afterwards, everyone was livid because we were all working and the whole of England was on holiday! (Thirties Woman MS.)

And if one pupil could persuade the school to forgo a holiday, how influential was Curry? In set pieces, where he could bring his powers of logic and debate to bear he was virtually irresistible.

Curry was very influential. He was the Chairman and held the casting vote. A very, very powerful arguer, very clever with his tongue, and he could always sway a meeting any way he wanted it to go. (Thirties Woman MS.)

Again, a description of Curry at a trying period in the beginning of the war reveals how his influence could be perceived as highly emotionally tinged.

Curry was quite outstanding in his handling of the Council. I remember how personally upset he was at some extreme demonstrations of rebelliousness. Somebody took all the cutlery from the dining-room and put them in a sack under a trap-door so the school couldn't eat, some boys cut all the curtains off the bathroom windows six inches from the top, and stealing was on the increase. Then one boy took a sackful of hens and put them into the Spanish maids' bedroom. Curry was upset because he felt he had failed, terribly upset. He called a meeting of all the children in the house with the boy present. He was desperate, I've never seen anyone so desperate. He said it was against all his beliefs, 'if people treat maids in this fashion then all my beliefs are shattered. It's against all my beliefs in socialism and in education'. (Thirties Woman P.)

To different people Curry was friend, father-figure, authority, or headmaster, attracting both affection and hostility. Both these last features were present in the third of the 'constitutional revolutions' which is in many ways the most revealing and in which several of our respondents were deeply involved during the early fifties. A series of events, fairly trivial in themselves, occurred which were exploited by a group of sophisticated boys to discredit the system of self-government. Many of the issues it discussed were petty and recurrent: two of the main ones were pocket-money and bedtimes. The Inspectors, for instance, noticed how tired the children looked and Curry decided to enforce new bedtime regulations which caused some resistance. In his 1947 book Curry averred that he had never used his veto or brandished it – on both counts he seems guilty of a certain amount of self-deception – but, in a way, he did not need to brandish it. Most children knew of its existence, and of what areas it would be enforced. This could be construed that the children's power was illusory (no one, for example, tried to send Curry to bed at seven o'clock as the Little Commonwealth did to Homer Lane!). One respondent claimed to have appreciated this while he was at school.

I thought Curry was one of the most astute manipulators of human beings, and for a boy of between twelve and fourteen to get that insight! I was on the School Council at one time and I can remember vividly Curry manouvering because Curry never used the veto – at least I can't remember him using it, but he always had tremendous skill at being able to dissuade a meeting and this wasn't always children but teachers as well. I can remember quite a number of occasions where teachers were sometimes, quite a number of teachers, on the side of a particular issue that children in the Council were putting forward and I can remember Curry being able to manipulate the whole gathering so that he never had to use the veto. I can also remember a meeting of the whole school at which one of the boys stood up and said that he felt the whole electoral system of the school was wrong and he said we should have proportional representation. And there were lots of 'hear, hears!' and what have you, then Curry stood up and using all sorts of analogies managed to sway the whole school against proportional representation. So during my years at school my main memory of Curry was a headmaster who tried to give the impression of absolute freedom but who, in actual fact, was a very astute manipulator of human beings. (Thirties Man MS.)

And in the fifties there was a group of boys who, according to one respondent, 'hadn't absorbed Curry's spirit' and who contrived a series of tactical manouvres to test the system in general and Curry's authority in particular.

Curry had tremendous pride in not having used the veto and it would have been a triumph to get him to use it. For example there was the 'Daily Worker' issue when we tried to get the 'Worker' onto the paper stand. 'Ian' and I planned it. In a way to get

Curry to use his veto on it as he was obviously dead aginst it but he got 'Cutforth' [member of Staff] to lead the attack on the 'Worker'. It would have damaged his prestige enormously if he'd been forced to use the veto but he made such a play of reason. So some absurd issues were put up deliberately to discredit it. (Fifties Man P.)

One method of undermining the system was to elect 'joke' candidates who were weak and ineffectual. Furthermore, the burden of responsibility had fallen disproportionately on the shoulders of a few who were elected time and again, until some of them became disenchanted with power and the absurd situation arose whereby the officers were presiding over their own misdemeanours. Then one key incident, concerned with damage to a girl's bicycle, occurred which the Cabinet seemed powerless to remedy

There was the whole business of 'Martha's' bicycle when some senior boys took it, rode it around, and wrecked it – this was brought up before the Cabinet which was somehow made a laughing stock by people like 'Ian' who were very sarcastic about it and a whole group of boys just jeered at it. (Fifties Man P.)

The upshot of this series of events was a desire on the part of general opinion for direct rule by Curry and he agreed to the disbandment of the Cabinet only with the greatest reluctance. Neill (1968: 25) has recorded a similar breakdown in self-government at Summerhill:

There was a time some years back when the school government resigned, and no one would stand for election. I seized the opportunity of putting up a notice: 'In the absence of a government, I herewith declare myself Dictator. Heil Neill!'

At Dartington the impetus for one-man rule seems to have come from below.

I think certain influential older students were determined to cause an anarchistic breakdown in the system which they did and so the only alternative was, a lot of people argued that this was what they wanted, that they wanted Curry to be a dictator. (Fifties Man MS.)

Eventually the lapse in self-government was resolved by a group of constitutionalists who reformed the 'Curryarchy' with a bicameral solution – a 'Moot', which anyone could attend, and an elected 'Agenda Committee' which prepared the matters to be debated.

The lessons of the constitutional crises, and of Curry's role in the machinery of self-government, have profound implications for the maintenance of order in the progressive community. They reflect, and almost run the full gamut of, the problems normally associated with an adult, participatory democracy – questions of adequate representation, of combating apathy, the tendency to oligarchy, of the powers of demagogues, of finding adequate personnel, and so on. The dilemmas of institutionalising 'freedom' are not to be underestimated and the whole question of the nature of authority and the role of the headmaster in a progressive school deserves sympathetic consideration. For he must act as the ultimate manipulater and unifier, ensuring that consensus is maintained and that the freedoms do not in fact become disruptive. At times he stands between the children and irresponsible deviance and then he is forced to exert his almost quasi-religious authority as charismatic father of an expressive community. The force of that authority could be considerable.

And Curry really said that if I didn't conform, and by conforming he meant stop being what he called 'anti-social', I would have to go. And I must say I frequently felt at the time that it would have been less painful to have been beaten and really being spoken to was a fairly terrifying experience, because Curry I think intended to brow beat you and he certainly made you feel that you were letting everybody down. (Thirties Man P.)

Chapter Six
The children's world

You keep implying that there might be social pressures of one kind or another but I didn't find this to be the case; Dartington was a world where people valued each other as individuals. (Thirties Woman MS.)

The pupil society

The regulation and consumption of time is often a vital factor in the functioning of total institutions which must cater for the inmates' needs for twenty-four hours of everyday (Punch: 1975). In many traditional boarding schools, for instance, time is minutely regulated in response to this organisational problem and leisure activities may be strictly rationed and their operation severely circumscribed (Weinberg 1967: 97–126). In contrast, the progressive school offers its pupils abundant opportunity for the spontaneous use of leisure time. One might anticipate, then, something of an atomistic institution populated by self-willing individuals, each pursuing their own specific interests. But what, in practice, were the norms and values of the pupil society at Dartington and how did they serve to regulate behaviour?

To what extent, for instance, were the children concerned with the socio-political radicalism with which Dartington was more or less identified? One woman recalled in the thirties that everything was discussed, that nothing was taken for granted, and that her predominant memory was one of constant, searching, discussion. Furthermore, Dartington in the thirties was positively involved in assisting refugees from Germany and Spain and this heightened general political consciousness. One sixteen-year-old respondent had to be rescued from Totnes station on his way to enlist in the Spanish Civil War. The bite seemed to desert debate within the school after the war and the radicalism became more diffuse and global.

I don't remember any current affairs, it would be more politics, world government and the United Nations and more wider issues than class distinctions. Dartington tried desperately to iron all these things out and say they didn't exist in a sort of way. While you were there there was no such thing as class. I think one tended to think of the yokels with Devon accents as a lower class than oneself, yes, because they were less educated. It was a question of education; meritocracy rather than innate class. (Fifties Woman MS.)

Before the war the internal clash was largely between communists and non-

71

communists whereas later it was more between the left and the centre. The results of the school's Mock General Election of 1950, for instance, were as follows:

The Liberals came top. This was entirely Curry's influence I'm sure, then Labour, Communist and Conservative. (Fifties Man MS.)

Weinberg (1967: 118) incidentally, cites twenty-nine mock elections or polls in public schools between 1945 and 1949 with the following results – twenty-three Conservative majorities, four Labour victories (by narrow margins) and two Liberal majorities.

We also have Curry writing to a mother expressing his concern over her son's membership of the Young Communists and questioning the virtue of young people joining organisations, 'as fanatical and single-minded as the Communists'. There was a small band of militant children in the fifties – they caused a furore over wanting the *Daily Worker* on the news-stand – but these only served to emphasise the relative apoliticism of the fifties Dartington generation. Indeed the *Daily Worker* issue in the fifties was more a test of Curry's authority whereas in the thirties the argument had been that all sides should be represented and that if the *Daily Worker* was taken then so should the fascist paper *The Black Shirt*.

Turning to spontaneous leisure activities, the pupils' general social life was characterised by long periods of chatty idleness (articulateness was highly prized) punctuated by eruptions of galvanic action. There was a good deal of continuity between the two generations in the range of interests – dancing was focal, as was swimming during the summer, and there was a jazz band, card and board games, roulette, the 'monkey game' – on apparatus in the gym, roller-skating hockey on the gym roof, soft-ball games such as baseball, and 'cocky olley' which was an American variant of 'he', and so on. The social importance of jazz among the fifties cohort presaged the pivotal role of popular music in the diffusion of a teenage culture in the wider society and, perhaps because of its American connections, Dartington pupil culture often appeared in advance of its contemporaries outside.

The most noteworthy feature of these pursuits was their susceptibility to rapid change; a novel idea, or a person with an exciting suggestion, was likely to be swiftly taken up and followed almost slavishly.

Monopoly first came out and there was a tremendous craze on Monopoly – the amount of prep that didn't get done on account of Monopoly, not only me but everybody, must have been enormous – it was an absolute obsession. And these games went on in the common rooms every single evening and the whole weekend. One was just drawn to it, everybody was, like moths to a flame. (Thirties Woman MS.)

Fashion also dictated what the Dartingtonian would wear.

> There were always crazes. We went about for a long time without any shoes or socks on, or with jeans rolled up, and then there was a craze for a certain piece of clothing, or girls had crazes for certain hair styles. (Fifties Man MS.)

The vulnerability of the pupil society to a dominant individual is a recurrent theme and it was evident that some children could take on an almost Pied Piper quality.

> It went in phases very much. You got somebody who was athletic who got everybody interested. You would have these terrific chases. Right over the whole roofs and everything – somebody would run away and everbody would chase after – we were about thirteen or fourteen and this would go on all evening. All up and down, in and out of the windows, and everywhere. Just because one person was very athletic he would do it and everybody else tagged along – just for something to do I suppose. But it was a phasey thing to do. If somebody was very keen on jazz then we would have these very jazzy sessions – everbody sitting around listening to New Orleans and all this. There'd be about two or three terms of this and then something else would come along. (Fifties Woman MS.)

One extremely interesting example of a pupil manipulating this situation for his own ends came when one perceptive young boy arrived at Foxhole and, being acutely aware of the status differentials in operation, deliberately set out to fill the role of an 'ideas man' by which he could entertain people and thereby win a prestige not normally allotted to someone in the lowest group.

> The 'C' group [the first year in Foxhole] boy had a terrible time. I was bullied when I first arrived. I remember at meal times I was invited on to a table with bigger boys and they would literally take food away from me or else tell me to go up and get food and then they'd snatch it away from me. I hated the size and noise, and the whole of the sex orientation in Foxhole. Or they'd take something from my wardrobe and I hated that. . . . At the end of the 'C' group year I could play games and invent fantasies with older boys. I invented a whole Foxhole aristocracy and awarded titles – I could say, 'You're the Duke of this' and 'you're the Earl of that' – which put me in a fantastically prestigious position. And I invented a language with Tim when I was in the 'B' group [the second year in Foxhole] called 'Borifian' and, again, people had to take exams in 'Borifian' so I had several social positions under my control by that time. But I still hadn't made the sex breakthrough which to me was much more important. (Fifties Man P.)

Coeducation

The lurid mythology that tends to surround progressive communities, with visions of sexual permissiveness, finds little credence in our interviews; on the contrary, indications point to the great restraint which the children exercised in sexual relationships. There was undoubtedly a precocious veneer of sexual sophistication, with four-letter words bandied about, but the reality was more often conspicuous by innocence, romaticism and responsibility. There were periods of relative licence – in the mid-thirties, shortly after the war, and the mid-fifties – the first two arising largely from problems of assimilating people coming late to the school and the latter probably in response to changing attitudes in the wider society. Curry (Bonham-Carter 1958: 212) reflected soberly on these changes with respect to sexual morality:

The problem is certainly extremely difficult and I sometimes think that at this stage of our particular civilisation it is insoluble, owing to the almost universal sexual hypocrisy among adults, the crude debasement of values promoted by so much advertisement and popular entertainment, and the complete lack of any agreement as to what would be an acceptable code, not merely among adults in general, but even among Dartington or 'progressive' parents themselves.

After a somewhat hearty, masculine, overtly emancipative beginning, when the rituals of courtship were somewhat decried, deep emotional relationships between boys and girls became acceptable.

I have heard, in the early days of coeducational boarding schools, that if the boys and girls fell in love it was regarded as 'silly', and attempts were made to inhibit any such manifestations by the scorn implied in that word. It has been suggested that this policy of repressing sexuality in the coeducational situation produced frigidity in some of the girls involved. I hope there is no coeducational school in which such a policy persists. (Ash 1969: 23.)

But apparently sexual intercourse, and promiscuity, was the exception to the norm.

There was bloody little sex I think. I never did, unfortunately, but if I could go back there now it would be bloody chaos! There were tremendous teenage love affairs, incredible we never made love, I don't know why. (Fifties Man MS.)

Where the couple were patently sensible and unlikely to get themselves into trouble there was no doubt that the staff were prepared to condone the relationship and to afford them a good deal of privacy. If there seemed to be any danger Curry would intervene and normally this proved effective; the arguments he used were that he was responsible to the parents, that one could not live as if the structures of society did not exist, and that the school might be closed if the scandal surrounding an unwanted pregnancy was made public. Some children who persistently threatened the social order by promiscuity or irresponsible sexual behaviour were asked to leave.

For one or two respondents the freedom to pursue an emotional relationship in a relatively enclosed community proved a source of considerable anguish: indeed with one it led to his leaving school early.

I had several girlfriends then one very serious affair which led to my leaving. She dropped me and I was very upset and moped around. In the end Curry said this isn't doing anyone any good so by sort of mutual agreement it was decided I should leave. This relationship certainly caused me a lot of pain. (Fifties Man MS.)

For many, relations with the opposite sex were part and parcel of Dartington life and were accepted naturally — one respondent, for instance, considered that being in love with someone was the most valuable aspect of his school career — but for some it caused emotional turmoil and disturbed their everyday existence. Some older boys, baulked by unrequited love, turned in somewhat predatory fashion to younger girls. Occasionally a highly sexually mature girl might break conventions by seeking partners in the younger age groups or even outside the school. One girl was attracted to soldiers billeted on the estate.

At this stage I was one of the baddies and my friend 'Sammy' and I used to wander around cut of school after dark to meet our American soldier boyfriends from up at the Hall. I couldn't have got pregnant from any of these boys but I was out late one night and in the morning the housemother rushed in and said, 'Quick Angela, tell me if anything happened and I'll fetch the douche!' We had a couple of school meetings to stop this because it worried Curry, he disapproved of it, he was worried for the sake of the school and perhaps the anxiety of being sued if a girl became pregnant. But he never put an absolute ban on going up there. (Thirties Woman P.)

Promiscuity, however, was not a feature of the school during most of the period that we are studying. Indeed, the norm was generally restraint short of actual intercourse owing to a very real fear of pregnancy instilled by Curry who, in effect, was the birth control (he used to say humorously that the school motto was 'no births, no deaths'). He possessed what one respondent called a 'subliminal advertising technique' which seemed to work in most cases. But there were other elements in the pupils' values which made for restraint; namely their romanticism, innocence, puritanism, and what amounted to self-imposed primary group endogamy.

Relationships were defined in romantic or even intellectual terms.

There was one rather lush looking girl who was extremely stupid and at Dartington of course intellectual ability was the most prized thing even in one's relationships with girls. You had to feel that there was some sort of intellectual rapport or you really weren't interested. (Thirties Man P.)

Apart from not viewing relationships in primarily physical terms (and obviously this did not apply to everybody) there was also the inculcation of responsibility by a sort of romantic utilitarianism where respecting a person's feelings became more important than respecting outside sexual conventions.

There was no moral code or anything like that. I think there was much more condem-
nation of people, of hurting people's feelings rather than how far one should go.
Breaking someone's heart so to speak would be thought a much worse crime than
merely raping them. (Fifties Man MS.)

Indeed, behind the apparent sexual precociousness there was often a strain
of conventional modesty (perhaps retained from some staid home
background).

We were filthy, I mean foul-mouthed, and used awful language. Yet I remember once
someone put a French letter down my dress but I promptly went to the lavatory, I was
appalled, shook it out behind me, pulled the chain without ever seeing it. We really
were in a way awfully modest too which sounds odd. (Thirties Woman P.)

One woman explained that in the thirties sex was taken seriously but again,
that sexual flippancy appeared as a surface phenomenon:

The boys all used to send for French letters by mail order. I mean most of them were
left down in the courtyard, full of water. This was a great joke. But it was really quite a
serious business at Dartington, but my husband would never understand this; but it's
difficult for you all to understand, those who haven't been there. There was this enormous feeling of respect about that kind of thing; but in a way we were sort of roman-
tics. I can remember at 15 talking endlessly about this, that you didn't go to bed with
somebody unless you were really in love, and to be really in love with someone you
had to be able to talk to each other and understand each other about everything.
(Thirties Woman P.)

At times the strength of feeling on sexual and emotional matters amounted
to puritanism. One woman said that at thirteen she started using make-up and
was accosted in a corridor by several senior girls who told her that it was
ridiculous for a young girl to wear make-up. Another elaborated the code
which defined what was acceptable among girls:

There were very strong taboos about wearing make-up, an exception at parties
possibly, and the standards about make-up were more specific than that. Lipstick was
slightly ridiculous but OK, powder was not because that was deception, you couldn't
necessarily tell if someone was wearing powder. Stockings were not to be worn except
at parties, to the extent that I said I wouldn't wear stockings every day at university
but that went pretty soon. But these things were pretty deeply ingrained. There was
this sort of puritanism, I remember several girls in the year ahead of us just happened
to become models immediately after they left and there was a very strong feeling
about this being a profoundly immoral thing to do and I remember somebody's moan
that it was just the same as being a prostitute and selling your body. (Fifties Woman
MS.)

Because of the intimacy in which children grew up at Dartington the peer
group became virtually a primary group. This led to something of an incest
taboo between contemporaries and to a great attraction for newcomers who

could gain a disproportionate influence simply from being a new face.

[Interviewer: Was it difficult growing up with boys to feel very romantic about them?]
You couldn't really, not really. When you'd seen them in the swimming pool and being weighed and measured and washed their socks and things like that which you did do occasionally you couldn't get frightfully romantic about them, which was very nice for a new boy coming to the school whereas we'd been there all the time. Someone new, or a new girl for that matter, they were very much sought after. (Fifties Woman MS.)

To a certain extent the nude bathing probably increased this feeling, for the children had probably swum and bathed together without clothes for years. Curry later came to defend the practice adamantly (after initial reservations) and it was not unknown for him to take a dip, as did some of the staff. And it may be that he considered it a crucial tension-release mechanism in a coeducational community. Incidentally, respondents themselves generally approved of the practice, some vehemently, and only a handful, mostly women, had reservations about it. Girls approaching puberty could find it embarrassing, but the real objection was that it became almost a shibboleth, or an instantaneous initiation rite, which limited the freedom *not* to swim naked. Indeed to legitimate the practice a whole counter-mythology grew up (some boys even timed themselves swimming and found they could swim faster without costumes) which held the wearing of costumes to be more erotic than plain nudity.

I can remember going back during the holidays when the Fabian Society was there and I remember the horror of having to wear a bathing costume, and the fear of it. I can remember that so distinctly, it was horrible, it was quite indecent I thought. I didn't go again, I thought 'oh no, this is awful'. I think there's something much more suggestive in wearing some of these costumes than there is to go without one but then other people don't see it that way and we have to live in society. (Fifties Woman MS.)

In this important section we have seen the strength of the norms surrounding sex at Dartington. Curry may have chosen to underestimate childhood sexuality because he had a curious notion that the sexual problems of adolescents were not acute during their schooldays because children developed more slowly in Northern Europe (Curry 1947: 71).

But certainly with English boys and girls in this climate, a substantial proportion pass right through school before encountering sex as a serious practical problem . . . conscious desire stops short of complete sex experience.

On the one hand emotional expression was encouraged but on the other its consequences were curtailed. Early socialisation was essential, and two potentially disruptive influences were always at hand to threaten the prevalent norms – newcomers who did not share those values and people from outside the community. This was one of the school's most vulnerable areas and one detects at times an almost exaggerated fear of its consequences. With responsible couples real freedom was extended but where it took a 'psychopathic, promiscuous, irresponsible, pregnancy-risking streak', as one respondent described it, then Curry intervened. That he had to do so comparatively infrequently was due largely to the norms of rationality and responsibility with which Dartington was imbued (as well as the other elements we have mentioned above).

One used to sit on the bank after a swim and one might get an erection, as boys will at that sort of age, and one would get embarrassed that this might happen to one. Only mark this well, not because of the display involved, that your private parts could be seen, but that you had irrational desires which you might not be controlling. (Thirties Man MS.)

Relations with and attitudes to the outside world

The educative value of a rural environment was emphasised by most progressive schools and by Dartington in particular. Yet the immense potential of the immediate locale and the region went largely unexploited; rather it served as an aesthetic backcloth to an almost self-contained community. When children ventured outside it was almost invariably for leisure or entertainment. Of course, the estate provided for many of their needs while the worlds of the estate and non-estate remained hedged with a strong, and sometimes virulent, mutual antagonism. Stories of nudity, illegitimacies, and black magic were legion in the Dartington locale and Joll (1969: 19) mentions the use of sexual slanders to discredit anarchist minorities while similar suspicions surrounded the Owenite communitarian ventures (Harrison 1969: 186). A. S. Neill said that when he asked some local boys why they were hanging around Summerhill, they replied 'for a free fuck' (Recorded Interview). Ash (1969: 79) puts the point somewhat more delicately:

The world-at-large has itself become much freer in its ways (has, in fact, itself become more of a child's world), so that the problem is less whether the local community can occasionally assimilate the unorthodox behaviour of the children from the progressive school in its midst as whether, reciprocally, the school can withstand the importation of behaviour – particularly such as stems from the autonomous youth-culture new to our times – which, because it is not moderated by the continuing responsibility for the school of those who belong to it, puts an undeniable strain on the informal structure of the school.

Curry maintained that because Dartington set no bounds the children had ample contact with the outside world and Ash (1969: 78) compares the progressive school favourably in this respect with the traditional school.

When the children did foray into the locality, however, their nonconforming behaviour and dress – one respondent recalled walking through Totnes in his bare feet, eating cornflakes out of a packet and singing – only served to heighten their consciousness of being different and special because of the interest they aroused.

Totnes was very Conservative with a capital 'C' and when we used to have our general elections in school we used to go down to the party political meetings in the village hall and I remember being turned on once by the brigadier somebody or other. I was turned on but we used to take it all quite seriously. We weren't very popular but 'Graham' used to be all day in the library reading Hansard for good questions to ask, and we used to get 'Oh! They be from Dartin'on 'all, you don't want to listen to they'. We used to be chucked out as often as not. Not chucked out but told to sit down, and come back when we were grown up. (Fifties Woman MS.)

There was even talk of dressing more 'respectably' and behaving more 'orderly' when off the estate but generally the self-awareness was inverted into a feeling that other people were different – to be scorned or, more often, pitied. Curry himself had noted that the children's remarkable tolerance for each other was not always extended to outsiders; and disdain seemed to be reserved particularly for other schools (with whom contact, except for occasional sports fixtures, was nominal).

[Interviewer: Was there much contact with other schools?]

We once showed some Public Schools boys around, I had letters from one of them for quite a long time afterwards, and I had the feeling they thought they'd arrived on the moon.

[Interviewer: What was the attitude to other schools?]

Oh, we pitied them from the bottom of our hearts. Dartington is the least snobbish place but I think we were impossibly pleased with ourselves at being there and sorry for everyone else who hadn't been there.

[Interviewer: Did you have affinities with other schools?]

Not really, we even felt that Bedalians were an inferior breed, we felt they weren't a true coeducational, progressive school, and perhaps had the worst of both worlds. (Thirties Woman MS.)

Particular venom seems to have been directed at the grammar school, which was practically a term of abuse according to one respondent, more than the public school even. One girl used to go beagling with cadets at Dartmouth and found them to be far more tolerant of Dartington than her fellow pupils were of Dartmouth. Two other pupils with contacts in Dartington village and Totnes, one in the thirties as a guide, the other in the fifties as a scout, described the conflict this engendered; the former spoke of 'this feeling of living in two separate compartments' and of slipping out of school in her guide's uniform hoping not to meet too many Dartingtonians on the way, while the latter said:

I was the odd one out in a way. I joined in the scout group down in the village but this was exceptional that anyone ventured outside the school and did something of that sort.

[Interviewer: What was the attitude of children in Dartington to your going?]

Oh, they thought that was quite peculiar. I'm quite certain I think the staff did too and I don't think Curry was too happy. Well he didn't object at all but it didn't fit into his scheme of things, you know uniformed youth organisations smacked too much of militarism for his liking. (Fifties Man MS.)

To a certain extent the estate was even viewed as 'foreign territory and never the twain shall meet sort of thing' by one respondent and the school remained the real focus of the children's world. The attitudes that this engendered are best left to the respondents themselves and it is worth quoting two respondents, one from each generation. Firstly, one respondent from the thirties documented the isolation:

[Interviewer: Was the social life self-contained?]

Completely. We went to the cinema in Totnes, otherwise a big gulf and, of course, we looked down on the people in the locality. We felt that the whole educational establishment of the country was wrong, and that the school was a pioneer, was a cause, for freedom in education and so on, which was opposed by two main coteries of educational conservatism – the public schools with their bearings and snobbery on the one hand, and homosexuality, and the local authority schools, grammar schools, with their authoritarianism, lower class snobbish conformism, restrictions, C. of E. etcetera on the other. And we felt equally antagonistic to the two and equally defensive. I always remember feeling so uncomfortable on walking to the cinema in Totnes, and passing a lot of kids from Totnes Grammar, one would tend to slip to the other side of the road. I don't remember any overt conflict, but they represented something, and we were very well aware of being a minority group representing a liberal, and to some extent unpopular, minority cause. It's very different now when most of the criteria are accepted – we were that 'dreadful school', aware of it, proud of it, nervous of it, all at the same time. There was this gulf, Totnes was a lower class town – there was Dartington, and there was a wilderness of local conservatism.

And secondly, a similar attitude was described for the fifties:

Basically, we felt the school was the centre of the world . . . when you walked into Totnes you would see all the grammar school boys and girls dressed up in uniform and we felt so superior to these people dressed up in an old-fashioned way. We really had this thing that we were the future of civilisation, and these people were stuck with old fashions and conventions and one should pity them. It was rather like one's attitude to religion, that it was something people believed in in the olden days, and one should be nice to the few old people who still do believe in it. It came as a rude shock at university to find that religion was still alive and virulent. It really shook me. (Fifties Man MS.)

Class and integration

From its inception Dartington offered generous scholarships for the children of estate workers to attend the school as day pupils; and, initially, young apprentices on the estate were considered a part (albeit a separate part) of the Senior School. Alone among virtually all of the inter-war middle class boarding schools, Dartington made structural provision for integrating working class children in the social and educational life of the school. There was, too, a strong egalitarian ethos that sought to stand above the traditional social restrictions of a class system and the estate almost approximated a sort of Devonian kibbutz. This important innovation in the structure of the school foundered on two rocks; firstly, the children themselves retained certain class values and, secondly, Curry saw the day pupils as a hindrance to the unity and reputation of his school. From very early on he complained continually about parents who were unable to satisfy the school that they understood its values and methods, and were prepared to cooperate sincerely with it. He would have liked to have excluded these parents and clearly this applied far more to the day children. (Manuscript Source, DHRO.)

At times the status or class distinctions from outside were simply reversed:

[Interviewer: Were there any social distinctions in the school?]

Oh yes. It was rather amusing because it was in reverse. The very rich children were more uncomfortable than the very poor ones because they had got a lot of money – 'old money bags!' – they got teased about it. (Fifties Woman MS.)

One girl actually made her mother buy her a conventional school uniform (a gymslip, a hat, and a coat) because she was conscious that other girls had superior clothes: she eventually solved the problem by wearing trousers and 'tomboy' clothes continually – the irony being, of course, the eradication of overt differences in clothes by the adoption of an informal uniform. Another girl, and girls suffered most from this, came from a lower middle class home in terms of income but suffered because her parents inundated her with clothes and belongings in order that she should have as much as the others; unfortunately, she was conscious of their inferior quality.

Related to awareness of class differentials was the position of day pupils who were generally from rural, working class backgrounds. One thirties respondent, a day pupil whose father worked on the estate, recalled the joy when Russell or Shaw visited the Hall because her father could expect a heavy tip. But she also remembered the distress when her mother was forced to work in the school:

[Interviewer: Was it a disadvantage in any way being a day girl?]

Oh yes. Well, kids would say 'you're not one of us'. Children can be catty and hard. At one time I can remember mother took a job in Foxhole washing dishes. Oh, can you imagine in that type of school and there's your mother washing dishes, do you know what I mean? Some of the children kept on about it as children will and it did embarrass me. I took it on the nail but I still remember it as if it was yesterday. If I had to wash dishes now I wouldn't wash them up in the school, I'd go away to do it for the sake of the children. And some of the professional types would say 'your father is only a servant and mine is so and so', you know. (Thirties Woman MS.)

While the class differences obviously contributed to the marginality of the day pupil it was also the case that they were mostly outsiders who missed out on the social world of the boarders. As far as the children were concerned, integration, however well meaning in intent, was never fully effective.

There was always the problem of the local day children who did not come from middle class homes. The fact of being a day pupil in itself made life rather difficult but there were ones who came from working class homes some of which had extraordinary attitudes. One boy turned up, probably under some scholarship, with a working class Brylcreem hair style and it was just unbelievable the amount of verbal venom directed at him and after a few weeks he changed it. Another boasted how dirty his comb was and that he never washed his hair and this culminated in a forcible hairwashing collectively organised. There was no question of day pupils eventually being assimilated, there were limits beyond which a day could not get assimilated and that's just all there was to it. Nobody was an outsider to the extent that they were ignored or systematically ostracised but they were just a set apart and certainly the day pupils were looked down on in principle. (Fifties Woman MS.)

The Elmhirsts' vision of complete social integration on their estate competed with Curry's aspirations for a glitteringly successful model school. The day pupils were often academically inferior to urban, intellectual children; their parents often disagreed with the school's values and also wished to remove their children early; but socially the working class children did not fit readily into the boarding childrens' world. In his reports Curry constantly argued against their inclusion in his school and obviously would have liked to have used the scholarships to patronise the intelligent children of progressive parents. The youthful forerunners of his cooperative commonwealth were, in practice, decidedly middle class.

Chapter Seven
The academic system and the staff

The readiness with which universities, and especially his own [i.e. Curry's], Cambridge, accepted boys and girls from the School, a fair proportion with open scholarships, against all comers, has served to prove a vital part of Curry's case, that a school that valued freedom and mutual respect so highly need not be a breeding ground for sluggards. (L. K. Elmhirst in Bonham-Carter 1958: 161.)

Academic

Dartington was never really in the forefront of innovations in the academic sphere; its pioneering role was primarily social. Curry (Bonham-Carter 1958: 218) admitted this and added:

I have never been able to get excited over teaching methods and I have felt that most gifted teachers, at any rate, arrive at their own methods. Nor have I been able to get excited about curriculum.

Bradley (1955: 196) expressed little interest in teaching and A. S. Neill (1968: 20) wrote:

We have no new methods of teaching, because we do not consider that teaching in itself matters very much.

Indeed, the stated goals of seventeen progressives (seven headmasters and ten house staff) interviewed by Lambert *et al.* (1971a: Chap. V) were on the development of the child's intrinsic personality, the generation of an atmosphere of freedom, minimisation of pressures, scope for emotional growth, for creative expression and cultural interests, and for the pursuit of happiness as an end in itself. As one respondent expressed it on behalf of his parents:

They always said to us the most important thing is that we should be happy. Whether you could read or write was insignificant. (Fifties Man MS.)

This low priority for academic innovations at Dartington was despite the fact that the school attracted a number of children of above average intelligence. The average IQ for forty-one out of sixty of our sample for whom scores could be found in the records was 130 (Median 131) with a range from 97 to 170. The test used by the school until 1969 was the Stanford-Merrill version of the Binet Scale which may have exaggerated the IQ of some children because it favours children with high verbal ability (Vernon 1962: 54). The

Malting House at Cambridge also attracted some intellectually gifted children and the IQ there averaged 131 in 1926 (van der Eycken and Turner 1969: 27). Dartington also enjoyed a generous staff–pupil ratio of roughly 1:5 in the late thirties and 1:6 in the early fifties, which compares with roughly 1:20 for maintained secondary schools and 1:17 for HMC independent schools although the ratio is lower for HMC mainly boarding schools (Kalton 1966: 62).

Yet 28 per cent of our Dartington sample left without passing any examinations at all, while many respondents regretted that their academic potential had not been developed more fully.

I just wished I'd had somebody who told me what to do and made sure that I had done it. There was nothing wrong with the school, the teaching, the principles, just that certain people were allowed to slide. It worked well if you had self-discipline, but I wasn't one of those – I should have been told what to do and what subjects to take, because I could have passed. But I didn't because I took the easy way out which you do if you are young and a bit on the lazy side. I left when father discovered that I hadn't done anything and felt it was about time I did. (Fifties Man MS.)

This lack of achievement appears to be a resilient problem for progressive schools as it is echoed in Lambert's *et al.* (1971a: Chap. V) research.

Their academic results are not so high as might be expected when their small classes and middle-class intake are considered . . . The informal norms of pupils in these and some other schools tend to place little premium on hard work and academic achievement for its own sake so that academic results are depressed.

On the other hand, other respondents were generous in their praise of the teaching so that evidently the academic system suited some people more than others.

Just look at the people who taught me. Chemistry was 'Webster', now Scientific Librarian at the Courtauld Institute. Physics was 'Decibels Peters', now Professor at Toronto. Biology was 'Urquart', now FRS and head of the Institute of Ornithology at Oxford. This was strong, potent staff academically. What children get three teachers of this calibre for First MB? (Thirties Man MS.)

In assessing the strengths and weaknesses of the school's academic set-up the following points must be borne in mind. Firstly, we have seen that the school did not believe in overmuch academic pressure prior to Foxhole where, it was hoped, the child's innate appetite for knowledge would cause him to attack the Senior School's greater academic demands with relish. Secondly, a high degree of self determination was increasingly expected of pupils as they moved up the school and, at times, the academic atmosphere approached that of a university. Thirdly, traditional sanctions were eschewed. Fourthly, competition was positively discouraged in terms of individual marks, class placings, or overt emphasis on results in internal or external examinations. Fifthly, and finally, the individual teacher was granted virtually complete autonomy to organise his academic domain.

Initially, the school did adopt some of the latest teaching methods, largely derived from the American experience of Dewey, Kilpatrick and Flexner, and the early years in particular were noted for a non-specialist approach of broad-subject groupings, using the project-method. In an early prospectus, for instance, the sourses of study were grouped around Gardens, Farms, Forestry, Building, Workshop, Crafts, Music and Drama, Publishing, Language, Social Studies, Health, and Accounts. The educative potential of the estate was obviously to the fore. One boy's 1929 report, for example, covered Music, French, Biology, Maths, Geography, Dancing, Drama, Philosophy, Pottery, Gardening, History, Social Studies, General Knowledge, English, and Games, while his later report also mentioned Psychology, German, Science–Electricity, and Design. The reality, however, was not always impressive and with Curry's arrival in 1931 the standard of teaching began to improve while the largely unsuccessful integration of estate and academic subjects withered away. There was a certain tendency to regard pupils as university material or else aspiring artists; there was some poverty in the alternatives offered to the less academic child, and particularly girls, with a rather limited and predictable 'domestic' group based at 'Highcross' (Curry's house). One woman, now in catering where she has to work constantly with figures, felt rejected in one class.

I regret dropping maths. He was probably a brilliant fellow but I remember being told, 'for God's sake just run away and learn to cook because you'll just get married'. And I learnt no maths at all, but, obviously, its still part of your job. But the stupid thing is ever since I've been married, I've been doing books and if I'd learnt a bit while I was there it might have helped now. (Fifties Woman MS.)

Bearing in mind, then, both the changes in atmosphere inside the school and the increasing academic competitiveness outside of it, we shall examine how pupils reacted to the doctrine of non-compulsion in the academic sphere and the concrete results in terms of the sample's examination results.

Freedom for the pupil in the academic sphere would be utilised in primarily two ways: firstly, there was considerable laxity about attending classes and, secondly, the child had the perogative to choose which subjects he wished to pursue. The former was never absolute. It depended upon individual teachers, the age of the pupil, and the prevalent norms (missing classes was common before Curry's arrival) – and was circumscribed particularly by the understanding that once a subject was chosen then attendance at those particular classes should be regular. The latter was usually decided after the first year in the Senior School and, while the choice was not meant to be arbitrary, there was a tendency not to interfere once the pupil had made his or her selection. The extreme case was cited by A. S. Neill (1968: 41):

Tom came to Summerhill at the age of five. He left at seventeen, without having in all those years gone to a single lesson.

Generally, children seem to have attended fairly regularly in those subjects they had chosen to study. But individuals could absent themselves for long periods; in one instance for several years.

I didn't go to classes in Foxhole for two years. I can remember going to one or two history classes, one or two biology classes, bookbinding which was the sort of things we'd choose in the afternoon and I can't remember any other classes at all. One or two geography classes. I stopped going. I don't know exactly when but nobody did anything about it at all. My tutor gave me one pep talk and said, 'you'll regret it later' and I said, 'I won't. Education isn't necessary'. (Fifties Woman P.)

Another respondent felt that her 'fallow period' had failed to respect the change to the Senior School and had extended right through her school years.

Maybe Curry was quite right, I had just got to untie myself, this was all that mattered – an extra fallow period, right along. He always used to go on about this fallow period, in the junior school you must let them go free otherwise there won't be fertile ground for anything. But with me it extended right up to leaving school. My imagination wasn't captured – and it was because I had no foundation to build on – no basic sort of education through all these different changes and different methods at every school I went to. (Woman Fifties MS.)

Another respondent was virtually illiterate while in his early teens.

I couldn't read at thirteen so in a way I'm very grateful to Dartington because at any other school I'd have been completely written off. But it was partly Dartington's fault as I was backward in other subjects too . . . the Middle School was buggering around, building camps and bicycling, so I got no direction at all. I didn't have a language and nobody directed me into one and this put me up the spout, as they felt there was no possibility of a university education. I don't remember any tutor, but I got no guidance on subjects at all, not at all. (Fifties Man MS.)

The freedom, to choose subjects and not to attend classes, could lead to an unbalanced attainment based upon short-term decisions whereby difficult or unpleasant subjects were simply avoided.

I very quickly determined that I didn't like maths so I didn't do it, also Latin so I didn't do Latin, and in the end I was cutting down and going exactly to classes that I liked going to. Individual teachers might say, 'What is the good if you turn up to this class when you missed the one before? How do you get the continuity of my lectures out of this?' And in fact it solved itself because you missed the continuity of it so you slipped out. The reason French didn't continue is that I lost a chunk of French in the middle and I could never catch up with the people who had attended. (Thirties Man MS.)

One girl dropped a subject before an examination.

|Interviewer: Did you drop some subjects in Foxhole?|

Yes, but I don't think I should have been allowed to drop them. Well, I dropped Geography the day before the School Certificate exam. and I had every chance of certainly gaining a credit because geography is a very easy subject and in a fit of pique with the teacher I just said I was going to drop it and so I did. Very stupid. (Fifties Woman MS.)

A revealing example of the difficulty of some Dartingtonians to knuckle down to long-term academic goals arose when the Dalton method of subject rooms and assignments was introduced; it flourished briefly, perhaps for its novelty value, and then withered. Theoretically, this type of teaching ought to have suited Dartington's approach of expecting to do basic 'research' work alone or together in the library for assignments: but, in practice, the system broke down and this happened on two separate occasions when the Dalton Plan was tried. Children got behind with their assignments, there were no sanctions to make them catch up, and the system collapsed. It seemed to be difficult for the staff to exert sanctions and pressure to motivate the children.

Well I think I always did at Dartington what I was interested in. Again perhaps this is a criticism of it, that one could have of Dartington and such kind of schools, that you can develop lop-sidedly. They had a tutorial system there, as you probably know, similar to the university and it depended very very much on your tutor as to how your sort of balance, your academic balance went. I had 'Patrick' and he was terribly nice, an awfully nice man but I think possibly I could have done with a bit more of a kick up the backside occasionally and he should have said, 'well, you should be working harder at history or English', or whatever it might have been. But because I tended to work hard on what I was interested in I enjoyed it, generally I enjoy academic work, I wasn't brilliant by any means, but I did only what I liked. (Fifties Man MS.)

There were children who revelled in the opportunity to work on their own and found no difficulty in setting their own goals and finding their own motivation. Also, ex-public school boys who came late to the school with habits of hard work were able to blossom in terms of academic success whereas the apparently more creative and multi-sided pupils seemed to find the environment too flexible and dissipated their energies unprofitably in too many areas. Similarly, one of the most fruitful experiments academically was that of moving the 'academic' sixth-form to the house called 'The Old Postern' in the late thirties where they lived an undergraduate style existence. But in a way their academic well-being was only guaranteed by isolating them from the other pursuits and distractions which were ideally meant to shape the well-rounded progressive.

It was an ideal place for someone who wanted to work and knew what they wanted to do, and at that time the teaching was absolutely first-class. When I was at the top of the Senior School we lived in the Old Postern, you had no set bed time and you could work on your own. It was a bit like a university. It was much livelier than my university in fact; there was no question at Dartington of going to a class and having someone read out of a textbook – I had to go to a university to discover that that sort of teaching existed. (Thirties Woman MS.)

One indicator of the success or otherwise of Dartington's academic system is the exam. results of our sample. But it cannot be emphasised too much that for progressives this is an external criterion which may be irrelevant in individual cases where social, emotional, or cultural development may be held to be more relevant. At the same time pupils did have to enter a society where a major means of assessment was, and is, external exams.

I always felt I was capable of more, also a little hurt that I didn't do as well as I thought I should, and also it did undermine my self-confidence. For all its progressiveness and everything there were still exams at the end and there was still the question of what you were going to do when you had left. (Fifties Woman MS.)

As mentioned above, 28 per cent of the sample left school without passing any examinations; but the major contribution to these 'failures' came from the thirties cohort where several men had their careers at Dartington interrupted by the war and where the pressure for women to pass exams was much lower than for the later post-war female generations (eight out of ten thirties women left unqualified). If we use five Ordinary Levels, or Schools Certificate, as the minimum criterion of a successful secondary education then over half, 57.5 per cent, of the fifties cohort left without reaching that standard. Furthermore, out of thirty-one respondents with IQs in excess of 115 some twenty did not achieve minimum university entrance standards while at Dartington. There is no systematic evidence in the school records about examination results. The Oxford and Cambridge Board were unable to provide me with a record of Dartington's GCE efforts because they do not record failures, because the grading system has changed, and because the work involved in getting at the original documents was beyond their normal scope in answering queries. With regard to the academic achievements of public school boys, Kalton (1966: 80) states that some 73 per cent pass six 'Ordinary' levels at GCE and 54 per cent pass two 'Advanced' levels. Of the 'control' sample only 7.5 per cent (three Bryanstonians in fact) left school without five 'Ordinary' levels or School Certificate. Hudson (Ash 1969: 171–80) summarises the evidence on achievement motivation and relates it to the progressive school. The progressive teacher faces the dilemma, he argues, of opting either to produce well adjusted individuals or brain workers but to do both is almost impossible because the social conditions which guarantee the former may militate against the latter:

I suspect that progressive schools make most children happier than authoritarian ones, but that they withdraw from them the cutting edge that insecurity, competition and resentment supply. I would predict that wherever we adjust children to themselves and each other we remove from them the springs of their intellectual and artistic productivity. Successful brainwork, demonstrably, is the outcome of dedication and single-mindedness, and happy children may not be prepared to make the effort that excellence demands.

Certainly it appears that quite a few of the Dartington sample found the academic permissiveness deleterious to sustained effort, concentration, and intellectual discipline. It was the subjects requiring these – Latin, Maths and Grammar, in particular – that respondents most baulked at.

I didn't do any maths after I was in the C group and I think that was a mistake on the part of the system that you could opt out of things quite so easily as that. I wished that I'd been made to do more, yes I mean it, made to do, especially now I'm a teacher which seems ridiculous that I can't do any sums further than long division. (Fifties Woman MS.)

In retrospect one respondent felt that he had been deflected from an academic career because of the inability to capitalise on his gift for mathematics.

I was just very good at maths, quite straightforward. If I'd been in any other school I would have ended up as a mathematician. There's no doubt in my mind about this and in fact my education didn't really fulfil itself and I didn't end up a mathematician. (Thirties Man MS.)

Another person arrived 'potentially brilliant' at Latin but later failed to pass School Certificate in that subject. Curry wrote to the father stating that parents who send their children to schools which deliberately avoid using the customary sanctions in regard to work must accept the consequences of this policy. English Literature, History, Geography, etc. were the popular subjects because the subject matter could be given a more immediate, intrinsic appeal and was not based upon a logical progression so that gaps in knowledge could more readily be tolerated.

At times the staff were almost in the position of selling their subject because the children could 'operate a tyranny' (as one respondent expressed it) on the teacher of an unpopular subject by not choosing to attend his classes. 'What is the best subject for me?' became transmuted to 'What subject do I enjoy most?' The effects on some children were to make them take some arbitrary and capricious educational decisions and to habituate them to by-passing obstacles rather than overcoming them. This temperament obviously has important consequences for the time when the pupil leaves Dartington for the wider society where it is more difficult for the individual to choose his own tasks and to set his own criteria of achievement.

The staff

Because it abrogates traditional authority the progressive school is dependent to a greater extent than other types of school on the quality of its staff: to implement its ideals and high aspirations requires warm and open personal relationships between the children and the adults. The implication of teaching in a radical school is that the member of staff has an ideological commitment to progressive ends. Indeed, it has often entailed financial sacrifice, as Kenneth Barnes (Child 1962: 157) has documented for the early days of Wennington.

For a while none of us had any pay; indeed for a term we all paid for our keep, but as the pupils increased we were able to draw a few shillings a week.

Also vocational demands of working in a nonconformist community are potentially great.

It was almost like accepting a priesthood to be on the staff at Dartington because they had to operate the system really for all one's waking hours because one was in and out of their rooms all day and late in the evening. I think they were probably very dedicated people. (Thirties Man MS.)

However, McConnell (1967: 171) claims a high level of commitment among staff at Eton where an assistant master might commonly work an eighty-hour week. Staff were also confined in their mobility by the independent status of Dartington which meant that their experience was not recognised in the state system and which restricted their alternatives to other progressive or independent schools. This was a major reason why the Trustees pressed for inspection and recognition in the wake of Fleming, although Curry found inspection difficult to countenance.

Curry hated being inspected. He was a liberal. 'What? The state being allowed inside this school. Never, Never!' But we said, 'No Bill, it's not fair on your staff'. (Recorded Interview with L. K. Elmhirst.)

Strangely, those who most approached the conventional teacher stereotype were often respected and effective by using their dominating personalities to enforce control.

In 'Belinda's' class you could have heard a pin drop, she kept us right underneath her thumb. She was an impressive, dignified person and you just didn't muck around in her class: she also demanded that your books were kept beautifully and if you didn't you got hell! People liked her but were also scared stiff of her. (Fifties Woman MS.)

Others endeavoured to carry along the children by the intensity of their own enthusiasm.

When 'Trevor' got on to ornithology or animal behaviour, he just lit up with excitement. I used to be engaged on making cages, you know he did all the early work on territorialism in robins, and we used to go out with him, and catch them and ring them. And because I was involved in this I got a kind of feel, I don't think I understood his research, but a feel for the enthusiasm that is implicit in good scientific research. So when I was fifteen, without knowing it, I appreciated what a good, scientific research worker, who is committed to his work, really does and feels about. (Thirties Man MS.)

Some found that their most effective sanction was to fall back upon sarcasm while all teachers had the power to exclude troublesome or unwilling children from their class – this often proved effective because it amounted to social ostracism. In other words it was lonely and boring to stay away.

There was too the occasional incompetent or misfit under whom the children had to suffer and plainly a nonconforming community may be self-selective in this respect. One respondent sketched a sympathetic portrait of a lively teacher who would probably have found it difficult to survive if asked to play a traditional teacher's role:

I was friends with Leon. He was a gas. He was such a mess. He was much more of a mess than I was even. Everybody loved him but, oh boy, what a mess. He kept trying to do crazy things like commit suicide and getting in towering rages with Curry. He was very taken with the whole spiritual side of life, his soul was burning like crazy all the time . . . he was profoundly interested in all moral questions and knew none of the answers. We asked him once why he didn't believe in Christianity and he said 'Because I would go to hell'. (Fifties Man MS.)

In some respects an even greater burden fell upon the house-staff than the teaching staff (though some staff were involved in both roles) because they carried out pronounced pastoral roles of neo-familial dimensions. The boarding situation placed a high-premium on the house-staff who were expected to be ever-present, unobtrusively vigilant, welcoming, homely figures who dispensed coffee, cocoa, advice, and implicitly, therapy. Their rooms became real foci for social gatherings and girls in early adolescence found them particularly valuable. Housemothers played almost overt maternal roles in the earlier years and a less explicit guide–counsellor–therapist–sympathetic listener role in the senior years. According to many of our respondents this extremely demanding function was well matched by the quality of people it attracted. Furthermore, in the structural provision of homely pastoral care agents, Dartington, and the progressive school, contrasted starkly with the somewhat cold masculine world of the public school. Indeed, the use of 'housemother' and 'housefather' as terms signifies a world of difference from the public school type of housemaster. The prominent role of women in the progressive schools is not matched in any other style of boarding except that found in schools for special populations, such as the handicapped, the sub-normal or the maladjusted.

From the very early history of the school there was a system of tutorships by which each child selected by ballot a member of staff to act primarily as an academic advisor but also potentially at least, as a sort of secular father-confessor. There were no hard-and-fast rules about how the tutorship was to be conducted but it was generally understood that the tutor and child would meet at intervals for consultation. They were to complement the real freedom afforded to the child with advice, guidance, and encouragement. In particular, they were meant to discuss choice of subjects, and to serve as a link between the children and the subject-teachers so that if a child was missing certain classes this would be passed on to the tutor who would try to exert some pressure.

How, in practice, did this system work? Through the eyes of a large number of respondents it left much to be desired. Its implementation was in-extricably linked with the personalities of the staff and some adopted a somewhat passive, almost negative role, whereas others were more forceful and positive. One man, for instance, recalled the constant presence of his tutor:

I can remember being constantly badgered by my tutor because I was failing to do my prep. and cutting classes. (Thirties Man P.)

On the other hand a near contemporary of his scarcely remembered any tutorials at all. The belief in non-interference in the child's freedom could mean that careers and further education advice was not readily available for fear of imposing a solution that ideally the child should arrive at himself or herself.

What is of interest to us is that the selection of tutors by children was defined to a great extent by a staff popularity-rating whereby pupils gravitated to a popular or 'in' tutor. One male teacher, for instance, was particularly popular among the girls.

Well he was rather beautiful and obviously very popular with the girls. (Fifties Woman MS.)

It may well have been gratifying for a teacher to be a frequent choice but the system could be unkind to the relatively unpopular teacher with few tutees. Also one tutor asked a pupil what sort of tutor he wanted him to be:

And he even used to say 'I'll be this sort of tutor if you want – if you want never to see me, that suits me. But if you want to have a tutorial once a week or more often, that also suits me'. (Fifties Man MS.)

And this really is the crux. From the best of motives teachers set out not to im-pose themselves on tutees; but should adolescents be asked to take decisions on their own in a situation where well-meaning passivity could verge on neglect?

Unfortunately nobody discussed the consequences with me for instance when I wanted to drop physics or biology. Nobody told me if you drop Latin you will not be able to go to such and such a university so I dropped Latin without realising the implications and this was something I very much regretted. (Fifties Woman MS.)

In brief, the evidence from many respondents raised serious doubts about the efficacy and efficiency of the tutorial system at Dartington — for many it provided very little guidance, scant encouragement, insufficient pressure, and was, in certain cases, neglectful of career and university opportunities. One explanation rests with the structural weakness of the staff role in a progressive school. For the progressive educator was expected to be almost a paragon and shouldered the burden of exceptionally high expectations. Furthermore, he or she could rely on traditional restaints in the learning situation but was enjoined to make what was taught seem worth learning. Yet the teacher's role had little overt definition as a somewhat passive or negative attitude might be construed as beneficial to the maintenance of the children's unhampered development and an active or positive attitude as almost infringing that development. The diffusiveness was further widened by the the necessity of playing the sort of role that different children demanded, namely to encourage those who appeared to need encouragement but not to interfere with those who did not. Furthermore, some staff were obviously more popular with the children than others and an unpopular housemother, for instance, might easily be deserted by her charges for a more popular member of staff. To a certain degree then there was pressure for the staff to court popularity particularly as the children could elect what classes not to attend, and this could mean choosing classes in congruence with the pupil's own values. But if they sought popularity in their general social roles outside the classroom how compatible was this with maintaining order inside the classroom? It must have been difficult to play two roles, the one permissive and the other authoritarian, in two different social settings. Thus while performance is dependent to a certain extent on the individual's personality it seems that the structural weaknesses and conflicting expectations of the staff role at Dartington could lead the individual teacher, tutor, or housemaster to resolve the demanding but diffuse expectations on him by accepting the socially popular but academically undemanding role demanded by the pupil society.

Cultural and craft activities

The school's policy in this area has traditionally been twofold; firstly, that extensive cultural provision should be part and parcel of the school's day to day existence (hence *extra*-curricular activities would be a misnomer) provided at no extra cost; and, secondly that there should be the utmost freedom of choice to participate – no child was to drink at the fount of culture unwillingly. This led to a characteristic dual theme in progressive education – neglected opportunities, regrets, and manipulation of the means for the wrong ends on the one hand, and intense enjoyment, fulfilment, and gratification on the other.

Dartington led the way, in keeping with other progressive schools, in employing an extremely wide range of recreational, cultural, and semi-educative pursuits to counterbalance the aridity of the public school's curriculum with its monotonous emphasis on Classics and Sport. However, the public school has altered considerably in this respect in recent years and Lambert *et al* (1971a: Chap. IX) detail the cultural facilities of one school:

One public school, for example, offered a choice of six sports, twenty-two societies, eight holiday trips and cultural opportunities which included the use of a large theatre, three Bechstein grands, a full sized indoor swimming pool, a weekly film that was on national circuit, and a library of fifty thousand volumes.

Dressmaking, bookbinding, music, woodwork, metalwork, painting, pottery, dance, drama, sculpting, choral and orchestral work, madrigals, ballet, play reading, printing, riding, farming, film making, sailing and other activities were available at Dartington, including societies organised around a specific interest and usually dependent on the enthusiasm of a teacher or senior pupil.

Particularly in the thirties, the cultural provision of the estate rubbed off on the school and it was difficult to remain immune from this influence.

I think it was almost impossible to come away from Dartington without a love of music and that is one of the things that I do thank it for. And there were all those extraordinary people at the Hall doing Dalcroze Eurythmics or rehearsing Chekov on the lawn. It was awfully difficult to escape this type of life. (Thirties Man MS.)

At the same time a by-product of the range of interests and the *laissez-faire* attitude to participation was that willpower could be eroded and an opportunity neglected much to later regret:

I was accepted into Dartington for music. My parents were very musical and I showed some talent for the piano when I was very young. But it was a disaster going to Dartington because it absolutely wrecked my music. It was all there, the Robin Master's Quartet, Ronald Anderson, practice rooms, people to help you with your practice. But I just did no work, it was a tragedy really. I was the sort of person who needed pushing. I might have been a good musician today if I'd gone to a school, say Eton or somewhere like that, where they do have good music facilities and push you. (Thirties Man MS.)

There were occasions of impressive cooperation and sustained effort when some active or energetic personality could set the lead. For example, the swimming pool was dug out, four girls constructed their own looms, some children built a potting kiln, one boy founded a sailing club, carol singers raised £80 in 1956 for Hungarian refugees, while one girl threw herself into entertainments.

In my last three years I produced cabarets, wrote the songs, did the choreography, general entertainment. I was always a good organiser so I would put up a notice 'planning half-term review – helpers please sign' and I would find as many as forty to fifty names. Curry even asked me not to do my cabarets during the summer term when exams were on but other times I was kept very busy with it and found it very gratifying. (Fifties Woman MS.)

Some of the more criminalesque elements manipulated the craft provision for their own ends and made keys for every lock in the building. There was, too, considerable apathy at times and the munificent facilities were not always exploited to their full potential. The progressive school is faced with the dilemma of accepting the regrets over wasted opportunities and the neglect of talent as an inevitable corollary of freedom or of attempting to close the gap by greater encouragement, stimulation, and individual guidance in utilising their cultural provision. For the enthusiastic individual who could supply his or her own motivation the facilities were outstanding; yet some children remained unable to take advantage of them.

I spent a lot of time on the piano which I took up late. A bit on the trumpet. Painting? No. Pottery? I messed around a bit with pots from time to time, and did some acting in the school plays. But I spent a fair amount of time just strolling around, eating bread and jam in the kitchenettes. It began to hang on you after a while and it got a bit boring towards the end. (Fifties Man MS.)

But perhaps the most revealing remark came from one respondent whose interest in potting in the Middle School did not survive the move to Foxhole because it involved a journey down to Aller Park to the potting shed.

I could never make the effort to cycle over to Aller Park to pot at intervals. Time was too valuable. Something social might be going on. (Fifties Man.)

Conclusion

Before turning our attention to the fates of our respondents after leaving Dartington we can briefly look at their feelings about the school. For instance, they were asked simply whether or not they were happy at Dartington. The vast majority, 92 per cent, replied that they were either 'very happy' (57 per cent) or 'happy' (35 per cent); the few who were not particularly happy exonerated the school (and mentioned personal problems or preoccupations with the problems at home) while only one respondent claimed to have been really unhappy with the school. Three-quarters of the sample said that they 'never' regretted having been to Dartington. However, this did not debar respondents from raising specific regrets and these were almost invariably centred on three problems. Firstly, some felt that their academic potential had not been developed; secondly, some found the notoriety of being in a progressive school difficult to bear when outside; and thirdly, some considered that they had been insufficiently prepared to meet the 'reality' of the outside world. But there was no questioning the unequivocal nature of their affection for the school.

|Interviewer: were you happy at Dartington?]

I loved it, yes, I loved Dartington.

|Interviewer: any regrets?]

Gosh, no. (Fifties Woman MS.)

In following the children into the wider society we should continually remind ourselves of four main elements in their background (which, of course, will have been differentially internalised by different respondents). Firstly, most of their relationships, including those with adults, were on a highly personalised, primary-group level. Secondly, the school had provided them with a warm and supportive environment, that for a minority may have amounted to a home substitute. Thirdly, they had developed a consciousness of being different or special. And fourthly, and in some ways most importantly, they had come to look upon authority as benign, and amenable to rational discussion. The problems that this could engender were described by two young women:

Dartington was different from and better than the outside world. But a worse problem than being better was being different: all the children were conscious that theirs' was not like 'ordinary' schools, and this caused isolation and snobbishness. On first leaving it was a terrible shock to my self-esteem that quite pleasant, normal people, not obviously perverted or maladjusted, came from ordinary schools. I also left with other unconventional assumptions but held them as prejudices, for instance that any punishment is wrong, corporal punishment is always sadistic, 'esprit de corps' is intrinsically a bad thing. (Fifties Woman MS.)

The only disadvantages of going to a school like Dartington is the fact that everywhere you go you are aware that people are noticing you and watching and seeing how you behave because after all you went to that awful school Dartington. We did get a bit fed up with that and we noticed that children who came from public schools could behave as badly as they liked; it didn't matter because after all they went to Winchester or whatever. (Fifties Woman MS.)

Part Two

Life after school

Chapter Eight

Leaving school

[Interviewer: How did you feel about leaving?]

Rather sad, sorrow. And rather wished I could have stayed on longer because it's a fantastic life. But it doesn't set you up for civilian life because when you are at Dartington it gives you no form of discipline, and when you go into the outside world life catches up with you with an almighty bang, and you suddenly realise you can't say, 'sod you, I'm going', because you've just got to do what you are told. And it took me a long, long time. I mean the Army wasn't enough. I had to have endless set-backs after the Army, countless things, and I'm still a bit like it now. I still have this attitude which has been allowed to breed in me and develop because of Dartington, that from the out-set the attitude has always been 'sod you, I'll go somewhere else'. And it's the wrong attitude, isn't it? (Fifties Man MS.)

The progressively educated adult may feel something of a stranger both in 'respectable' English society and in formal organisations. The conformity and proprieties of the former, and the hierarchy and impersonality of the latter, are at odds with the progressives' stress on individualism, nonconformity, non-competitiveness, and primary-group relationships. Certain public school vir-tues, on the other hand, are held to be positively functional in managerial and executive positions (Wilkinson and Bishop 1967: 29); in addition, there are firmly legitimated institutions in the wider society which offer support to the public school product, such as the Old Boy and London Clubs. The progressive culture generally is fragmentary and non-institutional in its loca-tion – except perhaps for Hampstead, university enclaves, and certain oc-cupations – and tends to be 'cosmopolitan' and metropolitan.

The expression of that culture is normally so distinctive, in dress, language, behaviour, and norms (Punch 1970d) that we would expect it to persist in an individual after exposure to it unless opposition or subsequent experience causes him or her to adapt in some degree to a more conformist life-style. The factors which might cause such adaptations are myriad, but we can examine some of the major areas, such as marriage, work, and friendships, which are accepted as normally contributing to adult socialisation in order to assess the extent to which they are likely to help or hinder reinforcement of the progressive life-style. The depth of internalisation of the progressive culture, the relative significance of the home and the school in the process of transmis-sion of that culture, and the extent to which the individual perceives it as con-flicting with 'reality' will vary from respondent to respondent and we have regrettably no objective means of assessing these differences.

Some Dartington pupils, for instance, will have returned to more conformist influences at home, some will have imbibed progressivism and found
themselves in conflict with the home, while others will have found reinforcement at Dartington for the norms and values of their home background. Most
encountered some institution or circumstance on leaving that did not fully
reflect, or indeed was antagonistic to, progressive values and it is this interaction with, and adaptation to, the wider society that we wish to observe in the
second half of this work. Michael Frayn (Sissons and French 1964: 331) has
satirised the ambivalent stance of the left-wing intellectual in our society and
his humorous delineation of the two major social types in the English middle
class provides us with indicators of what we expect both from a progressive,
and a non-progressive adult. He wrote of the 1951 Festival of Britain:

In fact, Festival Britain was the Britain of the radical middle classes – the do-gooders;
the readers of the *News Chronicle, The Guardian*, and the *Observer*; the signers of
petitions; the backbone of the BBC. In short, the Herbivores, or gentle ruminants,
who look out from the lush pastures which are their natural station in life with eyes full
of sorrow for less fortunate careers, guiltily conscious of their advantages, though not
usually ceasing to eat the grass. And in making the Festival they earned the contempt
of the Carnivores – the readers of the *Daily Express*; the Evelyn Waughs; the cast of
the *Directory of Directors* – the members of the upper and middle classes who believe
that if God had not wished them to prey on all smaller and weaker creatures without
scruple he would not have made them as they are.

For in its tolerance, diminished aggression, absence of competition, and its
counter-cultural values, Dartington probably renders some of its members
less equipped for the competitive struggle beyond its walls. Kenneth Barnes of
Wennington (Child 1962: 12 and 168) perceives this problem but counters it
forcefully:

If you take the detailed record of the subsequent history of the movement's pupils you
will seen an astonishing record of originality. It is simply amazing to see how many of
them have broken into new fields of thought or action in some way or another,
become leaders or pioneers in that particular field. I am not merely concerned, as I
might be if I were just working from statistics, with originality that can be measured in
a techological, or literary, or artistic field. I am thinking also of originality and
creativity in personal relationships . . . Not many children suffer frustration or disappointment in attempting to establish themselves in a career; but many tend to be
experimental rather than to settle quickly – they are enterprising and adventurous.
Observers often anticipate that children educated in this unusual community will have
difficulty in adjusting themselves to the less sensitive 'world' when they meet it. They
do have some difficulty, but precisely the difficulty I should want them to have. If they
merely adjusted themselves to the demands of an affluent and aggressive society it
would mean that our education was a total failure. The important question to ask is
whether the difficulty stimulates from them a vigorous, discriminating and construc-

tive response. In general, I think it does.

Here it is crucial to appreciate that difficulty on leaving is common in many expressive total institutions such as the public schools, service academics, and even Oxbridge colleges. Lambert (1968: 46), for example, has outlined the secular influence of the public school on its old boys.

The public school boy's commitment is of the affective and expressive kind, in which the school is regarded with deep feeling, as an end in itself, a profoundly experienced community by which he is formed, whose influence he later acknowledges and rewards, and whose pattern of life he sometimes seeks to perpetuate in adult life – in old boy organisations, club life, and other deeper conscious ways (man–woman relations perhaps).

Clearly some children from Dartington experienced significant problems of adjustment on return to the outside world, although this may be less the result of a progressive residential style than of the tendency in middle class residential institutions of all sorts to build up considerable dependency in the children they shelter. Because some middle class families may fail to develop a satisfactory role for the child and because their children board long from an early age in closed institutions, inevitably their emotional, spiritual and material needs are centred on the school and met within it. It is this that builds up dependence on the institution, although one could argue that certain elements in the progressive schools may accentuate it.

For example, the progressive child may actually be socialised to values that are counter to those of their parents where the latter are fairly conventional.

When I went back to India we had our confrontations and by golly we had them. I would pick on anything, everything they did was wrong – how they treated the Indians, what were they doing in India anyway, oh, I attacked their whole life. We argued bitterly from the moment I set foot in India, I started on them, on my father, on drinking whisky and on the club, and the white man. You can imagine, the whole thing. Until finally he got red in the face and livid, but this is boarding school isn't it? Hopeless! They tried their best. He got angry and mother got fed up. Eventually I went off and lived with another family. They couldn't really take it, because they hadn't grown up with us. (Thirties Woman P.)

Additionally, the progressive educational community tends to be inward-looking, and informal attitudes and values are frequently all-encompassing so that identification is almost inescapable.

I came with no preconceived respect for the ideals of the School: and yet in a year or two I became, as did most of my contemporaries, an almost fanatical adherent of all for which I conceived the School to stand ... Perhaps the most vivid recollection I have of the Bedales of 1908–12 is of my grief – I think I may say *our* grief – at leaving; or to put it another way, of the depth and completeness with which the school took hold of our imaginations. (L. Zilliacus of Bedales in Badley 1924: 159.)

These difficulties and dilemmas are frequently overlooked or rationalised in the progressive literature and assertion replaces evidence. In general, there is little known about the long-term effects of institutions on people who have passed through them. The following chapters constitute a small effort towards filling this gap and towards replacing the self-comforting assertions of progressives with evidence.

Pupils of ours have won Open Scholarships and gained places to a number of universities including Oxford and Cambridge ... We are proud of our academic successes, but we are just as pleased about old pupils who are happy and successful as farmers and gardeners and television cameramen ... We are in touch with a number of old pupils who went right through the school. Without exception these have turned out very well. They are happy and successful in their jobs and in their marriages, too, and they are interesting and agreeable company – what's more, they all have some constructive role in society. This is our answer to the people who ask 'will this sort of education fit them for life?'. (Eleanor Urban of Monkton Wyld in Child 1962: 122.)

Aim on leaving

The period prior to leaving Dartington, judging by many of the interviews, was characterised by vacillation, indecision, and uncertainty. The implications of earlier decisions to drop academic subjects came home to roost as people faced university or college entrance and found themselves deficient in some respect. At this stage people began to judge themselves by outside criteria and many found their accomplishments wanting. Many had little definite aim in mind and some were reluctant to leave. For a few there began a niggling disenchantment with the school that almost amounted to a sense of betrayal. This was particularly true of some girls who found their social potential exhausted by sixteen while the number of eligible older boys diminished.

In fact some 60 per cent of the main sample were either undecided or had no idea what they wished to do on leaving school whereas the remaining 40 per cent had some definite occupation or vocation in mind. But then 82 per cent of the whole sample did not proceed immediately to full-time paid employment. The majority went on to some form of higher or further education, the Armed Forces, occupational training, or travel. Their ages at leaving were 8 per cent at fifteen, 28 per cent at sixteen, 37 per cent at seventeen, and 27 per cent at eighteen. Overall, some 73 per cent of the sample had left before their eighteenth year which is the year when Advanced Level, of Higher School Certificate, was normally taken.

Most of those who were 'certain' about their immediate future came from 'congruent' homes and aspired to cultural–creative occupations for which Dartington could provide an ideal entrée. One or two of these respondents were unrealistic and failed to achieve their goal but most succeeded in following their chosen pursuit. Usually they entered a profession that demanded a high commitment – medicine, the arts, or farming – and there were seven cases of self-recruitment to parent's professions (three in medicine, three in farming, and one in the theatre). Almost without exception this sub-group entered some form of professional training. To a large extent, the 'certain' respondents came from homes which were congruent with the school and where the school could provide anticipatory socialisation for the adult occupational role.

I was ready to leave. The thing was I knew what I wanted to do and consequently I had an aim and this was just part of getting it accomplished. So for about six or nine months after I left school I worked on one of the estate farms, the Parsonage Farm, and lived in Foxhole. Then I worked at home for nine months, went up to Scotland and worked on a sheep farm for three months, then started at Agricultural College. (Fifties Man MS.)

The reverse of this also held true to a great extent in that there were far more 'aimless' children from 'incongruent' homes than congruent homes. Children of parents with 'organisation' occupations seemed to suffer in particular (cf. Roe's 1956 classification in Chapter 3 where the category 'organisation' comprised occupations such as director, accountant, higher civil servants, etc.). Also those who had been the shortest time at the school were most likely to be aimless as also were those in the age group leaving at seventeen. It would seem that an incongruent home disorientates the child as he or she is more likely to experience conflict between the school's and parental expectations. Further, that a child coming late to Dartington from an incongruent home may well be disturbed in some respect and that the late immersion in progressivism proves unsettling. There was a tendency for boys to leave earlier, so that nine boys in the fifties cohort had 'no idea' of what to do on leaving compared to five girls, and the limited vocational horizons at Dartington probably affected male pupils more than females for whom Art College, nursing, or teaching, were comparatively easy to enter at that time.

Several respondents roundly blamed the school for its introspection, insularity, and its failure to equip them adequately for the 'real' world. One woman claimed that once the staff in the thirties decided to hold classes on the outside world (with slides of women's magazines and recordings of popular music) but a near contemporary of hers outlined his opinions on the school's failure to relate to other than progressive values.

Yes, [Dartington was] out of touch with the outside world. Yes, I think the system is in fact not geared up to this. There was no case of positive help and guidance, of education for the world. All just sort of education for Dartington's atmosphere. You see they are concerned with the development of the child, but I think you come to a stage where a child, you know adolescence and becoming an adult, where you need to relate it to more than this childish society. And it needs to be able to develop its faculties and abilities. But Dartington was so much a Shangri-la, self-sufficient in its own way, it really is a Shangri-la and it took away from you the incentive, you weren't hungry at Dartington so one wasn't pressed, there was no need to make one's way in the world . . . If there was something you wanted to do well and good. 'Otto' [now an artist] was one of my contemporaries there and about once or twice a term he'd put on a smock and go up to the Art School and paint pictures and I'd say, 'what in the hell do you want to go up there for? Come, let's go and steal some apples or something' and I've heard it said that some children there would say, 'hell, have we got to go back to school now and do exactly as we please?' There was this vacuum somehow and it got quite boring sometimes. Put it this way, there's no stimulation coming in all the time from outside. You get, in a normal life, stimulation where there are irritants, opportunities, ideas, suggestions, or constant mixing which makes things work and gives children material to work on. But there you're in an artificial and in some senses a sterile atmosphere. It is the land of the lotus-eaters really where everything you need is easily satisfied. Except this. There's no bit of grit in the oyster. And I think it weakened them as people very much. It was the lack of stimulation and challenge and the insulation which does cause them to cling there afterwards. (Thirties Man MS.)

Some respondents went through a series of impulsive and short-lived aspirations (and this pattern could persist into further education or their careers).

Well I had various ideas. I started off wanting to be a physiotherapist and I had to have Chemistry. And I remember doing Chemistry for about a year, trying to catch up. And after this idea I think I wanted to be a games teacher. That was the next craze and then I decided to do primary school teaching and then I didn't get enough 'O' levels and so I went and did nursery nursing which I enjoyed very much. (Fifties Woman MS.)

Difficulty of leaving

The indecisiveness about the future among the majority of the respondents was probably one symptom of a certain reluctance to leave Dartington; for the people with little or no idea found it more difficult to leave than those with a set idea for their future. In fact, 17 per cent of the whole sample found it very difficult to leave and 35 per cent somewhat difficult but, conversely, almost half, 48 per cent, experienced little or no difficulty in leaving. What were the correlates of difficulty in leaving for the Dartingtonians?

Again (as with the 'undecided' subgroup) it was those who had been the shortest time at the school (and not, as one might expect, the longest) who found most difficulty in leaving and also it was the seventeen year old group who suffered most. It did not appear to be related to previous history of maladjustment, a disturbed background, parental marital problems, or type of home. A disturbed home background, for instance, did not make the respondent so dependent on the school that they found it more difficult to leave in a greater proportion than those with disturbed backgrounds who did not find it difficult. The significance of the seventeen year old age group experiencing difficulty may be that the normal leaving ages are sixteen and eighteen. Those who stay on a year longer have lost the support of their peer group, many of whom have left, have passed the peak of their social career, and probably do not have the motivation to complete a sixth-form course. Indeed, they may have stayed on another year simply to avoid leaving (one boy stayed for two years after School Certificate doing 'nothing, and it did get boring in the end') or to collect some more examination passes. Hence leaving school early before the usual age may have been experienced as more of an interruption than for those who had little alternative but to leave.

Certainly the attachment of some respondents to Dartington was that for a home substitute.

For me it was very difficult because this was the womb. This was home. Incredibly difficult, yes. I wasn't upset because I knew that it had to happen but this was where my heart was, let's put it like that. (Thirties Woman P.)

Several girls were able to work in the children's nursery at Dartington rather than leave the estate completely. Probably the girls were more outwardly emotional about leaving and one 'cried bitterly' on the railway station.

Curry said 'Never mind. If you're miserable and unhappy you can come back to us, don't worry. But I was miserable and I think we were all sad. (Fifties Woman MS.)

At the same time, there was a temptation for some people to linger and one woman recalled that her sister had to be given a slight jolt to make her aware of the reality of the situation.

[Interviewer: Did Curry's attitude to people seem to change at all when they left?]

My sister felt that, but she was certainly worse off than me about leaving, and they more or less had to say to her, 'you can't stay here forever'. And I think he may have been afraid that people would come and sort of live off the school and, of course, he would have found out that there are a certain amount of people who really live off Dartington and lead a slightly artificial existence. There are some I know that couldn't get on anywhere else, sometimes this can be nice but sometimes it seems to be a sort of retreat, an escape. Perhaps they could manage something if only they had a bit more of a push. (Thirties Woman MS.)

Some people went through a restless, depressed, anomic phase after leaving and several returned to visit the school in the first few years – one thirties respondent said people talked of becoming teachers so that they could return to work at Dartington. For many there was a problem of adjusting to the outside world and the difficulty arose for two main reasons – first was the latent conflict between the progressive life-style and non-progressive institutions and, second, was the consciousness of being different. One pilot respondent, now in business, pinpointed the first dilemma:

It was difficult for me to leave, in fact you hadn't been prepared and afterwards this made life difficult. *Education for Sanity* [Curry 1947] says why. I left with the notion that people behaved kindly and rationally and I lived my life as though they did. But I don't think that's correct. I think people are more competitive and aggressive and, in a way, Dartington is an unreal society. Now I'm much more competitive. (Fifties Man P.)

In another instance, one man was scarcely aware that his studied directness and premature assumption of an adult air was considered outrageous by other people.

Well I spoke to them as if I were an adult and this they found staggering and they couldn't get used to it. For example, I went to a party in Cape Town at which the admiral in charge of the Simonstown Naval Base – I think he was an admiral or higher, anyway a naval bloke with lots of scrambled egg on his sleeve – well, he was there and we sat down to tea and I was sitting next to him and I can remember, much to the horror of some people with me, saying 'What's it like to be in the navy? How much do you earn?' He was so staggered by this that he couldn't even reprimand me; probably from Dartmouth Naval College onwards he had never heard anything like it. So, this took me some adjusting. It wasn't a painful adjustment – more for other people really. (Thirties Man MS.)

With regard to feeling different one woman – and women were more likely to suffer from this – remarked:

This is something when you leave school. This is what you felt you had to stand up for – 'Oh, that's the school where they wear nothing all the year round', and 'Oh well, if you went there God help you' – and because you thought so much of it and so on you really had to stand up for it. There was quite a lot of prejudice in that way. (Fifties Woman MS.)

Another woman was asked if she felt different at college because of having been to Dartington:

Well, the girls tended to accept me. In fact I converted quite a lot, much to their parents' horror. But there was a feeling that you were slightly, I don't know what really, with a shady past is the only way I can think of putting it. 'Here's the girl who doesn't like the Queen'. This was from the parents of these girls. You know, not because I said anything about the Queen but just because I had gone to Dartington. I didn't like the Queen anyway! And 'you went to the school where you could do what you liked'. This used to really annoy me. (Fifties Woman MS.)

A woman wrote in a postal reply that her outrageousness was incongruous because it clashed with her otherwise middle-class mannerisms:

My tolerance for other people with views other than those of the people with whom I had been closeted for the seventeen years was non-existent. Now they were bosses and my colleagues and it was pretty hard to accept that they were even human. Also a small thing – my language was foul. I remember being on a bus with another Dartingtonian and looking up to see everybody staring at us. Had it just been the holidays we would have laughed it off but it wasn't, this was the real world and we would have to watch our language (had we been swearing in Cockney accents nobody would have noticed us!). (Fifties Woman Postal Quest.)

Yet another wrote of the necessity to justify continually her Dartington background:

Anyone who has been to a progressive school has probably all through the school years (and even after) had to defend the system against people who deride everything it means, has to be very wary in saying anything about mixed nude bathing, mixed sleeping quarters, freedom of speech (including swearing) and other little things which are taken so completely for granted by members of the school. One gets very much on the defensive and perhaps after a while certain points become set in one's mind in a certain unthinking and 'nothing can be wrong' way as a result of being on the defensive and trying to win over hardnuts by whitewashing or leaving out certain bits of information which to a conservative minded person might rankle. (Stanford 1958.)

Much depended on the social milieu in which the recent Dartington leaver mixed and its congruence with progressivism. One girl went to a West Country town.

I had nothing in common with people and I'm not a snob in any way but I just found that I didn't wish to know anybody. It's such a pokey little hole and I was that different girl – 'I fancy her, she's a bit different' – so I felt like a fish out of water, completely. (Fifties Woman MS.)

But what is evident, then, is that for about half of our respondents moving into the outside world brought an awareness of the conflict between the two cultures in which they moved. The progressive idealism of Dartington was well expressed by one man:

I think Dartington did try in a very class conscious society to give children an idea of a society which could one day be less class conscious and more like the one class society with such values as equal opportunities for all. So that Dartington gives you a liberal outlook. It also gives you a very much more sensitive attitude towards the arts . . . and I think the most successful thing about a coeducational school is the question of sexual attitudes. This is something I feel strongly about and I think you will bear this out with me [to his wife] that unlike the majority of English males I don't have any particular awkwardness with women. I feel you meet women quite equally the same way you don't feel some tasks are only for women and some only for men, you except either sex to do anything they feel capable of doing. (Thirties Man MS.)

Higher/further education

The majority of the main sample went on to some form of higher or further education or occupational training. Stewart (1968: 326) gives 84 per cent as the percentage of his progressive respondents gaining 'one additional qualification by further study', while 36 per cent of his respondents gained degrees or an equivalent. This is roughly the same as Kalton's (1966: 95) figures for public school leavers. But firstly, Stewart's figures are based on a 56 per cent response rate (after two schools had been eliminated for low response rates) and cover the years 1933 to 1958 without breaking down his figures in relation to the substantial increases in higher education opportunities in the later post-war period. Hence his figures must be treated with some caution.

Some 30 per cent of the Dartington sample attempted a first degree (six respondents, or 10 per cent, also took a postgraduate course) while the remainder of those who did not work straight from school attended Art College, Colleges of Education, Technical College, or Agricultural College. Six went to Cambridge, four to London, and four to provincial universities to read for first degrees, while two went to universities abroad. Three studied medicine and qualified as doctors. Five attended Polytechnics or the equivalent, five went to Colleges of Education (two as postgraduates) seven to Art Colleges, three to Music College, five to Agricultural College, two to Drama College, and one to a College of Printing. Of the main sample, 45 per cent studied for up to three years after school, 22 per cent studied for up to six years, and 10 per cent in excess of six years. Asked if they enjoyed the institution of learning attended after Dartington, 40 per cent replied 'yes', 45 per cent said 'moderately', and 17.5 per cent said 'not at all or very little'. These figures are expressed as the proportion of the sub-sample attending other institutions of higher/further education after Dartington. The women, in particular, tended to be more deprecatory than men.

For some respondents, the articulateness and *savoir-faire* of the Dartingtonian helped them adjust to further education. Progressive pupils, for example, tend to perform well in the interview situation (Child 1962: 168).

In seeking university entrance our pupil's ability to be responsive and at ease in an interview, and their wide interests, have counted heavily in their favour.

Also Skidelsky (1969: 33) wrote of former pupils from Bedales:

Bedalians are disconcertingly articulate and well-informed; and university interviewing bodies obviously go for them in a big way.

But for others it was simply a return to unenlightened, authoritarian pedagogy. The themes of the previous section reappear; namely culture conflict and a prickly self-consciousness. The fifties man who had been shocked on leaving by the virulence of religion at Cambridge was echoed by a thirties woman who had experienced the same awakening:

> It was a hell of a shock to me at college. First the emphasis on sport, and also religion. We thought it was archaic and outmoded and nobody realised that religion still had any influence in any way at all. (Thirties Woman MS.)

The same anti-authoritarianism, apparent before Dartington at traditional schools, reappears and we find respondents leading complaints about food, or poor digs, or getting into hot water for not calling the lecturer 'sir'! Some struggled to pass their exams over a number of years with motivation still hard to acquire; one man tried to pick up the threads of a musical education but claimed he had missed too much groundwork at Dartington; another took up boxing but not with the university.

> I wasn't interested in the competition so I joined the Battersea Boxing Club, you know dockers and that sort of people. (Fifties Man MS.)

Another hated the mono-sexuality of Cambridge and thought there was something wrong with a room without a girl in it; some claimed to have encountered racial prejudice and stereotypes for the first time; others set about 'converting' their colleagues to progressive ideals; and many found educational life after Dartington a disappointment and an anticlimax.

Three main areas aroused their critical comment – the dull formalism of academic work, the irksomeness of discipline and authority, and the hypocrisy with which other people behaved in relationships between the sexes. For girls, their directness was both an attraction for males and a cause of complaint from other females. Indeed, it was the women who seemed particularly prone to abandon courses before their completion; in all fifteen respondents did not complete courses (seventeen if we include apprenticeships) and, of these fifteen, nine were women while three women failed to finish two courses each. In a curious way the Dartingtonian was perhaps something of an innocent and, beneath the surface sophistication, was vulnerable to a world where social and sexual roles were played with less openness; for the ease of relationships between the sexes at Dartington was posited on the fact that, ideally, no one was going to take advantage of someone else. The impersonality, the callousness, the role duplicity, and overt sexuality of some people outside of Dartington shocked several respondents. For example one woman abandoned drama college after one term.

> I wanted to be a vet, but gave that up, then a journalist, then not really knowing what I wanted to do at all thought I'd go in for acting. But at the end of the first term I said, 'God! This is so damn artificial. I'm not going to be able to stick this' and threw it in. The kids were very way out and I'd had no experience at all. One girl wore very tight trousers, high-heeled shoes, and lots of make-up. (Fifties Woman MS.)

Another woman contrasted the warmth of Dartington with the impersonality of her college:

I always felt that school really was quite religious in a sense, in that people were always thinking about other people and doing things for each other. I felt this was much more religious and when I went to college I was simple horrified when I went into the college dining room and everbody sat down to their lunch. I think they collected it and they sat down. And nobody offered to get anyone else's lunch, nobody offered to clear anyone else's place, nobody offered to get anyone else a drink. It didn't seem to occur to them. There didn't seem to be any sort of feeling. I suppose these children hadn't really lived in a community like we had and there didn't seem to be any social feelings at all as far as I could see. (Fifties Woman MS.)

And, as another woman expressed it:

You didn't get so closely involved with them [people at College] as you weren't all sleeping together. (Fifties Woman MS.)

The importance of further or higher education is that it provided the first experience after Dartington of immersion in a traditional learning situation and a conventional community. Half of our respondents adjusted to this new environment perfectly well (some even found themselves better equipped to make use of the more adult responsibility than people from orthodox schools) but half found some difficulty in adjusting. Most survived, but a minority opted out for a variety of reasons, and institutions of further or higher education could serve as a buffer between Dartington and the occupational world and hence promote socialisation to more 'conformist' adult roles.

The Armed Forces

If there is one institution positively antithetical to the progressive ethos it is the Armed Forces. Militarism, aggression, instant obedience, traditional authority, uniform, enforced conformity, and the possibility of taking human life are nearly all anathema to the pacific humanism of progressive education. Yet conscription was a reality both for the thirties cohort who were involved in a war and for the fifties cohort who faced National Service. In all nineteen men entered the forces; of the remainder nine were deferred or ineligible, one served in a non-combatant unit, and two were conscientious objectors.

The proportion who objected from Quaker schools was 36.3 per cent according to Stewart's (1968: 334) figures, and for all his respondents it was 28.8 per cent. Probably modesty prevented any Dartington respondents from mentioning decorations (although one pilot respondent won the Sword of Honour at Sandhurst). The Bedales School Roll (1962: 317) however, mentions a list of military distinctions including a Victoria Cross in both world wars, five DSOs, three DSCs, and thirty-one MCs. Under the analysis of occupations in the Roll some 4 per cent of male Bedalians (62 out of 1,500) have made careers in the Services. Two Dartingtonians enlisted as regulars from the main sample.

The number of male respondents who found service life most unpalatable was exactly equal to the number of men who positively enjoyed the forces (six men in each case). Not surprisingly, it was the military discipline, and the boredom, which respondents complained about.

I hated the thing that Dartington never had and that was discipline. I couldn't stand it, I knew I was as intelligent as the chap with three stripes but he could call me all the names under the sun. I had horrible things said to me, which after Dartington where everyone was so damn nice to you. My reaction to begin with was to be scared, then I saw through their various stripes, decided I loathed them for their ignorance and went through hating everything. (Fifties Man MS.)

Not only was it irksome to be controlled but also it was distasteful to be asked to exert authority over other people. While two respondents were commissioned, and three were NCOs, there was a strong feeling that Dartingtonians should not accept commissions. For some respondents the Army was their first introduction to the caste hierarchy of English society and, instinctively rejecting the upper and middle classes, they tended to gravitate to the working class elements.

I quickly reacted against being officer material and decided in myself that I would be right at the bottom and I always tried to get myself into a barrack room with what were considered the untouchables, the lorry drivers and so on. Funny thing, I don't know why. (Fifties Man MS.)

One man actually avoided being an officer.

One of the things about the Dartington subculture was it would have been bad for me to accept a commission. For instance, we teased 'Simon' who did take one but really we considered it rather shocking. I disliked the idea of officers so I went into the ranks . . . I influenced two people in our billet to join the local Labour party and several middle class conservative people in the billets were very upset indeed by me because I was crossing class lines. (Fifties Man P.)

On the other hand there were several respondents who almost blossomed under a military regime.

I loathed the Army when I went in – I hated it more than my prep. school – and I could have cried when I left it. (Thirties Man MS.)

In another case, a pilot respondent found instant release among service discipline after Dartington. (Bettelheim (1969: 232) describes a similar feeling of relief among Israeli kibbutzniks on joining the Army).

I loved it. It was the *first time I'd ever been free* – no prep., no work to do, *no sense of any pressure to have to do anything.* And I remember this so clearly that one felt one had no responsibilities. I felt as though a tremendous weight had been lifted from me. The early weeks in the army I absolutely adored. This marvellous feeling of everything being done for you. (Thirties Man P. Emphasis added.)

Of interest in the accounts of this subgroup of male respondents was the sense of purpose, the stabilising influence of discipline, and the ability to concentrate and work when forced to, that the Forces seemed to provide for these particular respondents. But for most respondents conscription was unavoidable and merely something to be endured along the line of least-resistance, and then forgotten.

Chapter Nine
Work

In the previous chapter we dealt with some aspects of the short-term adjustment of our sample to the wider society after leaving school. In the following chapters we are concerned with their long-term adjustment as adults and one crucial area for examination is work. Occupation is one of the chief sources of an individual's status and identity in our society and adaptation to occupational norms an important source of secondary socialisation, especially for men. As the majority of our female sample was not in permanent paid employment we will have to rely, of necessity, largely on the data for men. We can look at the present occupations of our male sample, at the attitudes to work of all our respondents, at a brief consideration of the womens' jobs, and at the occupational adaptations of our male Dartingtonians. What work then were the male Dartingtonians pursuing at the time of interviewing? Using Roe's (1956: 151) classification of job types allied to a social class dimension we have a twofold table (Table 2) similar to that used in Chapter 3.

Stewart's figures (1968: 328–9) on occupations of progressively educated adults are not really comparable with our samples because they do not constitute a sample but only a 54 per cent response of his population and do not differentiate between men and women. In addition, he places teachers in the 'Service' category, which at 24.9 per cent was the largest proportion in any of his eight categories, whereas Roe herself placed them in the 'General Culture' category (a procedure which I have followed). However, his evidence does suggest how men and women from progressive schools are distributed occupationally. He noted, for instance, that 16 per cent of his respondents qualified as doctors or dentists while 14 per cent gained a qualification in education (over half of his 'Service' sub-group were teachers, or 18.5 per cent of all respondents). 'Science' and 'Service' sub-groups contained a high proportion of Quakers and he mentions that Quaker men are three times as numerous in the 'Service' category as men from non-Quaker schools. He concluded:

Without trying to lean too heavily on these figures we can see a broad distribution of careers with teaching and service highest of all, organisation and science close behind, and Quaker patterns of service revealing themselves predictably. Again the arts have a higher place than is usual, especially for the unattached schools.

With small samples widely distributed it is hazardous to place overmuch

TABLE 2. *Occupations of Dartington males and Bryanston control using Roe's (1956) categories and Registrar General's classification (Bryanston in brackets)*

Class	1 Service	2 Business	3 Organisation	4 Technology	5 Outdoor	6 Science	7 General culture	8 Arts and entertainment	Totals (Social class)
I	1	1 [1]			1 [1]	2 [4]			5 [6]
II		3 [1]	2 [5]	2	4		3 [3]	4 [1]	18 [10]
III (Non-manual)			1 [1]	[1]					1 [2]
III (Manual)				3 [1]					3 [1]
IV	1							1 [1]	2 [1]
V									
Total Roe categories	2	4 [2]	3 [6]	5 [2]	5 [1]	2 [4]	3 [3]	5 [2]	29* [20]

* One in Armed Forces = 30.

credence on the proportions for Dartington men but the four highest sub-groups were Technology, Outdoor, and Arts–Entertainment (all 17 per cent each) and Business (14 per cent). The Bedales School Roll (1962) provides additional comparative data on the occupations of former pupils of a progressive school but, once more, the evidence is not strictly comparable because of the idiosyncratic categories which the compilers of the Roll chose to adopt. It employs its own classification – The Professions; Commerce and Industry; Arts and Crafts; Domestic; Land, Sea and Air; Defence Forces – and reveals that most Bedalians are either in the Professions (roughly 25 per cent with 277 men to 236 women) or especially Commerce and Industry. Some 40 per cent work in the latter group where Bedales men predominate in ratio roughly 6:1. Occupations particularly attractive to Old Bedalians would seem to be medicine, dentistry, teaching, science, literature and journalism, business, engineering, arts and crafts, and farming. Obviously a progressive education has not incapacitated many Bedalians from filling formal occupational roles.

Two professions that do not figure largely in either Stewart (1968) or the Bedales Roll (1962) are the Church and the Forces. One might foresee this from the non-denominational or agnostic/atheist tenor of most progressive schools and from their strong pacifist strain. Kalton (1966: 95), however, records that 6 per cent of public school leavers joined the Armed Forces, two-thirds of whom entered one of the Forces Colleges, while the proportion going into the Forces from the independent boarders was 9 per cent (which probably reflects the high proportion of boarders' parents who are themselves in the Forces). Further contrasts with data from public schools emerge in Wakeford (1967: 229), where he writes of *first* occupations after school:

The most frequently mentioned first occupations were ... medical pratitioners; accountants, professional company secretaries and registrars; farmers; mechanical engineers; technologists ... and clerks, cashiers, and machine operators.

With regard to the *present* occupations of Wakeford's sample 34 per cent are employers and managers in socio-economic groups 1 and 2 (compared to 9.5 per cent of all economically active males in England and Wales in 1961) and 6 per cent are farmers.

The most sophisticated survey of public school men's careers is that of Bishop and Wilkinson (1967) who were able to trace in great detail the career success and 'elite' status of Old Wykehamists from the early nineteenth century to the mid-twentieth century. In an analysis of the occupations of 7,105 Wykehamists born between 1820–1922, by far the largest proportion went into the Forces (23.8 per cent) while 9.9 per cent entered the Church, 11.9 per cent the Law, 16.4 per cent business, 7.3 per cent government service, and 5.8 per cent were described as 'gentlemen of leisure' (Bishop and Wilkinson 1967:

64–9). Obviously the majority of Old Wykehamists have either been in business, the professions, or the Forces, while only 2.4 per cent were involved in the Arts. The major conclusion of Bishop and Wilkinson's research was that career success of Wykehamists was significantly correlated with that of their fathers; in other words the career success achieved by the Wykehamist status group had become increasingly hereditary.

Incidentally, when Millham and Bullock (1973) asked pupils in different types of boarding schools about the qualities that they thought were necessary to pursue jobs successfully, they found significant differences between the groups.

But what is interesting is not so much the actual varieties of response as the fact that the qualities thought necessary for successful employment matched the aims that the boys wished their schools to pursue. For example, the public school boys emphasised expressive qualities of academic excellence (62 per cent), moral rectitude (51 per cent), respect (72 per cent) and leadership (34 per cent) – all qualities pursued in their schools. The Dartingtonians, in contrast, suggested originality (56 per cent), wide cultural experiences (37 per cent), ability to work harmoniously with others (74 per cent) and flexibility (34 per cent) – all features valued in their ratings of what the school should achieve ... In other words, expressive goals are seen in both the progressive and the public schools not only as ends worthy in themselves but as necessary qualities for social and occupational success. Although the actual choice of occupations differs among the two groups of pupils, in both cases desired expressive qualities are oriented to a later elite status of occupation.

They were, of course, writing about pupils in the late nineteen sixties.

Women

While we are concerned primarily with the men's adaptations to work, for the obvious reason that employment is a major feature of their existence, it would be an injustice to a coeducational school not to consider (albeit briefly) the occupational records of the women on our sample. In fact, at the time of interviewing, two-thirds of the Dartington women were housewives with the home their main concern. But in one interview the following exchange took place with a married woman:

[Interviewer: So you haven't in fact worked since your marriage?]

Well, now we come to a very interesting point, you see. What is work? In fact I work bloody hard ...

[Interviewer: All right, sorry, I meant an occupation.]

Well, yes, I would like to have another job now that my children are grown up. This is why I would liked to have got my 'O' levels, my 'A' levels and what have you. It would have been nice and I do regret that. (Thirties Woman P.)

There were also four women who were not married, while six of the married women worked full-time (and seven part-time). With regard to the control women, three were not married, while the remaining seventeen were housewives (of whom three worked part-time). For most of our women then domesticity and a family were claiming their attention. If we classify the Dartington women on their main occupation (i.e. before marriage for most of them) then five were in teaching or lecturing, five in nursing, five in the arts, three in journalism, one was an analyst, while the remainder were in miscellaneous service or secretarial jobs.

Only two facets of the women's occupational roles can be dealt with here and they both represent polar extremes. Firstly, there was a sub-group who entered on an aimless, anomic stage after leaving Dartington and, secondly, there was an assertive subgroup who displayed considerable occupational resource.

Perhaps the most extreme case of the former was of a woman who claimed to have spent seven or eight years doing very little:

Just sort of mucking about, it's a sort of blank, not absolutely wasted but a lot of it wasted. (Thirties Woman MS.)

But there was a handful of women who found the retrictions of a conventional female occupational role difficult to bear and who seemed unable to settle in one particular job. One married pilot respondent found herself getting drunk every lunchtime for a year before she found a congenial occupation making documentary films centred on her childhood. A similar bout of boredom afflicted a respondent who, on the verge of a nervous breakdown, was rescued by a part-time teaching job. Despite the practical bent of the progressive credo several of the women found that they were not prepared for domesticity nor were they prepared for repetitive, mundane roles. Those who had taken secretarial courses, for example, were denigratory about them. Similarly, although Dartington placed an emphasis on women adopting a career, most women knew that work would not be a central life interest for them. Rather than accept traditional feminine occupations for which Dartington had unsuited them a small number of women drifted somewhat, not knowing quite what to do.

At the same time Dartington produced some determined and strong-willed women who, emancipated from some of the restrictive social conventions that surround women in much of our society, could be forthright and assertive in work situations. One woman designed exhibitions at an uninspiring museum.

They were very sleepy, so I threw my weight around as much as possible and got things done. (Fifties Woman MS.)

Another travelled on horseback in a Frontier Nursing Service in America, while another helped run a farm with some female friends in the Home Counties. Two particularly resourceful women ran successful businesses with their husbands. One started a designing firm with her husband and after five years they were employing ten people and had an office in London.

The business has grown tremendously since we started and it's done jolly well. I find the artistic stimulation the most rewarding aspect, when I've done a good design I'm very very happy. And living up here, its a very barren spot intellectually, I've been a cabbage and now this business provides an escape from that. I'd like to have a lot more people working for us and for the business to be a success, really, more than anything. (Fifties Woman MS.)

The other woman and her husband both worked and at the same time renovated cottages until they had enough resources to buy a catering business on the west coast of Scotland. After six years of 'very, very hard work, excruciating hard work' they have a business which employs ninety people in the season and has a six figure turnover. Several of our female respondents found it difficult to find their feet after Dartington, but when motivated found that they could apply themselves even when they did not completely accept the validity of the end as with this woman, who worked in advertising:

I liked being my own boss at the beginning; then I started getting promoted which was quite nice; then, at long last, I worked quite hard. It may have been a thing I didn't altogether approve of but at least I was digging my teeth in and doing some work at long last, and getting paid for it, and then I got a bit fed up with it. I can't take advertising seriously. I never could. It's all a big game. Nine years is long enough to play a game isn't it? (Fifties Woman MS.)

Men

Previously we have seen that the men in our sample valued self-expression and freedom from supervision and considered extrinsic rewards as of secondary importance. Yet, the latter we assume to be a major component of the value system of modern society with its legacy of the Protestant Ethic and nineteenth-century Smilesian self-help.

Money, wealth, possessions, and particularly the accumulation, retention and use of them, are a distinguishing mark of the middle class. (Lewis and Maude 1949: 102.)

Representatives of the conventional middle class as pictured by Lewis and Maude tend to work in formal organisations, with a hierarchical authority structure, bureaucratic norms of function, responsibility, and subordination, where entry is regulated by qualifications and where estimates of performance are prescribed. Achievement, competition, drive, and ambition are prized both for personal advancement and for organisational success (Sofer 1970: 158). Some people might view the regulation of conduct and values in the pursuit of such ends to be constraining but there are two types of middle class occupations which may remove the feeling of constraint by granting high autonomy to the individual. The first are the professions and the second are the less institutionalised, creative roles such as journalist, commercial artist, musician, actor, and so on.

If we accept that the Dartingtonian's occupational values are at odds with the predominant values of our society with regard to work then we hypothesise that the progressive men will fall into three main groups based upon their adaptations to the societal value system of capitalist enterprise (see Table 3). It is within this threefold framework that we wish to discuss the men's careers.

TABLE 3   *Male progressives' adaptations to conventional occupational values*

Accept

(i) assimilate conventional occupational values (but with initial difficulties)
(ii) assimilate conventional occupational values (little or no difficulties)

Ambivalent

(iii) accept conventional occupational values (but without relinquishing progressive values)

Reject

(iv) seek work compatible with progressive values ('successful' progressive)
(v) avoid competitive work situations; undermotivated ('unsuccessful' progressive)

But first it is worth scrutinising the work situations of our male sample as a group. Seventeen were in basically sedentary roles compared to thirteen whose work involved physical movement. Nineteen were in mainly 'cerebral' work compared to eleven who did physical work or plied a skill (including an actor and a musician). Seventeen were employees whereas *thirteen were self-employed*, which is surely a very high proportion and of great significance in assessing their adaptations. Eighteen did not possess a professional qualification compared to twelve who were qualified. Finally, the large majority were in positions of high autonomy compared to *only two* (possibly three) who were in low personal autonomy situations. This last fact is important because, while twelve respondents worked mainly within large formal organisations, few men were in positions where organisational or occupational constraints were maximised. Whether by accident or design, the Dartington males had avoided situations where they were directly subordinate to someone in a rigid

hierarchy of superiority–inferiority. In short, respondents had selected occupations which maximised their personal freedom and this is consonant with
their expressed values.

A. 'The accepters'

In this section we are looking at those men who have accepted conventional
occupational values and who are industrious, ambitious, and resourceful in
pursuing ends that would only be accepted in a lukewarm manner by es-
pousers of the progressive ethic. Some did have considerable difficulties in
accepting commercial discipline but now most were either self-employed or in
positions of high autonomy. Generally their fathers were professional or
business men.

One man, for instance, was a late arrival at Dartington from a famous
public school and is, in that sense, not a pure progressive. But now he is a
'trouble-shooter' for an industrial organisation and his main function is
revitalising unprofitable factories. Another (who chose 'career' as the activity
giving him most satisfaction), has built up a successful private investigation
agency but, again, there are aspects of his background which mark him off
from the progressive stereotype. He was more of a 'local' than a
'cosmopolitan' Dartingtonian – he came from the North of England, had
gone back there to live, had reassumed his regional accent, and had married a
local girl.

Another respondent's family had an extremely profitable business but he
decided to branch out on his own and now works in the accounts department
of a large firm.

I'd like the financial directorship of at least one company. I enjoy immensely the stock
exchange and gamble a lot on that. I enjoy immensely reading balance sheets and
working out whether it's worth putting any money in shares. It's all finance, it's
money, money, money, money, money, and all I do is make money. I even buy houses
to make money, all my life now is money, always will be. (Fifties Man MS.)

A sales representative, whose father was also a businessman, extolled his
firm in terms reminiscent of a classical 'organisation man'; after 'selling' his
firm's product to the interviewer he stressed the comfortableness of his niche,
the security, and the fringe benefits.

I get near enough to £2,000 a year. Then there are all sorts of things, such as expense
accounts, and it has a very good superannuation scheme, pension scheme, death
benefits. You know, sort of two and a half years of salary. At the moment if I stayed
with them all the time you'd get two-thirds of your salary on retirement which you
know is quite good. (Fifties Man MS.)

We estimate that nine respondents come in this category and, occupationally at least, they appear to be deviants from the progressive culture. Generally, there were factors in their background which might explain their predilection for commerce and industry. But the dilemma facing the progressive amid the steely asceticism of the Protestant Ethic was expressed by a pilot respondent in business management:

[Respondent] Dartington didn't make people hard enough for business . . .
[Wife] It doesn't!
[Respondent] People tend to be idealistic still, everybody there is too easy . . .
[Wife] You've found that out haven't you?
[Respondent] I'm beginning to shed consciously now the easiness of Dartington, I know I've got to be tougher to get on, if I want to earn more money. (Fifties Man P.)

B. 'The ambivalents'

Ideally, the ambivalent should lead an almost 'double-life' existence between an eminently non-progressive work situation and a highly progressive life style away from work. As this would constitute a position of some strain for many people, which presumably they would resolve by moving closer to one or other of the value systems, it is not surprising that the 'ambivalents' were numerically small. In fact there were four cases, mostly marginal, but there was one classic ambivalent among the pilot respondents.

This was a man who had had a highly successful career in industry, selling steel plants to Latin America, but still regrets a Third Class degree which debarred him from an academic career. At home he immersed himself in a rambling old house, surrounded himself with books, and in the interview he was disparaging about his colleagues in the business world.

You work with rather uncongenial people. People are entirely uninteresting and I feel I don't get enough chance to create. I've no doubt that the Dartington idea of intellectual achievement is something that I feel is lacking . . . there are long periods when you don't really feel that you are doing anything very much. (Thirties Man P.)

Of the three marginal progressives one was a high-ranking officer in the Forces. But his father was a novelist and now he sees himself also as much as a novelist as a military man.

It only requires an outward conformity and the writing is an antidote to service life. I don't look at them as being in any sense incompatible. Were it possible I'd like to write permanently but it's not practical. (Thirties Man MS.)

Another was in an occupational role that did allow for creativity but he worked in a large bureaucratic, international organisation. There was little

conflict between his two worlds of work and home but what was of interest
was his emphasis on out-of-work activities.

I have a highly cynical attitude to what I'm doing. I'm looking at it as a living. The disadvantage is having to work. The things which I would rather do are considered
useless in our society – I'd like to be sculpting, painting, and drawing. If I had to
describe myself in a jocular sort of way I'd say I was an anarchist.

[Interviewer: Working here is compatible with being an anarchist?]

But working for someone else isn't compatible anyway! (Thirties Man MS.)

Finally, a respondent worked for a government organisation which gave
him high autonomy but outside of which he pursued archaeology, film-
making, music, acting, handicrafts exhibiting, and bird-watching. Unlike the
'accepters', the ambivalents filled formal occupational roles but not at a cost
to their progressive culture; rather the latter was a primary satisfaction for
which work simply provided the means.

C. 'The rejectors'

The rejectors are people who appeared undermotivated in comparison with
the competitive values of modern society or who exercise their talents in 'unconventional' occupational roles which are congruent with progressive
values. For examples of the latter, there were among our respondents seven
men who were 'successful' progressives – an actor, a jazz musician, a
photographer, a classical musician, a journalist, a script-writer, and a teacher
in a progressive school. The three thirties men in this category all came from
'cultural-creative' backgrounds but this was not true of the four fifties men.

These men can combine their career with their hobby so to speak and can
largely define their own work situation. One of these, for instance, expressed
the independence that farming afforded him:

I've never worked for anyone. It would be a comfortable life working for someone else
and sometimes it's a hell of a strain on your own . . . I began to get terribly interested
in farming, it seemed to be an answer, and I had a little utopian idea that I would build
up this farm. (Thirties Man MS.)

Such artistic–creative professions form almost an interstitial, *déclassé* group
in society and nonconformity is tolerated from them. Rewards, however, are
often meagre and erratic, particularly in the earlier years and one thirties man
described the clash between art and security and how he had resolved it:

I've had a lot of offers to move from the ——— but for some reason I find it very
difficult to answer, especially in a concise manner, I've had very great reluctance to
actually step into them. Maybe because I've got a wife and three children to support
I'm reluctant to leave the comparative cocoon existence of the ———. What do I intend

to do in the future? I think it would be too depressing to say I intend to remain in this present job until I retire but I suppose it is probable. There are frustrations about being in a staff orchestra that are inevitable but on the whole I do it because I can continue to have some of the personal freedom as a human being that I could do as a Dartingtonian. I don't have to comply with nine to five working hours, I don't have to dress in any conventional manner, I don't have to make a great social effort to keep my job, and I can out of working hours lead the sort of life I want to. (Thirties Man MS.)

One could scarcely be more committed to progressive values than to work in a progressive school and one of our sample taught in a small, radical progressive school:

It's the personal freedom I most like and the involvement on different levels – with the children, my subject, and with a very interesting educational problem. (Fifties Man MS.)

In another case a respondent found success difficult to achieve even in a highly 'herbivorous' (though exacting) profession.

I'm fairly content with my career but it hasn't gone as far as I would like it to go; it's a difficult job I know but I would like to be a little further along than I am now. It's very difficult getting jobs, it's a very difficult profession; relating this to Dartington I don't know how much more successful someone with a fairly tough background of schooling, where they had been taught that the world is a hard place where you have to push very, very hard to succeed, which I think in this profession might have helped me. I don't think it would have helped me to be a better actor, but in a profession where so much depends upon push and luck, it's possible that the gentleness which perhaps I learnt at Dartington hasn't helped me in obtaining work.

[Interviewer: In what respects?]

Primarily in getting the work, you know banging your way into the man's office who doesn't want to see you, which I frankly can't do, and as work in the theatre is so much concerned with forcing your personality on people and impressing them, for the medium person such as myself the more push you have the more jobs you get.

[Interviewer: Do you experience this lack of push in other areas?]

Suppose I do, yes, if I feel strongly about something, in acting for example, I'm usually fairly adamant about it but less so perhaps than I was, you get tolerant as you get older; the excessive tolerance of Dartington, implied in their teaching, can hold you back, being over-tolerant. You know, drawing lines and taking decisions firmly is not one of Dartington's characteristics. Recently I have thought of possible alternatives, you see I'm thirty-five now, if you can't start to enjoy a reasonable standard of living by the time you're thirty-five, you could consider yourself to some extent a failure in that profession perhaps. I often wonder whether (a) one ought to have done something else in the first place or (b) is it too late to start something new? I want to get married soon and it's difficult contemplating marriage in my present financial circumstances. (Fifties Man MS.)

There was too the second subgroup of 'rejectors' who appeared to be non-competitive with regard to work. They tended to settle into the somnambulent crevices of paternalistic organisations or to choose occupational situations that provide almost a defence against the wider society. Five out of the six cases were from nonconforming or counter-traditional homes and four had fathers in cultural–creative occupations. In terms of examinations and motivation to work these are the 'losers' from Dartington – three left under a cloud, most left early, and at least five of them showed a distinct lack of motivation while at school. Four had elements of disturbance in their background.

Two of them are difficult to classify because, while they define themselves primarily as artists, they earn their livelihood from handywork. This places them technically in Social Class III Manual and their material rewards are not high. They are simply outside of conventional occupational values by which their position would be viewed as insecure, unremarkable, and of lowly status. One of them lets his flat for several months of the year and goes to Greece to paint. His jobs are spasmodic and he does not hold a national insurance card.

I started painting as a bit of a hobby and a chap who I happened to be very friendly with who is an artist was very impressed with it, so kind of since then I've put all my energies into painting. I've just been lucky, I've managed to keep things ticking over, my wife works a couple of days a week and we've just bungled along, so between us we average about twenty quid a week. I got a night job which was four nights on and four nights off which meant I had a hell of a lot of free time – that was working as a patrolman in some bloody Burglar Alarm Company. (Fifties Man MS.)

Of the others one was head of a maintenance section in a small steel-works and was tied down by his lack of qualifications, even though the firm had once belonged to the family.

I don't know where I'll go from here because although I've had ten years of this job on the practical side I still have not got any qualifications so getting a job elsewhere would be difficult so I don't know ... I've got no hidden urge to conquer the Himalayas or anything like that. (Fifties Man MS.)

Another man joined a large northern firm after university in a clerical capacity.

It's a bit of fun although I didn't seem to be fully employed all the time ... I tend not to be very busy – my superior won't admit he's got more people than he needs. (Fifties Man MS.)

Another man tried teaching but shied away from it (when his progressive ideas clashed with the demands of the staff and the difficulties of controlling the children) into engineering research:

I think teaching requires of progressive people to be very, very strong individuals and I don't think I've got this, I think I tend to be a bit retiring . . . By and large I haven't been happy in industry because of the discipline. This is why I drifted into research and development because it's very informal, you're not jammed in narrow guide-lines. (Fifties Man MS.)

Finally, there was one extreme example of a pilot respondent virtually using his occupation as a retreat and a barrier to interaction with outsiders:

It ties me down seven days a week because I let it tie me down. I don't like doing anything else because that's change and I don't like change. Social activities are sometimes an effort for me . . . I'm a stickler for mechanisation because I find that people are so unreliable. (Fifties Man P.)

For most male Dartingtonians the world of work demanded considerable adjustment for them as it was here that commercial values and the progressive culture were in potential conflict. Their values and behaviour placed a high premium on personal freedom and for those who could not guarantee this, irritation and under-motivation could result.

Chapter Ten

Marriage and children

And if, as sometimes happens, a school friendship ripens later into love, it could have no surer foundation or better guarantee of lasting happiness. (J. H. Badley of Bedales, 1924: 61.)

Marriage

Whatever state of free association that cynical critics might conjecture as the typical progressive relationship, the evidence suggests that our sample were quite content with the institution of marriage, for 90 per cent were, or had been, married. For Bedales the figures are 'sooner or later the proportion of girls that marry is around 77 per cent, while for the boys it is over 80 per cent' (Bedales School Roll 1962: 323). On the other hand, 10 per cent of the Dartington sample were single, two men and four women. The fulfilment and satisfaction from, or adeptness at, marriage of respondents – say to assess the claim of coeducationalists that children from a mixed school will make better spouses – would be extremely difficult to test empirically. Our intrest in the marriage patterns of Dartingtonians is, firstly, to describe them and, secondly, to relate them where possible to the progressive culture.

One indicator that contains deep-rooted and treacherous causes for the commentator, of respondents' acceptance of marriage (or, more specifically, individual marital partners), is the divorce or separation rate. Some 23 per cent of our main sample had marriages which split up; at the time of interviewing two respondents were separated from their spouses and six had been divorced. The number of women in this position was greater than the men, five to two. The Dartington proportion is similar to that for Bedales which has been estimated at about 10.2 per cent but this figure is not reliable because information was gathered partly by hear-say. Nor can we rely on official statistics because they do not contain separations. On the main sample there was one widow while four respondents had been married twice and one married three times. For most it was their first marriage for both partners. Of the small proportion for whom this was not their first marriage, four respondents had been married previously and in two cases it was the spouse who had been married previously.

It is almost certain that our figures for Dartington are not wholly representative for the same reasons that our sample is biassed. In what ways might this

126

affect our figures on marriage? Perhaps the most important omission concerns the number who marry non-English spouses as a fair number of Dartingtonians are domiciled abroad. Informally, for instance, one gets the impression that girls especially tend to marry Americans – this was true of two women among the pilot interviews and one on the main sample, while one heard of perhaps another dozen or so cases. Five spouses among the main sample were foreign by origin – a German, an Egyptian, an Austrian, an American, and an exiled White Russian.

In addition, some 13 per cent of our sample, or eight respondents, had married a fellow Dartingtonian; while out of 1,495 Bedalian marriage up to 1962 there had been sixty-three 'Double OB marriages', or roughly $8\frac{1}{2}$ per cent of the total (Bedales School Roll 1962: 323). One thirties respondent remarked:

There was quite a bit of inter-marriage amongst my contemporaries . . . They have clung together tremendously. I have heard it described as the umbilical cord. They seem characteristically unable to make their way in the outside world socially. (Thirties Man MS.)

But does this not seem to contradict the evidence of an incest-taboo that we encountered in a previous chapter? To answer this we must look at our seven couples (one man and one woman on the main sample are married to each other) more closely. Five of the males are in the main sample and the other two cases are females. In only one case did the relationship commence in school and only in two cases were the partners exact contemporaries. The more frequent pattern was for males to choose a partner several years younger and whom they barely knew while at school. In several cases the man had returned to visit the school and met his future wife there. Mr Dobbs, for example, went back for a visit shortly after the war and his wife recalled:

'Julian' was a new face and I expect I threw myself at him. Dartington was a very limited community during the war and you felt any new arrival that you hadn't seen before must be interesting [Wife of Respondent].

Similarly, Mr Kember met his wife at Dartington several years after he had left and found he could relax with her more than with a conventional English girl. In another case, one man had had no serious relationship except with women from Dartington, one of whom he married.

I went back once or twice and latched on to 'Veronica', my wife now. She was still at the school when I picked her up if you like. I'm really rather a babe in the wood. A closed circuit too, with all sort of Dartington girls. (Fifties Man MS.)

With such samples generalisations are perilous but it does seem that progressive women are more likely to be involved in a broken marriage than the men. In the main sample six women and two men were divorced or separated. In addition, of the Bedalian divorce figures, but again these are most unreliable as they rely on voluntary replies, 56 per cent were women and 44 per cent men (Grimson 1952: 16). Why should this be so? An oft-quoted remark on progressive education is that it produces manly women and womanly men. Progressive men may well have imbibed certain characteristics that make them highly compatible marriage partners – a facility for handling relationships with the opposite sex, an easy going manner, a certain gentility, and an adeptness at domestic chores – whereas women may be liberated from the constraints of a society which traditionally requires a subordinate, compliant role for women (though clearly less so). This may make the progressive women less amenable to a conventional marital role and more likely to avoid traditional partners (we have already noted their propensity for marrying foreigners and fellow Dartingtonians). One example of the progressive woman's forthrightness came in an interview when a woman was asked what had she most gained from Dartington:

I don't mind who I speak to or what I say to them either and I don't particularly mind how they receive it. By my husband's a lot more cagey – once I sent him back to the butchers with some meat and told him to stuff it down the man's throat and I'm sure he won't say anything of the sort but I would. (Fifties Woman MS.)

Finally, of the eight broken marriages seven of the respondents involved themselves came from homes where the parents had divorced or separated.

Spouses' educational background

Generally the respondents' spouses have had a selective education. Most had been to other than a senior elementary or secondary modern school; in fact the proportions, in order of size, were public school and grammar school (26 per cent each), 13 per cent at some other type of independent school, and 7 per cent abroad. Furthermore, the proportion of spouses who were progressively educated was 17 per cent with six wives and one husband having been to Dartington (in addition, one woman had a previous marriage to a Dartingtonian). Very few spouses of either sex had attended a coeducational school whereas the proportions of day to boarding experience were not dissimilar. Something like half of the Dartingtonian spouses, and of the control-group spouses, had been to university or college.

There is some evidence to suggest that Dartington women marry men with a traditional school background only where the husband's experiences make him abjure educational orthodoxy. One husband, for instance, who was present at the interview was asked how he had taken to military service after a previous period of conscientious objection he replied:

I went to a highly orthodox public school and the army was nothing compared to it. My wife's remarks on sheltered lives are nothing compared to an orthodox public school – that's monasticism if anything is, far more sheltered in fact, but not the same kind of lotus-eating as at Dartington. In an orthodox sex-segregated Public School you are sheltered all the way, everything is so controlled. 'Lanchester' had a very bad effect on my future life because it was so controlled, I've never really escaped from it even now. I can't face going to dances.

[Wife] But you're not interested in dancing.

Because I was never given the opportunity to become interested, I was physically distressed by it. Now one over compensates. (Husband of respondent. Thirties Woman MS.)

In another case, the husband had experienced a sartorial revolution in reaction to his schooling, and also partly under his wife's influence.

[Interviewer: How did you feel about 'Mountview' (traditional public school)?]

[Husband] Well at the time I detested it in a theoretical way – actually I wasn't terribly unhappy I was just plain bored. And I thought it was a rotten place but I didn't know exactly in what way. Afterwards, well it just seemed the whole place not only internally but externally as well was suspect. But it had become really a political view by then.

[Wife] I can add something to that. Two years ago if not to this day although it's become less salient, Ralph felt sufficiently strongly for his whole principle of choice of clothes to be to choose things unlike those he was made to wear at school and even if there were things he would have liked on other grounds, for instance he would not wear a white shirt even if he had a glorious tie to show off against that background or something. I've operated on that. (Fifties Woman MS.)

Wives, too, were occasionally revealed to have had difficult schooldays but less often than husbands. One wife, for example, had attended a vaguely progressive girls' public school:

I'm terribly mixed up about it – I was absolutely miserable but that was me rather than the school. I was terribly rebellious; partly of course I was undergoing a divorce between my parents at home and I think I would have been miserable anyway. And there was a terrific amount of favouritism. One was terribly frightened of the staff too – they used intimidation, extreme intimidation, particularly when I compare it to the way I speak to the girls at the school where I teach now. [Wife of respondent. Fifties Man MS.]

Occupations of spouses

The Dartington women tended to marry professional men – among the husbands, for instance, there were seven lecturers and four doctors. As for the four husband in Classes III and IV all of them ran their own highly successful businesses. Using Roe's (1956) eight occupational categories we find the two largest groups of husbands in Science and in General Culture. Compared to the women's fathers, there are less husbands in business, none in 'outdoor' occupations, and less in Arts–Entertainment. And by (Table 4(a)) choosing spouses mainly from Social Classes I and II the Dartington men and women exhibited a fair amount of social class endogamy (Table 4(b)).

Most male respondents' wives had worked at some stage since leaving school. Seven had worked in a clerical or secretarial capacity, two in Arts–Entertainment (one a ballet-dancer, the other a theatrical designer), two in voluntary work (one in marriage-guidance, the other for a charitable organisation), and there was one doctor. Next to secretarial work, teaching was the second largest occupational group – of the twenty-six wives who had worked six, or something just less than a quarter, had been teachers. A further five had professional occupations, namely, bank clerk, landscape architect, planner, scientific journalist, and publisher. Finally, there were three in miscellaneous occupations – riding instructress, *au pair* and waitress. Most were either not working or else only part-time at the time of interviewing because they had young families to look after.

Spouses' compatibility with the progressive ethic

It is trivial, but true, that people seek partners with compatible backgrounds and values. If we accept the picture of the Dartingtonian as something of an outsider in English conventional society then we expect him or her to marry a 'progressive' person, marry someone who does not fully accept conventional values (counter-traditional public school men or foreigners), or else accommodate their own progressivism if marrying a traditional or conventional person. Occasionally a spouse was present at the interview, and what they said about Dartington was often revealing as to the extent to which the relationship reinforced, or detracted from, the spouse's progressivism.

Several husbands, for instance, were derogatory about their Dartington wives' academic attainments; one, who was serving in the Forces, was reported by the respondent to think her 'pretty stupid'.

He just thinks I fooled around and didn't learn anything, which is probably quite true. Quite often he has to help me with my correspondence – I'm a hopeless speller because I learned to read very late. (Fifties Woman MS.)

In another interview a distinct clash emerged between the respondent's and husband's values – he being a professional man, ex-public school, and in her eyes something of a culpable 'carnivore' (to use Michael Frayn's useful typification).

TABLE 4 (a) *Husbands' occupations of Dartington women (Reg. Gen. classification)*

	Dartington	Badminton Control	(Wives' fathers occupations)	
			Dartington	Control (Badminton)
I	14	6	7	3
II	5	7	15	10
III (Non-manual)	1	1	3	1
III (Manual)	3	–	2	–
IV	2	–	1	–
V	–	–	–	–
Totals	25*	14*	28	14†
$n=$	26	15	28	16

* Plus one in Armed Services.
† Plus two in Armed Services.

(b) *Husbands' occupations (Roe classification)*

	Dartington women's husbands	Dartington women's fathers	Control women's (Badminton) husbands
1. Service	3	6	1
2. Business	2	6	1
3. Organisation	4	6	4
4. Technology	3	2	3
5. Outdoor	–	3	–
6. Science	6	1	1
7. General culture	7	3	1
8. Arts–entertainment	1	4	4
Totals	26	30	15
$n=$	26	30	15

I hate the TV, loathe it – my husband comes home in the evenings and sits down in that chair and stares at the thing until it's time to go to bed and I could scream. I hate the thing. I'll always look at a discussion or something like that but he always looks at these beastly westerns . . . And another thing I've never been sort of terribly interested in material possessions and my husband's terribly keen on them but I suppose it's the way I've been brought up. (Fifties Woman MS.)

Not unnaturally, however, there was more frequently an indication of a normative fusion in marriage whereby the partners bolstered each other's progressivism by selection procedures of varying degrees of consciousness. For instance, one woman had married an anarchist: after expounding his views on the potential future of Dartington as a revolutionary model for a new, pioneer, coeducational, non-punitive, approved school, his wife remarked:

Our views on education are so parallel – Malcolm really is an old Dartingtonian, except that he didn't go to school there. (Thirties Woman P.)

One sensed, in fact, that Dartington women often 'converted' a deviant conventional husband whereas, conversely, the Dartington men seemed to attract women who reinforced their progressivism by the union. It was noticeable, for instance, that whenever a man had married a 'non-supportive' wife – say from an overtly working class background or with a secondary-modern education – then that wife discreetly made herself scarce during and after the interview whereas 'supportive' wives did, on occasion, threaten to dominate their husband's interview.

Children

Perhaps the most crucial, demanding, responsible – and some would say fulfilling – role that many adults are asked to play is that of parent. How our Dartingtonians perform as parents should attract our especial attention, for it is here that we can observe the progressive ideology being transmitted to the second generation. Indeed, what our respondents do with their children constitutes something of a test for that ideology; firstly, it is an indication of the extent to which our respondents retain progressive values; and secondly, it should reveal in what areas conflict may arise between their progressive heritage and the perceived interests of their own progeny. Two areas will be examined in particular; namely, socialisation and education.

All but two of the married respondents on the main sample had children, and between them the fifty-two men and women had produced 129 – or just less than an average of 2.5 each. Most of the children – 61 per cent – were aged ten or under with 32 per cent between eleven and twenty and the remainder were over twenty-one years of age (only one was older than twenty-five). In other words, about a third were adolescents.

One fact does emerge with clarity from the interviews; namely, that the Dartington sample were greatly concerned with, and engaged in, the fates of their children. Indeed, some of the almost obsessive maternal qualities that we noted among respondents' parents reappeared among some female respondents; for example one woman remarked:

I think we would go to a lot of trouble to move to a good area and so on. And of course, we would be absolutely intolerable parents in the PTA and things like this. (Fifties Woman MS.)

While another woman expressed her interest in educational matters:

I take the education magazine *Where* and I read everything I can get hold of on the subject. I listen to everybody's views, and I've been passionately concerned in their [the children's] development right from the beginning. I've found it fascinating and its one of the few subjects I can still absorb at a tremendous rate. (Fifties Woman MS.)

Briefly, the methods of socialisation were permissive and intra-punitive but with frequent qualifications expressed in favour of a more firm approach than many of their parents had adopted. Some 43 per cent, for instance, said that they used corporal punishment (by which most meant smacking and then only infrequently) compared to 5 per cent of the Dartington parents. One woman expressed the gap between theory and practice:

In theory I am firm, quiet and patient. In practice I blow my stack. (Fifties Woman Postal Quest.)

There was, too, an apologetic tone when respondents admitted resorting to the hand because this conflicted with the progressive philosophy; but one woman was not so squeamish:

'Maria' [fellow Dartingtonian] asked me once if I slapped them and I said yes. And she said 'We're not supposed to from Dartington are we?' And I said 'I don't give a damn. They need a smack now and again'. (Fifties Woman MS.)

Finally, a substantial minority of respondents explicitly acknowledged the influence of Dartington in shaping their attitudes to child-rearing and education.

[Interviewer: Do you have any conscious ideas or philosophy in bringing up your children?]

Same as I was brought up. It wouldn't occur to me apart from getting cross to force any particular attitude or social pattern on my kids. I'm not worried if they have an accent or speak with a plum in their mouth, if we'd stayed in Australia the kid would have grown up with an 'awful Australian accent' [respondent drawls] – so what? No pressures. If they can make the grade all right, I don't care when she takes her exams – sixteen, seventeen or eighteen.

[Interviewer: Do you feel influenced by Dartington?]

Yes, I do. The lack of rigid class aspirations, I'm not worried about their accent, about a rigid time schedule, I haven't got my child booked in at a school, with the years ticked off and exams to pass. (Fifties Man MS.)

With regard to their expectations for their children's education most plumped for some facet of progressive ideals – such as freedom to develop (15 per cent) or personal happiness (50 per cent) – but a minority insisted on the importance of examination successes for their children. Over half of the children of primary school age were at state schools but a third were at private schools; very few indeed were at progressive schools (of junior age) and even less at preparatory schools.

The sample had forty-eight children of secondary school age or older. Over half of these had been to state schools – grammar, secondary-modern, or comprehensive. Not many had been to public school (in fact, no sons had been to a public school) but just less than a quarter had been to an other independent school. The proportions going to single-sex and coeducational schools were virtually equal but the majority had attended day schools and of the subgroup who boarded half were at Dartington. The Bedales School Roll (1962: 326) mentions 248 children of Old Bedalians who have been sent to Bedales; the editor calculates the percentages as 11 per cent of sons and 15 per cent of daughters who are sent to their parent's old school. The public boarding school was evidently avoided by respondents for their children in favour of state day schools but with private boarding schools as a second preference. What influenced respondents in making these choices?

It is possible only to summarise the extensive interview material on children's education. While there was considerable individual variety one common factor arose frequently and that was a fair measure of satisfaction with state primary schools but a great deal of soul-searching with regard to the merits of state secondary education. There are objective reasons why this should be so such as the fluctuating standards of state schools from area to area, the ferment surrounding the comprehensive issue at the time of interviewing, and so on. But, in addition, the respondents have experienced a unique education, where most were extremely happy, and this doubtless remained the model for many people against which other schools were measured. However, left-wing opinion had attacked private education and the effects of boarding so that there are ideological reasons why respondents should ponder deeply over secondary education; while, even more to the point, many could only have afforded private education by considerable sacrifice.

Some respondents were insistent on high academic standards, in compensation perhaps for their own lack of attainments. This was certainly the case with a respondent whose aspirations for his children were as strong as his regret at Dartington's inability to develop his own talents:

My main concern is that they should be stretched intellectually to the maximum – surely this is the time to do it, in youth, it's so difficult to work on it later on. (Thirties Man MS.)

Others were less insistent in this respect and gave priority to individual development and personal happiness.

I'd rather have lower academic standards and have them happy at school. (Fifties Man MS.)

Many respondents stressed the differences between the sexes in what they expected from education. Several were determined for instance, to see their girls educated coeducationally (women were particularly insistent on this) but were prepared to sacrifice their sons to single-sex schools. With secondary education there often arrived too a whole new emphasis in the organisation of the school — selection, a narrowing of the curriculum, and an increase in authoritarianism — which was potentially in conflict with the more liberal views of the home. Large classes, boisterous children, compulsory religion, corporal punishment, and undue academic pressure began to emerge as areas where respondents' children encountered difficulties in the same way as respondents' themselves had baulked at the traditional school as children. In brief, many respondents were in a position whereby they acknowledged the defects of state education but were reluctant to patronise private education for social and political reasons. Ironically, those reasons were applicable as much to Dartington as to say Harrow, Bloxham or Rossall.

One major element in the public school's effectiveness is that its social world is in some degree circular and self-perpetuating and that its institutions are largely self-recruiting. Yet only three respondents from our sample had used Dartington as the main secondary school for their children (or some of their children), although the majority had considered it. In fact, *65 per cent had considered Dartington* compared to 35 per cent who had not. The major considerations were cost, dislike of boarding, and an ideological preference for the state system. But deeper issues intruded. Many former pupils pictured the school as they had known it in the Curry era; without him it just was not the same school. Indeed, some of the children of old Dartingtonians, imbued with their parents' classical Curryism, clashed with the 'revisionism' of Curry's successors and there occurred expulsions, withdrawals, and recriminations.

Quite a few respondents had visited Dartington with their husbands or wives and viewed its later development as a betrayal of its original ideals. One or two explicitly said 'yes, but only if Curry was still there'. At the same time, some people felt Dartington more appropriate for a girl than a boy (at which Curry would surely have turned in his grave).

Yes, for the girl. We don't think much of girls' schools. No, for the boy; he will go to Eton. I don't know why, just that we are rather conventionally minded over boys' education. (Fifties Woman. Postal Quest.)

A telling qualification was a widespread dislike for boarding and its disruptive effects on home life; people were determined to have their children at home and not to repeat their own unhappy experiences in this respect. Others would not use Dartington even if they could afford to because they disagreed with private education on ideological grounds while others compared Dartington's facilities unfavourably with the better state schools. But, behind the discussions, the aspirations, the criticisms, and the rationalisations, lay the bare economic fact that most respondents simply could not afford to pay the fees at Dartington. Indeed, several regretted that no special financial provision was made for the children of former pupils. Ironically the school had priced itself out of the pockets of its own alumni who mostly do not earn enough to support it. This was certainly true of earned income; for without capital, private income, or a covenant, few of our respondents could have contemplated sending children to a boarding school on their salaries (cf. Chapter 9). At Dartington in 1967, for instance, the fees ranged from £465–£534 (List 70) while the average for a group of progressive schools in 1965 was £456 (Stewart 1968: 315). Thus two children at boarding school for only five years would have cost a respondent in 1968 something like £1,000 p.a. in fees and £400 p.a. in 'extras' (in 1957 the *Financial Times* calculated the extras at £100–200: Glennerster and Pryke 1964: 11) making a total of £7,000.

The dilemma of the adult Dartingtonian is that the radicalism to which he or she often espouses has turned against privilege in education even where it is progressive. Yet state education at the secondary level contains many of the facets of a traditional, authoritarian education which the progressive parent is likely to reject. Furthermore, the school to which they are committed has moved away from its pure form under its original guiding light to a less radical position. How they are to resolve the academic and ocupational success which they wish for their children with the conventional values largely attendant on attaining those goals is their major problem; one self-employed engineer expressed this progressive parents' dilemma:

I'd like my children to be able to live in the way that I am now and to have my values, moral values – if only I knew what they were! I wouldn't like them to lead unstable emotional lives, I'd like them to have good emotional relationships – that sounds pompous – they should have higher education, and it would be nice for one's ego if one was an engineer. I want them to be in a good competitive position in relation to the rest of society but I wouldn't like them to be Freemasons or members of Lloyds. (Fifties Man P.)

Chapter Eleven
The progressive life-style

Yes, Dartingtonians are distinctive. They are more liberal in outlook, less conformist, they think very deeply about things, are socially conscious, though not politically, but caring about the conditions of the world. None have got stuck in a rut or got middle-aged outlooks. (Thirties Woman MS.)

In this chapter we wish to examine some of the data, and some of the observer's impressions, about respondents' life-style. The progressive culture purveys a distinctive life-style which isolates its practitioner from respectable bourgeois society and, indeed, signifies his or her social distance from that society. Unfortunately, there is a paucity of ethnographic material on this radical wing of the middle class. Indeed, apart from Pear's (1955) *English Social Differences* there has been no attempt to map out a social typography of groups in relation to a wide range of considerations such as income, occupation, accent, dress, leisure, culture, education, and so on. Lewis and Maude (1949) have done something of this order for the conventional middle class but this work and that of Pear's are both now badly dated.

In Michael Frayn's humorous typology (see Chapter 8) of the English middle class we would expect Dartingtonians to be classical 'herbivores', i.e. members of the creative, cosmopolitan, *avant-garde*, libertarian, radical intelligentsia. Even where a former Dartingtonian is not strictly a member of the intelligentsia he or she is likely to hold them as a reference group because the school certainly reflected an expressive cultural and intellectual ethos. And Progressive Education, let us remind ourselves, stresses norms of creativity and individuality, preaches political commitment (implicitly) and social involvement, and provides an opportunity for manual skills and cultural involvement. What elements of this ideology and background are in fact displayed by the samples' life-styles as adults?

Recreational and cultural interests

Asked about their general cultural and recreational pursuits respondents gave a picture of normal leisure interests such as the cinema, television and reading, but with a significant proportion engaging in cultural activities. One-quarter of the sample, for instance, still played a musical instrument (which one suspects would be much higher than in middle class society generally) and there was evidence of a utilisation of manual crafts and skills. But it was

137

noticeable from the replies that many respondents led a very home-centred existence. They were generally not 'clubbable' people and avoided formal associations.

In fact nearly half of the sample were joined to a social club or voluntary association (43 per cent were and 57 per cent were not) but of these very few took an active part in the society's functions and leadership. This can be compared with Parkin's (1968: 16) sample of members of the Campaign for Nuclear Disarmament who one suspects share many of progressive education's counter-traditional values.

It proved to be the case that 84 per cent of adult respondents were involved in at least one formal organisation, whilst 35 per cent of the total were members of three or more.

What clubs or societies were mentioned? There were Amnesty International, Homosexual Law Reform Society, International Alliance of Women, St John's Wood Preservation Society, Divorce Law Reform Association, Noise-Abatement, Women's International League for Peace and Freedom, Mental Health Association, Vegetarian Society, the Soil Association, Penal Reform, CASE, CND, the Guides, the Scouts, Home-Bound Wives, Graduates Club, baby-sitting cooperatives and residents' associations.

Of the five people who said that they played a highly active role in clubs or societies four were women, as were five out of the nine respondents who were 'moderately active'. Men, on the other hand, seemed particularly reticent and one man summed up a general suspicion of formal associations:

I have some sort of recoil from joining clubs and organisations, I don't know why. I suspect it's because I mistrust ready-made theories and normally if you join something like that, a religious or political organisation, you involve yourself in accepting some arbitrary beliefs and ideas and this would put me off. (Thirties Man MS.)

In saying that they were not 'clubbable' types, quite a few respondents intimated that they did not want to be associated with a conventional bourgeois stereotype. One man, for example, lived on a Home Counties farm but explicitly dissociated himself from the local hunting set.

Things like the local hunt leave me cold – a lot of 'nouveaux riches' exhibitionists jumping around in red outfits. (Thirties Man MS.)

One respondent was particularly insistent on this point of not accepting conventional status connotations when he was asked if he possessed a motor car.

Yes, I have a car. I run a beat-up old piece of fully depreciated capital. I couldn't care less about having a conspicuous article. In fact I'd rather have the money in capital than in class-aspiration furniture. I'm not interested in what people bloody well think. (Fifties Man MS.)

Similarly, respondents found it difficult to perceive themselves in terms of social class.

I'd ask you to place me. I haven't the faintest idea. I can't bear the thought of being put into a category or fitted into a class. I can speak King's English, I've had a private education, own a bit of property, I'm a tradesman practically aren't I in using my camera? Artist? So what is it? Am I middle class? Father is upper middle so I'm branded aren't I? Branded by what I'm bred out of up to a point. Mother's lower middle, that will bring me down. I quite often meet people like the local squirearchy in my work. Country set? One gets on with them but I've nothing in common except land and farming. But not through the hunt, cocktail parties, balls, or any of that sort of trash. (Thirties Man MS.)

[Interviewer: Where would you place yourself as to social class?]

I couldn't really do it, you know. I'm not being awkward but I have absolutely no class identity at all – no identity in an ideology, nor aspirations to the glorious middle-class. (Fifties Man MS.)

Finally, one respondent gave up in disgust in attempting a self-definition:

[Interviewer: Where would you place yourself as to social class?]

These are really sweet questions! We're middle-middle. We're just one of those boring people who are middle-middle. By that I mean we're middle class but we are not bourgeois. Damn it, its an impossible definition. (Fifties Man MS.)

Politics

Peace, world-government, internationalism, and other humanitarian and often left-wing sympathies, have permeated the values of many progressive schools and Dartington more than most. The progressive literature has an elitist streak of preparing a new type of citizen (cf. Curry in Blewitt 1934: 56) and one area where we can test the involvement demanded by their ideology is that of politics. Firstly, where did respondents place themselves with regard to the national political spectrum (left-wing or right-wing)?

The main sample expressed preferences which were slanted somewhat towards the left-wing of the political spectrum with over half in the 'left-wing' or 'left-of-centre' categories. However, one man remarked:

I'm not on the national political spectrum. I don't believe anybody is good enough to represent 50,000 people. I think there are great holes in our political system. If I had to describe myself politically I suppose in a jocular sort of way I'd say I was an anarchist. I have written 'abstain' across the ballot paper but not in '66. With that proviso, my voting is the best of three bad 'uns, and so I vote Labour. (Thirties Man MS.)

There was also a noticeable concentration of responses in the three centre choices (left-of-centre, centre and right-of-centre) with 61 per cent of the Dartingtonian responses falling within them. This predilection for the centre is borne out by voting patterns in the 1966 General Election where as many as 28 per cent of the main sample voted Liberal. Butler and Rose (1969: 320) found that 10 per cent of the electors they surveyed regarded themselves as Liberals in 1966; also the Liberal vote had dropped considerably since the 1964 election. While this may make the Dartington subsample of Liberals look large we must recall the small size of our sample compared to opinion polls; also different forms of question, e.g. making the wording conditional on the likelihood of the Liberals gaining a majority, bring out much higher proportions supporting Liberals. By far the largest proportion of the sample, however, voted Labour although there was still one-sixth of the sample which voted Conservative (seven men and three women).

Some 18 per cent of the main sample, less than a fifth, had been politically active (canvassing, driving at elections, standing in local or national elections, or belonging to a political party), and only two respondents had been active to any great degree. This contrasts with Parkin's (1968: 39) data where 73 per cent of his sample 'indicated electoral support for Labour', (though many would have preferred a CND candidate). In addition 51 per cent were members of a political organisation or party and this meant 'predominantly the Labour Party'. The two most politically active people that the writer encountered were both women, one a communist, the other an imperialist. The former has been to work-camps in Cuba, been on every CND march (and even marched behind the CND banner with a group of London printers in a May Day procession in Prague), attended the meetings to organise the Grosvenor Square demonstration (of March 1968), and performed a good deal of work with overseas students. Both her parents were active members of the Communist Party. The latter respondent, who was not on the main sample, was organising secretary of the League of Empire Loyalists for four years and she remains the Honorary Secretary, stood unsuccessfully as a parliamentary candidate (as had her father), and snatched the microphone from Anthony Eden, then Prime Minister, at a Conservative rally in the fifties.

Then I shouted into the microphone before I was hustled away, 'You are throwing away the British Empire which is the greatest force for peace the world has ever known', or something like that. (Thirties Woman P.)

Not only were the majority of respondents not active but many of them regarded party politics in a disdainful light of which voting Labour was seen largely as the lesser of two evils and voting Liberal an affirmation of independence from a sordid wrangle. One thirties man described himself as a 'sort of left-over, sentimental left-winger' and there was a rather diffuse, nostalgic humanitarian radicalism about some of the replies by which people wanted both to display left-wing sentiment and to emphasise their independence of party affiliations. The solution for some was to avoid the extremes and vote Liberal.

Well I've always voted Liberal which I suppose you think is a non vote. I tried being a Young Conservative and it made me sick. I only went once or twice and I couldn't stick that; it made me very bolshy. I really can't stand being too Labour either so that I'm centre of the path. (Fifties Man MS.)

Indeed Parkin (1968) argues that the radical middle-class espousal of internationalism and humanitarian moral absolutes avoids a confrontation with left-wing ideologies that centre on material and economic ends which would effectively challenge the intellectual's own status position.

Those respondents who voted Conservative were often quite repentant about it as if they appreciated their deviance from progressive norms. Sometimes, economic interests were given as the intruding factor.

I'm socialistically inclined voting Conservative. I agree with all the socialist ideals but I vote Conservative hoping that they will carry them out more efficiently. I suppose the answer is that having a certain private income I think that the Conservatives are more likely to retain it and keep up the private enterprise. (Fifties Woman MS.)

In another case, the respondent's wife ensured that her husband voted appropriately:

I don't know, methinks they [the political parties] are all a shower. I think I'm left or left of centre but I tend to think they are all a shower. I find everyone at work is violently Conservative which is very depressing.

[Wife: This is Yorkshire, don't forget, a very philistine county. Yes, it's very depressing. I'm more left and they're not all a shower.]

I voted Labour in '66. I didn't have any choice [laughter].

[Wife: Pressurised! I've always voted Labour ever since I remember voting.]

I once voted Conservative [laughter]. (Fifties Man MS.)

Religion

Among the Dartington sample only two respondents were regular church-goers. Altogether 27 per cent attended church, with varying degrees of regularity, compared to 55 per cent of the control group. The Dartington proportion was slightly less than that of their parents and for most of them attendance meant simply on festivities or ritual occasions. Few people were really convinced Christians and of these most had been converted after Dartington. As with voting Conservative, those respondents who went to church acknowledged their deviance from progressive expectations.

[Interviewer: Do you still go to church?]

Yes, I'm a Sunday school teacher. Probably Curry would turn in his grave if he heard that! (Fifties Woman MS.)

Similarly, many respondents who conformed to the church ritual of matrimony, and 54 per cent of the sample had done, saw the contradiction between not attending church nor believing in religion yet still getting married in church. Not infrequently family pressures were blamed:

I didn't bloody well want to get married in church. I don't give a damn about it because I don't believe in God, much to the vicar's consternation. So I had to promise to bring up the kids as Christians. There was pressure from the in-laws so we had 'Jane' christened but I don't think I'll have the other one done. (Fifties Man MS.)

A very small minority of respondents did seriously consider religion or were converted after Dartington and in most of these cases they turned to Catholicism. One or two showed general interest in the spiritual, others thought it might give their children something to believe in, while others almost seemed to be searching for something positive and definitive. One pilot respondent had become a Roman Catholic after school, has had eight children, and has endeavoured to send them to Catholic schools.

[Interviewer: Did you have a dark night of the soul previous to the conversion?]

No I just steadily moved in that direction. It just seemed absolutely the logical thing to do, and you know once I was a Catholic I appeared to be at home and I just felt at home ever since. (Fifties Man P.)

Another Dartingtonian, a woman who was not interviewed, was also converted to Catholicism and has since become a leading advocate of birth-control from within the Church (her campaign has attracted some attention in the press and she has been refused communion at Westminster Cathedral).

Another respondent had similarly moved towards the Catholic faith after school and appreciated the need for tighter control in contemporary progressive education because of the growing lack of inhibitions in society.

[Interviewer: Do you resent the authoritarianism of the Church?]

No, it's not worried me in the slightest degree – the kind of things on which it is authoritarian are the kind of things on which I have always felt there is an authority. The Childs said they were changing a lot of the freedoms at Dartington because before in the early days there had been the framework of a stable society to help exercise all kinds of controls over our behaviour. I know it was true because when I was at Dartington we had very, very strict standards. They weren't strictly for moral reasons but we would have been absolutely terrified to experiment on drugs, that was unthinkable. So that the Church's kind of authoritarianism, from abstract first principles – this is right or wrong – seemed to me to be completely right and appropriate. (Thirties Woman P.)

The overall intuitive impression of the interviewer, then, was of home-centred, 'privatised' individuals avoiding formal institutions and political–social activism. They were often not overtly materialistic and mostly displayed a comfortable frugality. Externally they might appear fairly conformist – most were buying their homes, owned one car, and usually went on holidays abroad – but generally they seemed withdrawn and soft, as if they had swopped push and advancement for tranquillity and personal happiness though occasionally at the cost of feeling slightly unfulfilled. They were often defensive about money, material possessions, and implications of social aspirations which were frequently denied in strong language. The caricature of some latter-day William Morris making his own furniture, avoiding the use of machinery such as cars, 'phones, and televisions, and listening to uplifting music at the end of a day's manual labour, proved largely imaginary. On the contrary, our 'Children of the new Era' have largely turned their backs on the burden of reforming that world which Progressive Education initially so strenuously denigrated. Rather, in the privacy of their own home or in the company of like-minded individuals, they can indulge in symbolic progressive rituals that stress social distance with the conventional middle class.

Long-term adjustment

In the previous section we described some aspects of the main samples' life-style. Now we want to re-examine some of that evidence for the light it sheds on the final strategy which individuals have adopted as adults in adjusting to society. The implications of a progressive education are that ideally its alumni will not be compulsively institution-centred because the school will have stimulated their individuality rather than their loyalty and hence have made it easier for them to move into the outside world than children from a traditional school. It is important, then, to look at respondents continuing involvement in the school world and at aspects of their life-style as clues to the extent to which individuals have conformed to, or deviated from, the culture and ideology of the school and the progressive sub-system in the wider society.

It is possible, in fact, that the consciousness of being a Dartingtonian came only with the entry into the outside world. Musgrove (1971: 29), for example, felt that identity with an institution was often forged after discharge.

When they have given so much throughout their schooldays, Old Boys will seldom admit that it was not really worth it; in retrospect the experiences of schooldays will acquire a remarkable potency. Guardsmen, like Etonians, are created in the ten years after their discharge. The power of schools may be long delayed, operating through a process of retroactive socialisation.

When respondents were asked to define the characteristics of the archetypal

Dartingtonian, several rejected the concept by stressing the individualism that the school sponsored but many readily identified a string of characteristics that were deemed to mark the adult Dartingtonian.

[Interviewer: Are Dartingtonians distinctive?]

Oh yes. You can usually spot them. You can pick them out just like that in a room full of people. Not necessarily a Dartingtonian but someone with a similar atmosphere anyway. It's very obvious in the first few years after you've left because they're very natural, easy to talk to, swear a lot, and we're broadminded – I don't think you'll find many narrow-minded people from Dartington and we defend the little ones, the ones who get hurt, we look after people less better off than ourselves. (Fifties Woman MS.)

Equally, J. H. Badley of Bedales (1924: 209) was prepared to sketch the qualities of an Old Bedalian:

But the influence of the school on one who had passed through it can hardly fail to leave certain convictions, sufficiently strong to affect his outlook and manner of life, e.g. one is the realisation that happiness is not dependent on extent of possessions, still less of luxury, but rather on a certain simplicity of life, on health and enjoyment of the open-air, on comradeship and on the nature and range of one's interests and the possibility of doing creative work, with some other motives and interest than only that of private gain.

In talking of adjustment, then, it is clear that many correspondents still strongly identified with Dartington. They perceived qualities in themselves which may have been mythical or exaggerated but which they traced consciously to the school influence.

[Interviewer: What are the traits of a Dartingtonian?]

I think the greatest trait most Dartingtonians have is, some would call it permissiveness, I don't think it's that, it's a kind of liberalism in thought, what's the bloody word, tolerance. I think an awful lot of tolerance. But then that always doesn't work, because we are all intolerant of fools. I'm very intolerant of fools and the rest of the Dartingtonians I have met are, but they won't admit it. I mean in the army or the war I never met one person I could talk to, no I did meet one and she's still my friend. My husband was in the army and we've moved around as army wives, and I certainly wasn't tolerant, I mean we had the greatest contempt for the army at Dartington don't forget. My husband says I'm pretty intolerant and he could be right but one gets more intolerant as one gets older. I mean my father was a Labour man, and always has been, but now he says 'Bring back the cat' and he really means it! (Thirties Woman P.)

Generally, they agreed that there was something distinctive about the adult Dartingtonian which usually meant an expression of counter-traditional values.

Yes, there's something fairly strong, not the old school tie sort of feeling, but certainly there's something about my contemporaries, some quality in common, or lack of something perhaps. They have a sense of humour, tend often to laugh at and deride the more conventional features of England – aristocracy, the Queen, political parties, etc. – sometimes on a low level, sniggering for sniggering's sake. On a higher level, standing back and seeing things from a different point of view, that is a characteristic of all Dartingtonians pretty well, unless they've been swamped by their home background. (Fifties Man MS.)

At the same time they claimed to feel somewhat vulnerable in competitive company.

I can't spell. I am not ambitious or competitive or 'pushy' in my career and am still hurt and surprised when my colleagues behave in this way. I think I am easily taken advantage of. (Fifties Woman. Postal Quest.)

One woman claimed to have increasing consciousness now of her progressive background more than in the years immediately after leaving:

I'm more conscious now of being a Dartingtonian, in marriage guidance counselling, because I meet a lot of people interested in Dartington. It never fails to produce a lot of interest. It used to be, 'Oh, not that extraordinary place!' But now people show tremendous interest, and envy I think. I may have used it occasionally to shock people, but I'm very proud that I was one of the first. (Thirties Woman MS.)

Indeed, another woman wrote that she rather enjoyed the educational cachet of notoriety conferred by Dartington:

Dartington is different and I like being a bit different. (Fifties Woman. Postal Quest.)

Additionally, most of our respondents enjoyed being at Dartington and felt that they had gained something positive from having been there.

It's very difficult to say exactly what I gained from Dartington. The atmosphere of the arts was important; the fact that the whole estate was concerned, that there were arts and music and people in the school were encouraged to take part, in the audience or actively. I think this is quite important. It made a great impression on me that I saw the Shankar Indian Dancers at the Barn Theatre at Dartington, thirty years before the arrival of popular Indian culture into this country. And now we have the son of Shankar – who is the great sitar performer, and I've seen his father; and the whole bringing of Indian culture to England thirty years before the pop world. The Ballet Tours dealing with modern ballet, or attempts at theatre. I can remember 'Thunder Rock' the play about the lighthouse keeper which was then being presented in the West End and at Dartington as an *avant-garde* play. It attracted people like Norman Slutsky the metalwork man, the Robert Master's Quartet and Kinloch Anderson, and all this is important. (Thirties Man MS.)

Generally, they considered themselves well-adjusted.

[Interviewer: Are you satisfied with the education you received at Dartington?]

As regards social integration, terribly satisfied. I was happy, that was the great factor, and I integrated into society perfectly well, it wasn't traumatic and it isn't traumatic. I'm not a homosexual, thank God, I don't beat my wife, and I don't have to wear rubber knickers, so I'm well integrated. I don't have impossibly high goals with no chance of achieving them. The all-round education was first class but academically not very good – it was of course during the war and there was the lack of good staff. (Fifties Man MS.)

With regard to attachment to school, Bedales, for example, had formed a London Old Bedalians Club in 1917 and has published a regular compendium of data on former pupils much in the manner of public school Old Boys' Associations. The financial support, business contacts, and organising ability of the latter are often invaluable to the school whereas Dartington has not needed its former pupils as a body in this respect and they have never exerted a formal and cohesive influence on the school. Dartington would doubtless have scorned such an institutionalised extension of itself as smacking too much of public school camaraderie. Yet from almost the earliest years some Old Dartingtonians displayed a gregariousness not unlike the much parodied public school men. Curry (1947: 31), for example, wrote about a boy that Dartington did not 'cure' of his difficulties:

Even though he left us at fourteen or fifteen he always tells me that he looks back upon the school as the only real home he ever knew. For that reason he loves to come back.

Shortly after the war an *informal* Dartington Former Pupils' Association was set up which arranged periodic reunions. In examining the material on contacts and reunions we must continually bear in mind that those people who do not wish to retain contact with the school are not represented on our sample, and therefore our sample is biassed towards those who do wish to re-main in touch with the school and its informal old boy and girl network. It appeared that three-quarters of the sample are in touch with fellow Dar-tingtonians, that a large majority have visited the school since leaving (30 per cent recently, i.e. within the last three or four years), and that over two-thirds have attended reunions at some time since leaving (10 per cent recently). Compared to many public schools this would appear unremarkable but it should be seen in relation to the progressive school's non-institutional ethos.

One woman explained that her friends at boarding school were virtually her only friends:

I was always very close to them because they were the only friends one had because I really had no close friends at home. They were literally the only friends one had of one's own age so I kept very much in touch with them. (Fifties Woman MS.)

This probably accounts for that small number of former pupils who used to return avidly to the school shortly after leaving for visits which eventually became a problem and had to be controlled; Curry decided in the interests of the smooth running of the school that Old Dartingtonians be allowed one free visit per year but that this did not apply to their guests, who, furthermore, were only welcome from Friday evening to Monday morning. Apparently an old boy had been responsible for diluting some pure alcohol from the laboratory for consumption by some of his former school-mates. One respondent consciously restricted his desire to return:

Dartington was much more important and secure than anything else which made it difficult for some people to leave. Well, not so much for the girls, because they got fed up at the end and wanted to leave and get away. But for the boys, yes, they always wanted to come back. And I deliberately rationed my return trips – I used to go twice a year or something like that, I went quite often – because I so hated the other boys who had come back and upset the whole society by coming back after they had left. They would wander around or try to get off with the girls and that sort of thing. (Fifties Man P.)

Another man returned regularly and eventually married a fellow Dartingtonian who was herself brought up on the estate there.

[Interviewer: Was it difficult for you to leave Dartington?]

Well, I used to like going back, I think I had so many friends there, because I didn't actually have a girlfriend at the point of leaving so it was as if there was a love thing there. And it was going back to this, 'Matthew' used to say this, I can't actually remember the words properly but it was that there was something about the place, that there was a feeling, or certainly this was how I felt, that there was this tremendous pull or magnetic attraction, and the very, very happy atmosphere. It used to cost me a lot of money but I used to go back and stay at the Cott Inn.

[Wife: Particularly in your case because you were more lonely at home, being an only child, it was your second life, it was your home.]

Well after I left I went back regularly at intervals for eight years. And really now, because through marriage of course, I am most probably the most regular ex-Dartingtonian to keep visiting. But I love it you know, we go down there on average three times a year, we are going down again in about a fortnight . . .

Well just before you go I'll show you photos of how Dartington used to be. Partly because of 'Miranda' coming from Dartington it means more to us than just Foxhole and the school, and all the way along I get this overawed feeling when I am at Dartington, that the school is just one part, one operation, and there are so many things going on at the place. (Fifties Man MS.)

One female respondent claimed that once a former pupil had climbed uninvited into her bed during the middle of the night when she was at Foxhole much to her consternation. Another respondent wrote to Curry asking if he could visit the school for a couple of days because he was missing it very much and felt 'school-sick'.

Many respondents return to the locale or visit the estate as much as the school. The Dartington Music School in the summer provided courses or employment for some of them while A. S. Neill has also written that the grounds of Summerhill are peopled by former pupils during the summer vacation. A small proportion of respondents have visited the school regularly, some annually, but one or two pilot respondents went several times a year.

I still can't keep away from the place now and go back every year to the Summer School. Last summer I took a house down there for a month. (Fifties Woman MS.)

Another woman explained that her visits did *not* imply that she was dependent on the school:

I don't feel at all dependent on the school. I adore the place, it's a very beautiful place, and I'm very fond of music and I like a lot of the people there, so I go down not only to see the people I was friendly with at school but to go to the Summer School at the same time. It meant so much to me, it was the place I spent longest, I've never been anywhere else for that long, and I just think the place is beautiful, and I love the way they look after it. I didn't go last summer but I have a feeling that I must go once a year. I shall go again this summer. (Fifties Woman MS.)

Husbands and wives were frequently taken to see Dartington, almost as an initiation (one respondent spent his honeymoon nearby), and one described her reaction:

|Wife|: Years ago when we first met we went down there. I think the grounds are incredibly beautiful. I'm sure if I'd spent my childhood there I'd want to go back, it's that kind of place, particularly if you are rootless. You could easily dig in roots. Because it does have something. (Wife of Fifties Man MS.)

In contrast, some respondents felt disillusioned or let down on returning especially after Curry had left and one woman said she felt acutely afraid of not being wanted there. Some 40 per cent of respondents still kept in touch with members of staff some of whom were still at the school. In short, our evidence points to the strong hold which the school still exerts over many of the respondents on our sample. The control group were almost equally attached to the school and old pupil network but then they have formally administered Old Boys' and Old Girls' associations which are organised from the school and which are much more comprehensive than the Dartington association.

Finally, one respondent held a somewhat jaundiced view of reunions:

One goes to these slightly traumatic, harrowing reunions. It's rather like going to Madame Tussauds – one sees a lot of people around slightly balder, slightly paunchier, with terrible problems usually, and all rather disappointed in life, perhaps they expect too much. (Fifties Man P.)

In the previous section we observed that there were some respondents who did not conform to the progressive stereotype either by voting Conservative (ten respondents) or by being church-goers (seventeen respondents). In both respects they were in a minority compared to their fellow Dartingtonians and their behaviour was, on the surface at least, not consistent with Dartington's values or general left-wing progressivism as espoused by many of the sample's parents. In what respects can their adult actions and norms be traced to influences in their background?

Of the twenty-seven respondents involved, four both voted Conservative and went to church which means we are dealing with twenty-three individuals who had 'deviated' from ideal progressive norms. Earlier, in Chapter 4, on the parents, we noted that there were twenty-six home backgrounds that were 'incongruent', on one or more of three indicators (politics, religion and socialisation) with what one would expect from parents patronising a radical school (that they be left-wing, agnostic–atheist, and permissive).

In fact eighteen of our 'deviant' Dartingtonians are from incongruent backgrounds and five are not. Of the ten respondents who voted Conservative, six had a parent who also voted Conservative and in the four other cases the spouse voted Conservative. With regard to church attendance, seven respondents out of seventeen had parents who also were church-goers and of the ten whose parents were not, seven had spouses who went to church. In other words in the majority of deviant cases there were elements in the home background or the marital partner which might explain the respondent's deviance from the left-wing, progressive norm.

Another important area of adult socialisation is that of work and we can examine the occupations of the 'incongruent' men and of the 'incongruent' women's husbands (in the two cases where the woman was unmarried the father's occupation has been used). Using Roe's (1956) eight categories we see that the deviants' occupations tend to be grouped under 'Business, Organisation, and Technology' but not under 'Arts–Entertainment' or 'General–Culture'. Many of the occupations are professional or semi-professional (such as managing director, insurance agent, and quantity surveyor), but with a strong commercial bias, and these are probably less likely to support a radical left-wing ideology than say journalism, teaching, or arts–entertainment occupations.

Another indicator of general social attitudes is choice of newspaper. Among the deviants seventeen regularly took a daily newspaper; of these twelve took *The Times*, the *Daily Telegraph* or *Daily Express* compared to four who read *The Guardian* (one took both *The Times* and *The Guardian*). It is clear from this and other indicators that the deviant sub-group had been exposed to influences – in the home, or by occupation or marriage – which are potentially contrary to the liberal ideology of the progressive subculture. Either Dartington did not impress its social and political liberalism on them because the die had been strongly cast by the home or else adult resocialisation has led them away from the progressive norm to a more traditional and conservative one. This suggests that the distinctive life-style of the intelligentsia impresses itself on the child and while it may be positively reinforced by a progressive education it is the home background which is dominant; conversely, the children from 'incongruent homes' may well have reverted to the behaviour and values of the non-progressive home following a progressive education that was out of keeping with the social–political ideology of the parents. It does appear from our admittedly meagre evidence, that a modern education probably failed to 'convert' those children who were not already attuned to its liberal social values.

The control group

Ideally, if one determined to assess the effect of an institution on an individual, there would be no substitute for a longitudinal study which traces the neophyte's progress over a number of years, testing periodically, and holding the findings constant against those of a control group. But the availability of suitable control-groups in experimental research designs can constitute a considerable problem in sociological research because of the multiplicity of potentially intervening variables and the difficulty of ensuring comparability between two groups of people. This is equally, if not more, true of educational institutions which frequently have a heterogeneous population and which reveal an almost infinite variety of institutional practices and recruitment patterns. As implicit comparisons are unavoidable in a discussion of the effects of Progressive Education it seemed necessary to have a control group, and interviews were conducted with twenty men from Bryanston and twenty women from Badminton. To a certain extent the progressive ethic itself can be used as an absolute against which respondents can be seen to have either deviated or conformed. Basically, however, one needs to observe the differences between children of progressive parents and those of traditional parents who have passed through a radical educational environment. But *a priori* one assumes that, say a Masonic stockbroker, will not select a radical education for his children and therefore the clientele of a radical school will be highly self-selective; in advance it would seem unlikely that the school itself would produce sufficient individuals from orthodox homes who could be used as a control. In addition, there was the practical problem that to obtain sufficient information to match individuals would have involved a preliminary interview which was not feasible given limited time and resources.

One did consider using siblings as a control, i.e. brothers and sisters who did *not* go to Dartington. The two people matched would have shared the same home background but different educational experiences. Two objections presented themselves to this solution. The strongest was that the reason why one sibling was sent to Dartington, and the other not, could be an indicator of considerable differences in parental attitude to the two children; for example, perhaps one was a 'problem' child. Also one would have introduced a wide gamut of educational experience in that some siblings may have gone to a traditional boarding school, others to a state day school, while some may have been educated abroad. The picture was complicated by the fact that respondents had altogether thirty-one full brothers, thirty-four full sisters, eighteen half-brothers, nine half-sisters, seven step-brothers, and eight step-sisters, and there was one foster sister.

It seemed advisable to restrict the control to a comparable institutional base; but what school was comparable? In a study of an independent progressive school, where parents have the opportunity to choose a minority education (which is looked upon as deviant by the remainder of the educational system, state and private), the educational radicalism of the home is crucial. There seemed little point in choosing a traditional public school for the control as many indicators, such as parents' religious and political affiliations, would almost certainly be the polar opposite of the radical parent. Neither could one choose a state boarding school because, although comparable on the important variable of coeducation, it would have had a much broader social class intake. Summerhill, another radical school, would not have had the necessary records and would probably not have cooperated; besides many of its clients are American and the English parent who chooses Summerhill might have only duplicated our findings for Dartington. One seemed in danger of choosing a group which would either be too different or not different enough.

A compromise solution was to choose two mildly progressive schools whose parents were likely to be more liberal than the traditional upper middle class and whose children's educational experience had affinities with the more radical progressive sector. Badminton and Bryanston suggested themselves and both agreed to cooperate. They supplied fairly full and up-to-date lists of former pupils as all former pupils are automatically contacted by the Old Boys' and Old Girls' associations. Twenty men and twenty women were selected from the leavers of 1950–4 to coincide with the Dartington 'fifties' sample. All had spent a minimum of three years at the school. A reasonable cross-section was taken from across the school houses to make the sample fairly representative. However, it was decided to confine the sample to people living in London and the Home Counties because our main sample was heavily biassed toward the South-East, and because there seemed little to be gained intellectually from drawing a widely scattered sample.

In essence, one was controlling for two basic factors; a fairly comparable social class background and a not too dissimilar educational experience. Both the fifties cohort and the Badmintonians and Bryanstonians came from predominantly upper middle class homes, spent a minimum of three years at an independent boarding school considered progressive to a greater or lesser degree, and left school between 1950 and 1954. Both the control schools differed from Dartington in an important respect, namely they were single-sex; and this is an indicator that they were somewhat less progressive than the coeducational Dartington. However, both were originally considered progressive though have moved to the right educationally since the war (especially Bryanston). In strict terms 'control' group is a misnomer as the control population has been selected on only a couple of crude indicators. In effect, the parallels between the main sample and the 'control' group will be used to illuminate a few broad facets of the research with the proviso that such comparisons have to be treated with caution and that only crude and very general conclusions can be drawn from them.

Briefly, we can look at some aspects of the adult lives of the Bryanstonians and Badmintonians in order to compare them with our data for the Dartingtonians. None of the control group, for example, expressed considerable difficulty on leaving school and generally their passage into the wider society was much smoother. Furthermore, they displayed less of a tendency to shy away from formal roles and establishment positions. Nearly two-thirds of the controls, for instance, went to university and for over half of them this meant Oxbridge. Then with regard to National Service, fourteen Bryanstonians entered the Forces of whom no less than ten were commissioned. Occupationally too the control men were less likely to be in cultural-creative jobs and more likely to be in 'Organisation–Technology' positions.

The Badmintonians were slightly more radical than the Bryanstonians but politically both were considerably to the right of the Dartingtonians with regard to self-placement on the national political spectrum and voting preferences – 42 per cent of the control group voted Conservative compared to 10 per cent of the Dartington sample. The controls were also mainly *Daily Telegraph* or *Daily Mail* subscribers rather than readers of *The Guardian* or *The Times*. Indeed on nearly every indicator the men and women from Bryanston and Badminton were more conventional – say on religion, socialisation of their children, or political feelings – than the radically educated Dartingtonians.

In effect, it seems that the control group suffered far less from the cachet of rebellious notoriety that followed a Dartingtonian on leaving their benign cloister. They were similarly attached to the old school and former pupil network but then both control schools had comprehensive and formally administered Old Boys' and Old Girls' associations. In essence the control group had enjoyed a mildly progressive education which set them slightly apart from the ultra-traditional public school but which did not confer on them the rich and expressive counter-traditionalism with which an Old Dartingtonian or Old Summerhillian tends to draw attention to his or her educational un-iqueness. As a consequence, the control group reported far less anomic strain in adjusting to society and most of them had readily assimilated, socially and politically, to conventional bourgeois society. They also earned more money than the Dartingtonians!

The progressive adult: conclusion

The expectation surrounding the progressively educated child was that he or she would mature to become a new type of man or woman. On leaving, however, there was a tendency for the progressives' gentle, non-competitive, almost other-worldly ethos to make adjustment to the 'realities' of the wider society abrasive for some respondents. Males in particular were handicapped for filling conventional occupational roles. At the same time, women were liberated to a certain extent from traditional inhibitions; this could lead to a certain forcefulness and to selecting counter-traditional partners – such as foreigners, Americans, manual workers, fellow progressives, or renegade public school men.

But perhaps the greatest potential burden that the children of the new era had to shoulder was as precursors of a new, improved social order. Imbued with an anti-authoritarian and anti-institutional ideology they were faced with the task of reforming a society where the institutional centres of power are for-mally structured, hierarchical, and bureaucratic. In addition, my evidence does suggest that the progressive adult has been somewhat enfeebled for the role of crusader. A pioneer of minority opinions needs to be resilient, com-bative, self-reliant and tenacious whereas the progressive environment seems to sap those very qualities. The internationalism, the tolerance, the pacifism, and the attempt to stand above prejudice was poor preparation for the heat of political battle where life can be vindictive and acrimonious and where success is bought with painstaking application to the minutiae of political organisation. There were few respondents in conventional leadership positions of power compared to the over-representation of public school men in the elite positions that Bishop and Wilkinson (1967) have convincingly demonstrated.

Much of our evidence is descriptive and impressionistic and one cannot draw a strong causal connection between the school and adult life because of the possible multitude of intervening variables. Nevertheless, Curry (1947: 109) himself was aware that the modern school might be accused of producing 'neurotic misfits', however, he felt that it was less important that the individual fit easily into society than that he was free from serious internal conflicts.

Since sixteen I have not been well-adjusted. Since then I have been firmly persuaded that our economic and social number is bad, our international order outrageous, and most of the current views on religion and sex preposterous and superstitious. (Curry 1947: 124.)

And in that sense he admitted that he was not 'well-adjusted'. In addition, other progressive educators have stated that despite their espoused non-interference and individualism the progressive school undoubtedly influenced its charges.

We have no wish for uniformity, whether in dress or speech, in creed or opinion. Yet there is something that marks them as Bedalians and remains a bond between them (Badley 1924: 209.)

Respondents themselves continually drew attention to parallels between their education and their present life and some even appeared to achieve a sort of catharsis in revealing their feelings on the subject during the interview. On some occasions it was even quite difficult to get away!

Finally, we have previously had to rely on speculative generalisations about the effects of progressive education which range from the self-congratulatory to the slightly mocking.

Neill's products often have creative gifts and warm-heartedness but they cannot get up in the morning to use them. (D. Holbrook in Skidelsky 1968: 42.)

The American historian Graham (1967: 67) generalised from her research on Progressive Education:

The progressive school in emphasising the development of individuality has often failed to develop an adequate social outlook. It has cultivated open-mindedness, but students are not moved to social action or fired by great beliefs or causes. Students are critical but indecisive, interesting and well-poised as individuals, but self-centred.

The subject matter of this work contains treacherous pitfalls for the researcher with few guidelines. It has been said that priests used to promise life after death and that teachers now promise life after school. But among the sea of assertions about the relationship of school to the 'after life' there are only a few islands of empirical evidence (Jencks 1975 and Newcomb *et al.* 1967). Rarely, apart from access to elite networks, has access been gained to adults in relation to their previous institutional experience. In ranging widely, this study has inevitably been forced to generalise on the basis of weak evidence. But, rudimentary and qualitative as my data admittedly is, it does, nonetheless, begin to marshal facts in an area where previously there were few.

Chapter Twelve

Conclusion: Dartington, the progressives and the anti-institution

The progressive retreat

Progressive education ... [which] for some time past has lost its way ... Undoubtedly it has been weakened, diluted by the disintegrative forces to which it has been subjected ... The educational debate of recent years has passed the progressive movement by ... [it] has run a grave risk: the risk of stagnating within its very own bounds. (Ash 1969: 11 and 120.)

The independent progressive school movement ceased to grow after 1940, when Kilquhanity, Monkton Wyld, and Wennington were founded. In the United States progressive education declined precipitously after the war and became something of a laughing-stock. In 1957, the point where my analysis of Dartington Hall School must end, the school was only rescued from a period of stagnant tranquillity by the internal upheavals surrounding the trauma of Curry's resignation and replacement. Its idealism tempered by the Cold War period and its recruitment corroded by inflation, Dartington was no longer in the van of modernity and its nadir echoed the unhealthy state of the English progressives who have never recovered the élan of the inter-war years. Then, Blewitt (1934) had mentioned three general values which united the early progressives; namely, a rejection and substitution of the public school model, an espousal of the needs of the individual child, and a belief in fostering a changed world. Dartington would have subscribed wholeheartedly to all three. In addition, it had pretensions to be a 'research station' (Ash 1969: 200) and a laboratory school from which other schools could take their lead.

If it is extremely difficult to assess the effects of schooling on children (Lambert *et al.* 1971a, Chapter IX and Young 1965: 8), then it is even more problematic to trace the influence of Dartington and the other progressives upon education in general.

But first, as a framework for assessing Dartington's achievements and failures, it might be instructive to sketch some conditions under which we would expect the progressive school to flourish. Ideally one assumes that to function effectively the school should possess a healthy congruence with the progressive radicalism in the wider society in order to gain encouragement and reinforcement for its minority values; stable and supportive parents who wholeheartedly agree with the school's ideals and are prepared to give their children an exclusively progressive education; a headmaster who can hold the community together administratively and also inspire commitment yet without infringing the progressive libertarian philosophy of maximum freedom and minimum restraint for the individual; a staff of balanced, mature, responsible, sensitive individuals who do not seek out progressive education because of their own emotional inadequacies and who can maintain the delicate balance between judicious guidance and non-interference; and, finally, children who are emotionally secure, socially sophisticated, 'divergers', with the ability to use fruitfully (i.e. as the progressives themselves would wish) the freedoms offered. As Curry constantly lamented in his reports to the Trustees his school never fully enjoyed all these advantages and, not surprisingly, there was often a considerable divergence between ideal and reality.

Evidently some parents held either undue or conflicting expectations of the school. But, more crucially, the majority of our sample only turned to Dartington when orthodox education had failed or been found wanting for their children; in effect, something like a half of our sample's homes had indicators of traditional attitudes (on politics, religion and socialization) while probably a half of the homes were divided on the decision to send the child to a progressive school. Widespread parental support for the school's values was not entirely agreed and conflict did arise on occasion between the home and the school. A significant proportion of the children were difficult and insecure; for example, one-third of the sample suffered from a broken home (divorce, separation or death of parent), while many reported some form of material or emotional disruption in the home or previous background. Coupled with these facts, many of the children arrived at Dartington already habituated to the authoritarian restraints of traditional education which meant that they could not always adapt themselves successfully to the freedoms offered. And, while some of the staff were excellent, the school did attract some inadequate people who rarely stayed long as well as a few not quite first-rate people who stayed too long. In addition, there were austerities and post-war inflation to contend with which afflicted most private schools and which limited adaptability because mere survival was now at stake.

In what areas then, does Dartington seem not to have lived up to its expectations? In effect, Curry *was* Dartington and while Dartington is fairly representative of the radical progressive school, Curry held two views which separated him from fellow radicals. Firstly, he hoped to achieve high academic attainment among his pupils and, secondly, he espoused a great respect for reason (unlike the emphasis on the senses among Neillites). With regard to academic standards, Dartington can hardly be said to have scaled the heights despite some highly intelligent children. Not only that, but Curry disclaimed interest in teaching methods or curricular reform (which is precisely that area that has probably had most influence in changing orthodox education) and this one feels was a failure. Like many innovators and utopians with a conception of how differently things can be done if only the resources are available, Curry constantly demanded exceptional and ideal conditions for his children, such as a generous staff–pupil ratio, specialist cultural facilities, well-qualified staff, single-rooms, a narrow ability range, and, ultimately, he almost wanted to ignore economic considerations in order to have complete freedom to choose children. One feels that something more is expected from this investment in an educational environment which was, and is, the envy of England.

To talk almost of 'returns' in this way may seem to violate progressive ideals but Curry himself wanted to sponsor good academic results, cultural attainments, and to hold up progressive education as the ideal; in effect, he wished it to demonstrate that individuality and freedom could be purchased with no diminution in conventional standards of attainment. But academic results were, and continued to be, mediocre despite the small classes and almost individual attention. Use of the cultural facilities could be sporadic and on occasion debilitating of disciplined cultural attainment. Many of our sample criticised the inability of the school to motivate them to fulfil their academic, and/or cultural, potential and the general *laissez-faire* attitude of non-interference and non-compulsion does seem to have had a deleterious effect on the children's achievements in conventional terms.

To balance against these points, we can look at Dartington's achievements. Probably the most important feature to emerge from the evidence is that Curry and his staff endeavoured to be humane and to espouse a genuine respect for the individual child at a time when traditional education was still enmeshed in what Lytton Strachey called 'licensed barbarism'. The extent of coeducation was greater than at almost any other school and sexual discrimination was notably absent. Much of the cruelty and brutality among children was diminished though never eliminated. Relationships between adults and children were often frank, open, and devoid of unnecessary social distance. For psychologically disturbed or sensitive children, to whom orthodox education was irksome if not crushing, there can be little doubt that Dartington was highly beneficial. In effect its latent function was to serve almost as an 'approved' school for difficult middle class children, in most respects it performed that function admirably by providing a benign, warm, supportive, non-punitive, therapeutic environment.

Some of Dartington's failings and strengths are common to many progressive schools, but it differed from all of them in one important respect – money. Behind Dartington there was always the resources of the Elmhirsts and of the Dartington estate whereas many progressives have subsisted on a shoe-string. This makes Dartington's failure to innovate perhaps less excusable than for some of its smaller, impoverished, brethren. In practice, it almost appears as if the progressives felt that simply to demonstrate progressive education would be to open the flood-gates of a universal demand for their educational blue-print. Presumably this is what Neill (1968: 19) means when he stated that Summerhill was no longer an experimental school but rather a 'demonstration' school. Consequently, progressive phrases about 'science', 'experimental' and 'innovation' have an empty ring.

Furthermore, hopes of influencing the traditional public school can hardly be said to have been realised. Resilient, firmly entrenched, and subtly manipulative, the more adaptable public schools could implement curricula or cultural innovations from the progressive sector without fundamentally altering their structure while the ultra-traditional public school was almost invulnerable to external pressures. Eton, for example, can claim many of the features of the progressive school (individual rooms, excellent art and craft facilities, an international clientele, children sharing in domestic work, etc.) yet within the framework of inexorable exams, uniform, games, chapel, and monosexuality (McConnell 1967). Additionally, some public schools have successfully bent before the wind of new patterns of child-rearing in middle-class families and of the commercially stimulated youth-culture by reducing certain areas of institutional control and by altering patterns of boarding (Millham and Bullock 1973).

The irony is that, if anything, Dartington ended up by sharing the same drawbacks as the traditional boarding school by which Curry seems to have been mesmerised. For, according to Weinberg (1967: 165) the chief problem of boarding school life chosen by a group of public school headmasters was 'the closed nature of the community and distance from the outside world'; also Wakeford (1969: 178–9) outlines the features deprecated by the Public Schools Commission in traditional boarding styles – the loss of warmth and affection, separation from peers, restriction to an isolated and artificial community, the lack of privacy, and the emphasis on conformity to a predetermined pattern of behaviour. And yet the progressives placed their faith in a residential environment. For example, at a Cambridge Conference on the 'Place of Boarding in State Education' (1965: 45) many delegates agreed that as a miniature community a boarding school could set higher moral and religious standards than the outside world. And this was exactly the position adopted by several contributors to Child's (1962) Symposium; for example, Hu and Lois Child of Dartington wrote (ibid: 52 and 146):

Young people are subjected to a ceaseless barrage of sex propaganda in the Press, in films, in the theatre, in advertisements, in the sexy novel, much of it exalting sexual satisfaction as the most important of human gratifications. Add to this the almost universal availability of cheap contraceptives and it is small wonder that the forces battling for restraint are on the retreat ... The illegitimacy rate, the incidence of venereal disease, the rise in the divorce rate, with all that this means for the unhappiness and maladjustment of children, all point to an unhappy state of affairs, as does also the incidence of neuroses associated with sexual disorders ... How then can we cope with this problem in a boarding school? . . . The answer lies in the fact that we are a community, and a small community, which can develop an ethos of its own. . . . Total membership of a community rather than the partial participation in community life of the day pupil was and is thought of as a vital part of the educative process.

Introspective and moribund, the post-war progressives lost track of educational radicalism in the wider society and became like beleaguered garrisons viewing the outside world as hostile and predatory. In America, for example, Progressive Education had been extremely influential between the wars but had become a term of opprobrium by the middle fifties. The fate of the Progressive Education Association (PEA) described by Cremin (1961) and Graham (1967), revealed that a diffuse educational philosophy, which promised much initially, was found wanting when circumstances had changed; it led eventually to an inability to define its aims, to a certain anti-intellectualism in practice, to an increasing gap between theory and practice, and to capture by social radicals in the thirties. Its own internal squabbles led the PEA to introspection at the neglect of its earlier concern with social problems. For example, Graham (1967: 163) accuses the movement of ignoring the education of immigrant children, slum youngsters, and rural youth as well as not facing up to the vital question of desegregation. From a membership peak of 10,000 in 1938 the PEA declined until an important ballot vote in 1947 brought in only sixty-eight replies; the Association was declared insolvent in 1949 and was formally dissolved in June 1955 (Graham 1967: 149–50). Not only had progressive education apparently failed to adapt to the realities of post-war America – a heavily industrialised, racially divided, immigrant absorbing, rapidly changing mass society faced with the burdens of world leadership and international rivalry with the Soviet bloc – but it became a scapegoat during the backlash against radicalism in the forties and during the intense reappraisal that America undertook in the mid-fifties. But the most crucial factor in the movement's collapse was that it had simply failed to keep pace with the transformation of American society rendering many of its ideals obsolescent (Cremin 1961: 347–52).

While no corporate movement has been shaped by progressive education in England, the New Education Fellowship, which was founded in 1920, most closely approximates the spirit of the movement and it too experienced a contraction and a change of emphasis occasioned by the war. The independent schools were central to it in the inter-war years and they still advertise in its journal *The New Era*. The English section was influential too in the international movement which had its heyday in the decade 1925–35 when it held well-attended conferences (the Cape Town conference of 1934 attracted 3,000 people for instance) that were addressed by people such as Jung, Buber, Adler, Tawney and Mumford (Boyd and Rawson 1965). After the war, the conferences were never again pre-eminent, the dozen journals were reduced finally to one (*The New Era* with a current international circulation of 2,000–2,500), financially the movement was impoverished, but, most vitally, the strong psychological orientation with the emphasis on the individual child was transmuted into a concern with questions of a more social, economic, and political tone (the NEF has been closely connected with UNESCO). These concerns led the NEF to abandon the independent progressive school in order to concentrate on the state schools in post-war England (Boyd and Rawson 1965: 185).

No new independent progressive boarding school has been founded since the war. The present position of these independent progressives is best approached through Ash (1969) who described the Colloquy which Dartington sponsored in 1965 as an 'educational confrontation' (ibid: ix).

A Colloquy? Rather a confrontation! For what began as an intended meeting of minds between two groups each considering themselves to be educational progressives ended up in an irreconcilability of attitudes that was distressing, perplexing, and ominous.

The contestants were the 'traditional' progressives of the independent boarding sector who were roundly attacked by the 'new' progressives who championed the state day comprehensive school. Whereas the schools in Blewitt (1934) opposed the public school, the 'traditionalists' at Dartington (i.e. largely the 'radical' progressives – Dartington, Wennington, and Monkton Wyld) were united primarily in their opposition to the comprehensive school. In fact, the bitterness of the exchanges was probably occasioned by the belief of the old progressives that they were the suitors with someting precious to offer the state system and they reacted with chagrin when their advances were rebuffed.

In brief, the confrontation exposed the parlous condition of the old progressives; they found it difficult to agree among themselves and were practically forced into making a *volte-face* on some of their original ideals. The new progressives accused them of being

An insignificant backwater: protected, precious, unreal; no longer the vanguard to achievement, but rather a curiosity, something apart. (Ash 1969: 120.)

Defensively, the old progressives refused to countenance any change in their traditional structure; in fact they were forced into a conservative corner where King-Harris (headmaster of St Christopher's Letchworth) passionately repudiated an experimental role for the progressive schools; Hu Child of Dartington opposed changes in the curriculum, and in boarding provision, and Kenneth Barnes of Wennington regretted the use of the epithet 'progressive'.

I think it is unfortunate that we are forced to justify the term 'progressive'. It is not a label I welcome, and I doubt if we can find a definition of it to satisfy us all. (Ash 1969: 12)

The two strongest arguments pursued by the traditionalists were firstly that the progressive school existed to serve a minority and should be allowed to exist in order to guarantee parental choice (the classical defence of the public school!) and, secondly, that they stand for the ideal of treating each child as a unique individual. The latter could not be equated necessarily with social equality where giving every child equal opportunity was not synonymous with treating each child as a person. In effect, the progressives of the independent sector were revealed as being extremely cautious and conservative and as deeply wedded to their 'traditional' structure. This placed them, according to the new progressives, as bed-mates with their original arch enemy, the elitist, exclusive privileged public school.

Indeed, the progressives were as equally threatened by the Newson Commission on the Public Schools as the public schools themselves and Dartington took active steps to accommodate itself to the wind of educational change, including the holding of the Colloquy and the sponsoring of this research. About the same time, Royston Lambert was appointed headmaster and his proposals for altering the school once more returned Dartington to its role in experimenting in the social structure of the school. (Lambert 1969). His ambitious plans included shared teaching with the local comprehensive in Totnes, links with state school pupils from the West Riding of Yorkshire, variations in the length and type of the residential experience, and a workbase abroad in Sicily. As an indicator of how the middle-class, rural boarding school might integrate with the state sector, say if the Newsom Reports' proposals of 50 per cent state places being taken up in independent schools were ever implemented, Lambert's schemes were suggestive and radical. Indeed, one argument for the continued existence of the independent sector has been as an experimental wing of the state system. Is this then a possible future for the independent progressive school?

This seems unlikely: apart from the school's own reluctance to innovate and the fate of the experimental schools in American education (Miles 1964: 499) their physical, constitutional, and ideological position make them of limited relevance to the state day system in which the majority of the country's children are educated. The absolutely central question in contemporary education is the allocation of resources; the people who hold the purse strings are accountable for expenditure and therefore educational priorities tend to be determined by administrative structures, public and private demands, by the needs and demands of the majority, and by local and national political interests. It costs somewhere in the region of four or five times the amount to keep a pupil at Dartington as it does to keep one at a secondary modern school; to give every child at a secondary school in 1966 the benefit of a year at Dartington would have cost the state £1,680,000,000 or practically the whole educational budget for that year. (DES Statistics 1966/67). The progressives would have never faced the problem of resources if their ideas had been adopted by the state.

If they had confronted the issue then they would have realised that resources involve competition for power. But the progressives were utopian and almost other-worldly and simply did not have the temperament to perform as an influential pressure group; they had little or no conception of strategy, tactics, publicity, organisation, patience, or persuasion. They rejected the state educational system because they distrusted the power of its centralised machinery, because they were personally not prepared to conform to social convention, and because they wanted wide freedom to 'experiment' with the child. But in adopting an anchoretic role in rural communes they cut themselves off from the very people they espoused to influence. Having withdrawn from the problems of working in the state system to an artificial environment it seems inappropriate, if not naive, to demand that the state follow their lead.

At times, the progressives are exasperating in their arrogance, their pretentiousness, and their dogmatism. These may be part of the characteristics of people drawn to educational radicalism and partly the result of the courage, enthusiasm and intransigence necessary to pioneer a nonconforming community. Nevertheless, one feels that English education would have been impoverished without the challenge to orthodoxy of the progressive radicals. Their role has been one of heretics and outsiders providing a beacon for the left-wing in education and a fate to avoid for the right-wing. Imperceptibly and piecemeal many of their ideas have penetrated the Colleges of Education – Susan Isaacs, for example, has had a tremendous influence on progressive ideas in the training of teachers (Van der Eycken and Turner, 1969) – and the primary schools (Plowden Report 1967). Because of the demands of university entrance, occupational selection, and the deeply ingrained academic disciplines, however, their influence on the secondary schools has been slight. (Boyd and Rawson 1965: 130–50). And, in their own right, they certainly cater for a need among intellectuals for their children to be educated in a style that contrasts with the traditional public school.

Finally, Dartington, in common with its fellow independent progressive schools, proved reluctant to carry out a programme of evaluation for its 'experimental' education. Before adoption of an innovation can take place a serious evaluation of the design must take place together with a policy for implementing it in the schools; rarely does this happen (Miles 1964: 495f). Indeed, for a number of reasons, the progressive school may feel threatened by research because of its marginality and its desire for legitimation.

However, its influence has probably worked far more through its spirit, through its literature and ideas, and through its raising of some of the timeless issues of the aims of education than on an experimental or institutional level. Had the progressive school succeeded in being adopted as the universal form of educational provision then it would have made itself unnecessary; the fate of progressive innovators in the state system, such as Duane at Rising Hill (Berg 1968) and MacKenzie (1970) at Braehead, may suggest that the independent progressive school is still a necessity if orthodoxy is to be challenged.

However, to challenge and to implement are two separate processes; and we would argue that to become a serious contender for the national educational system the progressives require a strong and convincing case. But they have never displayed much appetite for undertaking the objective appraisal and critical evaluation of their own educational assumptions that this would demand, while the modest evidence of this research indicates that, in many respects, their case is far from proven. Nevertheless, the legacy of the radical innovating schools does provide us with a valuable record of one of the most ambitious attempts to alter the conventional structure of school. And in Dartington we have an excellent socio-historical case study of one of the crucial forerunners of what might be called the 'anti-school'.

The institutionalization of an anti-institutional ideology

Only the creative process is anti-art; art itself is moribund . . . only the anti-school is valid . . . We must hope that the progressive school can somehow achieve its own perpetual revolution. Clearly, this revolution is one that must use the ever unpredictable resources of children's personality as its dynamic. Somehow, then, the progressive school if it is to be a continuing entity – if it is not to blow up – must survive the effects, wayward as they may be, of this dynamic. (Ash 1969: 64–5.)

Most social groups or collectivities, other than those of a most impermanent kind, seek to perpetuate their existence and identity over time. The modern formal organisation, for example, tends to adopt a rational, bureaucratic structure in order to ensure its survival and aims at continuity, impartiality and efficiency. In addition, Schon (1970) contends that formal organisations are often 'dynamically conservative', that is to say they fight like mad to stay the same. Some social groups, however, set out deliberately to combat this innate tendency to dynamic conservatism and form what I call 'anti-institutions' (Punch 1974b). The desire to escape what is perceived as the deleterious consequences of a permanent social structure and the attempt to capture the absence of constraint in an association with an anti-institutional and an anti-authoritarian ideology is what I mean by an anti-institution: it is an attempt to live perpetually on the margin, resisting the encroachments of formalisation.

It is the attempt to retain the spontaneous, immediate, concrete nature of 'communitas' (Turner 1969: 127) against the fate of 'declining' into the norm-governed, instutionalised, abstract nature of law and social structure. For once a collectivity threatens to become permanent it tends to cater for continuity and survival and much of its energy may go into routine activity, maintaining social control, and planning a sequential programme. Permanence seems to demand formalisation and radical institutions no less than conservative ones, as Michels (1949) found to his distress, seem subject to the iron laws of institutional life that the structural arteries harden as recurrent needs are foreseen and calculated mechanisms, roles and subsystems, are adopted to meet them. The radical progressives were conscious of the constraints and limitations of orthodox forms of association and were determined to avoid congealing or ossifying – as Curry used to say 'Dartington has no traditions, except that it has no traditions'. The progressive school apparently relinquished the safety and comfort of traditional authority and endeavoured to solve the paradox of institutionalising freedom for the individual child. Crucial for any stable collectivity's survival is the problem of social control: how to get its authority accepted as legitimate and how to cope with deviance. With conventional restraints removed did Hobbesian anarchy prevail; and, if not, how was the war of all against all prevented? For, reviewing his own experiences in running a progressive school, Bertrand Russell (1968: 154) came to pessimistic conclusions:

Many of the children were cruel and destructive. To let the children go free was to establish a reign of terror, in which the strong kept the weak trembling and miserable. A school is like the world; only government can prevent brutal violence.

At Dartington Curry seriously tried to work a participatory democracy of rational individuals that would solve the perennial problem of how the individual could engage in social activity without compromising his freedom. Rousseau believed that the answer to that dilemma was by the creation of a 'corporate communion where each simultaneously discovered himself in the closest possible solidarity with others' (Wolin 1961: 371). In practice, this tends to mean either despotism or religious zeal, for without one or other of these two forms of social cement self-interest tends to prevail. Where neither of these forms of social control operate in a communitarian enterprise anxiety and insecurity have to be overcome. Potentially Dartington embraced a communal existence that was continually threatened, perilously balanced, and that consciously made self-generated uncertainty a structural feature.

For example, there must be a modicum of consensus, i.e. an explicit or implicit social contract, for a group of people to agree to cohere over time. In the progressive school, however, the contract has to be reforged with each generation and therefore the school is potentially exposed to a cyclical threat as continuity is not guaranteed; particularly since anticipatory socialisation to the special values of the progressive school is far from complete because of its peculiar recruitment pattern. This insecurity was exacerbated at Dartington by a set of institutional contradictions which made it vulnerable in the area of social control. What are some of those forces? Firstly, there is the fundamental paradox that it both wished to have its values accepted yet without wishing to impose them. Secondly, it both attracted and catered for difficult children who are exactly those people most likely to threaten its delicate social order. Thirdly, it ostensibly held out no precise stereotype to be followed by children although self-selection tended to minimise diversity among the staff, and among other pupils, with whom a child might identify. Fourthly, it professed to encourage the free expression of personal emotion and yet demanded a high level of almost adult responsibility. Fifthly, and this is central and fundamental, we have seen that Dartington (in keeping with the radical sub-set of progressive schools) had features that made it approximate to a 'total' institution (Goffman 1961) – i.e. physical remoteness, a mutual antagonism with the outside world, a high proportion of boarders, a small-size and broad age-range, and a zealously guarded independence.

To understand how the democracy functioned at Dartington involves a consideration of the challenges to its social order and Curry's response to these threats. It is also worth mentioning some of the external pressures that Curry had to contend with such as friction with the estate managers, a conspiracy of parents to oust him, mounting financial pressures, deteriorating relationships with the Trustees, and hostility from the locality, the press, and the educational establishment. Internally, our evidence for Dartington indicates that the progressive school can be subject to periodic crises when the social order is threatened and has to be reinforced because the safety of routinised authority has been abandoned in favour of paring institutional restraints to a minimum and of encouraging the children 'to do their own thing'. The problem then becomes of what happens when reason fails; how is authority then to be exercised? Ironically, it was when the children were perhaps most 'progressive' (that is childish, irrational and emotional) that they were most dangerous. Harrison (1969: 188) for example, noted with the Owenite communities that the idea of deviation was barely considered and that there were few psychic resources within the community for dealing with fundamental disagreements. Dartington was similarly vulnerable, but when disagreement arose the vital mechanism for inducing consensus was the self-government. Here reason and discussion would guarantee the individual's freedom in a communal setting.

In practice, several respondents reported that Curry manipulated the Council or Moot. One could argue that as the final authority in a periously balanced community he was forced to manipulate both in the interests of certain pupils who might suffer at the hands of the strong and to preserve his own school. His burden was the necessity of total supervision, twenty-four hours a day, every day, over children for whom he was legally responsible and over whom he acted *in loco parentis*. Furthermore, an underlying authoritarianism can be detected in his personality – note the tone of moral absolutism about so many of his utterances for example – and also Curry appears to have had an increasingly inflexible conviction of what constituted virtue. His ideological conviction not to impose his values led to a faith in rationality almost as if rational argument would prove irresistible. The School Council, for instance, could absorb sporadic challenge within its own terms of reasoned debate but the tolerance limit was reached when the challenge was persistent and *unreasonable*. Under those circumstances Curry abandoned his professed aims and exercised his undoubted charisma.

But charisma can be a precarious form of authority as it continually threatens to become routinised. Curry realised that there were occasions when all that stood between a 'Lord of the Flies' anarchy was himself, and in response to this he seemed to cultivate a mystique. The dilemma was that Curry could not relinquish authority to anyone else for fear of severing his ties with the pupil society and hence he was *forced* to intervene when disorder occurred. To a certain extent, rules may obviate the necessity for the continual personal repetition of orders, but without conventional sanctions at their disposal and with little real authority the staff had to rely on Curry's authority to reassert the equilibrium.

One weekend everyone got going with fire hoses and soaked the place which was pretty irresponsible. It made a terrible mess and the staff got in a terrible state because they couldn't stop it and I feel it was really an awful lot of people joined in whereas it had originally been a few people who had started it and who were being rather stupid. Curry was fetched and just came and talked about it; he could always deal with that sort of thing. (Fifties Woman MS.)

Paradoxically, however, the very use of sanctions may undermine authority and be subject to the law of diminishing marginal utility. At each intervention Curry was putting himself at risk for the charismatic leader must always be successful. Hence Curry took considerable pride in allegedly never using his veto in the Council. But frequent intervention could become merely tedious and routine and it was essential to re-create and perpetuate the illusion that a powerful personality bridged the gap between reality and the collective illusion. As soon as some children penetrated the illusion then Curry fell back on the illiberalism and disguised authoritarianism of the charismatic leader. In the last resort he could not permit the children to choose an alternative to his definition of virtue; morality was posited on collective unity, an external enemy, and the survival of the school. And, if necessary, he was prepared to force the children to be free. In short, the *volonté générale* became the *volonté d'un*.

Probably the most insistent theme of the radical progressives is an adamant refusal to 'mould' the child; and yet the apparently open society of the progressive school can fall victim to norms as rigid and all-embracing as those of traditional informal schoolboy codes. This has been noted by progressives themselves. For example, H. B. Jacks of Bedales (Child 1962: 37) remarked:

If you encourage children too directly and too emphatically to think for themselves, to be independent, critical, liberal-minded, you can quickly produce a kind of liberalism on principle, which is die hard to the last degree. There have been occasions when I have encountered at Bedales an attitude of 'Oh no, we don't do that here. We're different'. As someone said once, the conservatism of a progressive school is the most conservative of all.

While Coade of Bryanston (1966: 152) wrote:

I know at least one progressive school where tradition has become as tyrannous, restrictive, and illogical as at any of the older foundations.

Behind the diminution of overt institutional control the pupils were subject to considerable informal pressures that set normative standards defining limitations on dress, behaviour and values. Millham and Bullock (1973), for example, generalised about their experiences of contemporary progressive schools:

The community is inward-looking, and the need to achieve a consensus and the quasi religious nature of the progresive ideal tends to stifle real debate both within the school and on the larger estate. There is no coherent, vigorous anti-group, the radicals' nursery, such as characterises almost all other leading education establishments and greatly enlivens the intellectual world of the public schools. Informal attitudes and values do tend to be an all-encompassing and inescapable influence on the children . . . Despite such communities' apparent liberalism, therefore, and their radical stance, the power of the pupil society, the tendency to recruit from certain limited social groups and for the children to be introduced to progressive values from an early age, invest these egalitarian communities with elements of expressive totality. These values are pervasive, in that they cover many areas of life and are strongly held, and in the closed nature of the schools the informal control that can be exerted by ostracism and rejection can become highly coercive. In a society where you are very dependent on others emotionally and materially, exclusion is extremely painful.

There seems to be a parallel here with aspects of the children's world in the Israeli kibbutz. For varying reasons the children in both institutions tend to be vulnerable to the dictates of the peer group; Bettelheim (1969: 225) for example, argues that 'kibbutzniks' are often rudely self-assertive as a group because they can express collectively what they are being asked to suppress individually. And, if true, this might also be true of the displaced aggression at

Dartington with its water fights, food-throwing, and broken windows. But while the inflexibility of the progressive code was a direct antithesis of the movement's aims it became an important element of social control, controlling deviance and spelling predictability. In effect, the unintended consequence of the 'Progressive Ethic' was that its individualistic, anti-authoritarian ideology produced at times an almost tribal closeness. The paradox was that on the one hand the staff tried to espouse the classical progressive doctrine of non-interference while, on the other hand, the children, faced with this potentially normless situation, embraced progressive values with an almost religious collectivism. Ironically, the 'anti-institution' became institutionalised.

Indeed, deviance may have been more difficult in the progressive school than in the traditional school. For, without formal roles, positions are filled by individuals and attacks on authority become personal attacks; and who was going to challenge Curry? And, as for the 'kibbutznik', it is almost impossible for the progressive child to stand alone against the group. The exceptional unity of the school can be seen in the absence of almost any manifestation of an 'informal system' which is generally considered to be ubiquitous in formal organisation. Skidelsky (1968: 58) correctly observes that the progressives saw only the negative side of the sometimes brutal world of the subterranean schoolboy culture without recognising its positive virtue of protecting the child from the encroachments of the adult world. At Dartington the almost universal norm of other total institutions that inmates 'never rat' did not operate and what would have been considered informing elsewhere became an acceptable practice. By allowing the pupil society little if any autonomy it could be argued that the progressives forged a social environment that, in some respects, was potentially more insidiously 'total' than many authoritarian regimes.

Indeed, Bettelheim (1969: 230) described the closeness engendered in the kibbutz as like the initiation societies of preliterate tribes. And the 'freedoms' at Dartington could breed insecurity and in response to this the children appeared to develop a ritualised non-conformity, where even the obscenity and lawlessness was stereotyped (Turner 1969: 93) and where ritual gave visible expression of public morals lest there be any doubt about private conscience (Douglas 1966: 128). The cruel irony was that on occasions the children preferred security, and even domination, rather than the perpetual burden of making their own decisions. At Dartington, the children of the 'new era' were willing to surrender voluntarily that freedom which their mentors had fought so passionately to establish. Curry, the supreme individualist and rationalist, was forced into a paradoxical and ultimately tragic position whereby he purchased a communitarian, educational experiment at the cost of betraying his most cherished ideals. For the price he paid in taking young children into a total environment, was to mould unintentionally a pubescent totalitarian democracy where the immature individual, faced by the burdens of freedom internally, and the animus of hostility externally, escaped this onerous dilemma by submerging himself in compulsive conformity to the group and, at one difficult point, by electing Curry 'dictator'.

Conclusion: researching alternative education

This book recounts a case study of research on one particular English progressive school of relatively long-standing and considerable resources. Hopefully it contains some pointers to the dilemmas and difficulties that might be anticipated in evaluating contemporary alternative educational provision such as Free Schools and some action-research and community development programmes in Compensatory Education. Clearly, many alternative educational schemes of the last decade in America and Europe have been concerned with disadvantaged groups in the delapidated schools of inner-urban areas; and certainly not with middle-class children in a private, rural boarding school. Nevertheless, there do seem to be similarities of ideology and associated attempts to set up 'anti-institutions' that suggest comparable, if not greater difficulties, of evaluating these experimental ventures. Indeed, in some cases their broad socio-political aims threaten to make them unresearchable while their anti-rational ideology raises problems for rational models of discourse. Some of the spokesmen of the new educational radicalism acknowledge a debt to the old progressives while others appear to be unaware of their legacy. Yet, while the vocabulary has changed, there are remarkable similarities in diagnosis, disposition and precept. With the advantage of having scrutinised the legacy of Dartington and the progressives we can now examine innovative educationists who advocate a drastic restructuring of school in the light of the difficulties encountered in attempting to appraise a diffuse ideology, a complex anti-institutional structure, and the long-term effects on former pupils.

Contemporary radical education is, if anything, more strident in its claims than its English progressive forerunner and draws on a strong anarchistic, anti-bureaucratic, and anti-technological theme. The late nineteen sixties and early seventies, in fact, witnessed the proliferation of alternative institutions – such as communes, Claimants Unions, counter-cultural self-help agencies, the Peace Movement, and student protest movements – that often had a deep irrational, even anti-rational, ethos. There was often a hostile attitude to outside evaluation, to the keeping of files, to non-affective hierarchical relationships, and to the power implicit in expertise. Some free schools, particularly black schools in the urban ghettoes, had a high degree of socio-political socialisation that parallelled the new commitment of alternative institutions as well as having a programme of very formal instruction (Graubard 1972). But those experiments most comparable to the early progressive movement were Free Schools for middle- and working-class children with a motif of freeing the children from a stereotypical moulding education that allowed little self-expression and individuality and that was irrelevant to the real needs of working-class children. (R. and B. Gross 1971).

So far the author has supervised several studies by graduate students of this type of Free School in England and, for a number of reasons, they proved quite difficult to research. One project, for example, investigated the spearhead of the movement in England, namely the now defunct Scotland Road Free School in Liverpool (Swirsky 1972). The area is replete with all the physical and social problems attendant upon urban obsolescence and decay overlain with slum clearance and redevelopment. Many children from this district feel rejected by, and in turn reject, the state school system. The immediate aim of the Free School was to free those children from an educational establishment that stands for a cynical and exploitative society, while its long-term aim was to refurbish the culture of the fragmented working-class community and, in effect, transform society. But, apart from these vague aspirations, there was little formal articulation of aims apart from a belief in lack of structure. Because it was not a boarding school the Free School was even less formalised than the progressive school and had even less tolerance for a research role.

A consequence of this combination of the Free School's commitment to political change and its lack of a formal structure and boundaries seems to be that one can only research such an anti-school if one believes in it. This is because there is practically no place, or no rationale, for a disinterested observer role; one is either committed or one is simply not accepted. The graduate student who researched the Scotland Road Free School, for instance, took an active part in the life of the school; it was just not possible, she claimed, to stand and watch without being drawn in. She was openly sympathetic and participated in teaching and the few activities which took place. Perhaps being called upon to join in can be seen as a form of testing behaviour to test the researcher's bona fides?

At Scotland Road the researcher had the difficulty of deciding which were the real goals of the Free Schools. One of its founders claimed.

We don't have any definite aims – we just create situations. (Swirsky 1972: 31–7.)

Was the venture simply a negative reaction to the failure of state schools or was it a positive enterprise with realisable ends? If it was the latter how could the researcher appraise those ends? In effect, for the diffuse, global ideology of the Free School to be evaluated it would require a longitudinal community survey of some twenty to thirty years to see if the school had acted as a powerful aid to change, advancement and improvement in the local community and if it had produced a structureless institution that did not impose values on its pupils.

In brief, it might be suggested that closer scrutiny by research would reveal that many Free Schools are even more precarious structures than the marginal English progressives and, as such, must devote their energies to survival rather than self-scrutiny. Indeed, Kozol (1972: 421) asks if there is not almost a self-destructive instinct, arising from an underlying fear of long-term commitment among the staff of American free schools, that militates against continuity and deep involvement. The rapid turnover of staff, the frequent collapse of radical experiments, and the struggle for resources and survival do not bode well for the researcher aiming at a systematic study. In addition, the ideology aims to foster hostility to research and evaluation because left-wingers (some of them ex-sociologists who view academic Sociology as a tool of capitalism!) are now much more conscious of the way in which research can be used and controlled by the established order.

As if the political, methodological, and institutional problems of such alternative educational provision were not enough, there is the added burden that schemes, such as Headstart, Follow Through, EPA, and Community Educational Projects, are reviled by the far left of educational radicalism because they still work within a pernicious system while posing as an alternative to it. In this sense, they are worse than the established schools because they pretend to have the interests of 'deviant' children such as blacks, minority groups, and working-class groups, at heart while in practice they work to fit the child to the system rather than restructure the system to fit the child.

The most radical and influential educational counter-ideology of the last few years has been that of the 'de-schoolers' who would argue that many government sponsored and semi-official alternative educational programmes are a form of empty radicalism because they are still concerned with the institutional process by which children are educated − 'school'. They continue to segregate one particular age group of the population from others in specially designed and equipped premises where they are placed in the care of professionally trained adults, where time, social grouping, and activitity are organised, controlled and processed, and where the process of learning is fragmented into a sequential programme of subject areas called the curriculum. In contrast, the de-schoolers, notably Illich (1971), Reimer (1971), and Goodman (1971) argue for the dismantling of the very concept of school.

In a sense the radical free schoolers' emotional rejection of structures leads them to the same conclusions as the de-schoolers but the latter have erected their attack on the school establishment into a persuasive intellectual counter-ideology that, in effect, amounts to a utopian vision. It is held up as the path to salvation for a society on the verge of self-destruction and has gained almost immediate currency as the latest dogma of educational radicalism. But, while de-schooling remains largely a rhetorical stance, there are indicators that similar problems of evaluation would be raised if one attempted to appraise a de-schooled education.

To begin with there is the problem that the de-schoolers are divided among themselves. On the one hand there are those with some experience of teaching the underprivileged (Kozol, Holt, Kohl, and Postman and Weingartner) who argue largely for internal de-structuring of the orthodox school; while, on the other hand, there are the more global ideologues (notably Illich, Reimer and Goodman) who see de-schooling as nothing less than a socio-political mass movement for fundamentally altering society. Together these writers paint an apocalyptical picture of cultural and environmental decay in which the mass-production techniques of compulsory education play a sinister role in processing people for an exploitative, consumer society while also noting the similar role of education in colonial as well as ghetto exploitation. But when it comes to proposing alternatives there are wide differences of opinion between the authors and few indicators of how a de-schooled society might be brought about (or even what it would be like). The difficulty for the researcher, then, would be to decide which brand of de-schooling represented the authentic version and which aspects of the ideology where mere rhetoric and which were statements of realistic aims that could be used to hold up against actual practice.

Furthermore, the value system of the de-schoolers goes beyond its liberalism and emancipative ethic to demand, in the name of putting 'humanity back on the main path' (Reimer 1971: 134), the taking up of political positions which may require acts of civil disobedience including draft-dodging (R. and B. Gross 1971: 105). There is the basic contradiction, which was also apparent among the classical progressives that the de-schoolers affect to free the child from one set of imposed values only to reveal at every step their commitment to a radical set of counter-values. This brings the problem of whether disinterested research can take place in such an environment which might put considerable strain on the researcher. There might be the dilemma, for instance, that is encountered in observation with deviant groups in criminal sub-cultures, of being technically an accessory to a misdemeanour and of facing possible legal action.

To state the problem of evaluation in its most extreme form, would not the destructuring of school – so that it becomes a process without walls, without compulsory attendance, and without a regulated time sequence – make observation almost impossible? With education taking place in a coffee bar between two computer-matched partners might not the observer feel uncomfortable as the conspicuous and impassive third party? Indeed, would he be granted access to the confidential data about individual's interests compiled by the computer (Illich 1971: 94). If not what would constitute his data for there would be no curriculum, subjects, tests or grades? Rather he would have to decide whether or not de-schooling was producing

an actively enquiring, flexible, creative, innovative, tolerant, liberal personality who can face uncertainty and ambiguity without disorientation. (Postman and Weingartner 1971: 204.)

and whether or not it had created an environement espousing objectivity, tentativeness, self-sufficiency, contingency, open-endedness, flexibility, inventiveness and resourcefulness. In addition, the de-schoolers themselves warn that charlatans, demagogues, proselytisers, corrupt masters, and simoniacal priests might have a field-day at first (Illich 1971: 100). How, then, would the researcher decipher the frauds from the pure of heart? Finally, how would the investigator chart the success, the failure, or the influence of a 'just world' as ushered in by a cultural revolution? For, as Reimer (1971: 99) asserts:

The riddle of mass education demands the unfolding of a mass education movement; only a great cultural revolution can take us beyond the cultural crisis of our times.

This book has argued that there exist a series of radical, innovative 'experiments' on the periphery and beyond the boundaries of educational systems. These ventures often make large claims to be viable alternatives to orthodox education. They currently exert a good deal of influence over educationists and thinkers concerned with the inefficiencies, inequalities, and alleged inequities, of state educational provision in certain areas. Yet, surprisingly, this range of educational alternatives has not attracted the sort of comprehensive evaluation which contributes to our knowledge of the structure and functioning of these 'anti-institutions' and nor have the lessons of their extensive experience been appraised for the benefit of contemporary innovators and experimenters who may be duplicating their errors. Rather the literature is clouded by rhetoric and special pleading.

The author has conducted a limited sociological study of one radical, English progressive school. That study encountered conceptual and methodological problems, field-work setbacks, and an ambiguity to evaluation among the research school which seem to indicate that there are even graver problems in researching an 'anti-institution' than in conventional organisations. In tentatively generalising from that experience to the potential difficulties of evaluating the success or failure of contemporary alternative educational provision, it is suggested that the ideas of some free-schoolers and de-schoolers raise almost insoluble problems for a positivistic sociology. As it is, there is widening controversy concerning facts, evidence, validity, values, theory and empiricism in the Social Sciences (Phillips 1971) which has led to scepticism about the broader significance of research findings and to pessimism about effectively evaluating the implementation of social policies and innovations. The sorts of doubts raised by that controversy are amplified by the difficulties of evaluating 'anti-institutions' because their diffuse and wide-ranging aims amount to the formation of social movements espousing long-term social and political change.

But the realisation that research is an imperfect instrument does not necessarily mean that it is not worth doing. Rather, the current appreciation of the deficiencies of much research that aims to follow a natural-science model should alert us to half-concealed, and perhaps more theoretically interesting areas for research. In Educational Sociology, for instance, there is a growing awareness of the difficulty of isolating specific variables or of having adequate control groups because everything seems to vary at once. In consequence, there have been a number of fresh theoretical perspectives, such as the use of theories of Symbolic Interaction and studies in the Management of Knowledge area (Cosin *et al.* 1971 and Young 1971), which have widened the scope of the discipline away from its earlier peoccupation with the differential distribution of educational opportunity and with narrow conceptions of educational attainment.

Similarly, with regard to alternative education, the dilemmas and difficulties of researching this area should not obscure the fact that radical schools are often ready-made 'experiments' in alternative structures with rich potential for the sociologist. They make more visible a host of explicitly sociological questions that have been neglected in educational research. In particular, they direct our attention to, for example, the sources and nature of educational ideologies; convincing explanations of social processes; the institutional barriers to innovation; the subtle ambiguities of emancipative structures; the role of charisma in educational leadership; to the mutually manipulative interaction between the worlds of pupils and teachers; the political context of educational policy making; the lack of fit between education and society in different periods; and the belief system and social context in which research itself is carried out.

In effect, the Sociology of Education and its accompanying research have displayed too narrow a focus. This narrowness has kept it a relatively underdeveloped area, working within a narrow set of criteria compared to mainstream Sociology. The perspective needs broadening because, for all its volume, educational research has rarely faced up to the complexity of social processes in educational institutions or to the intricate relationships between education and political-economic structures and values. For, from Plato to Rousseau to Illich, the debate on the ends and means of education has been far more wide-ranging than is allowed for by the studies employing relatively crude tests of attainment. I would argue that a broadening of perspective, and of our understanding, in educational research is necessary if we are to get to grips with, for example, alternative educational ideologies and structures that are theoretically interesting but which are not readily amenable to the methods of positivistic Sociology.

This sociological portrait of Dartington and of its former pupils, for example, has ranged over a broad canvas. As such it has probably stretched the qualitative data to generalisations that are difficult to validate. Nevertheless, it has endeavoured to outline tentatively the ambivalences and dilemmas of a radical educational community viewed as an 'anti-institution' and of the paradoxes of trying to produce a culture-free individual. The difficulties of innovating in these two areas, in the social structure of the school and in the socialisation of the child, should not be underestimated. A sympathetic understanding of these difficulties is necessary in appraising the empirical evidence for Dartington. Otherwise it becomes too easy to be harshly critical of the long, subtle, complex, and sociologically interesting process by which Dartington changed from the buoyant and ambitious radicalism of the nineteen thirties to being, after the war, a somewhat muted and introspective progressive retreat.

Bibliography

Ariès, P., 1962, *Centuries of Childhood*, London, Jonathan Cape

Armytage, W. H. G., 1961, *Heavens Below*, London, Routledge and Kegan Paul

Ash, M., 1969, *Who are the Progressives Now?*, London, Routledge and Kegan Paul

Badley, J. H., 1924, *Bedales: A Pioneer School*, London, Methuen

Badley, J. H., 1955, *Memories and Reflections*, London, Allen and Unwin

Bamford, T. W., 1967, *The Rise of the Public Schools*, London, Nelson

Berg, L., 1968, *Risinghill: Death of a Comprehsnsive*, Harmondsworth, Penguin Books Ltd.

Bernstein, E., 1967, 'Summerhill After Fifty Years', *The New Era*, Vol. 48., No. 2

Bettelheim, B., 1969, *The Children of the Dream*, London, Thames and Hudson

Bishop, T. J. H. and Wilkinson, R., 1967 *Winchester and the Public School Elite*, London, Faber and Faber

Blewitt, T. (ed.), 1934, *The Modern Schools Handbook*, London, Gollancz

Bonham-Carter, V., 1958, *Dartington Hall*, London, Phoenix House

Boyd, W. and Rawson, W., 1965, *The Story of the New Education*, London, Heinemann

Brown, J. A. C., 1954, *The Social Psychology of Industry*, Harmondsworth, Penguin Books Ltd.

Butler, D. and Stokes, D., 1969, *Political Change in Britain*, London, Macmillan

Chazan, M., 1973, *Compensatory Education*, London, Butterworths

Child, H. A. T. (ed.), 1962, *The Independent Progressive School*, London, Hutchinson

Coade, T. F., 1966, *The Burning Bow*, London, Allen and Unwin

Cosin, B. R., 1971, *School and Society*, London, Routledge and Kegan Paul

Cremin, L. A., 1968, *The Transformation of the School*, New York, Knopf

Curry, W. B., 1934, *The School and a Changing Civilisation*, London, John Lane, The Bodley Head

Curry, W. B., 1939, *The Case for Federal Union*, Harmondsworth, Penguin Books Ltd.

Curry, W. B., 1947, *Education for Sanity*, London, Heinemann

Curry, W. B., 1958, 'The School', in V. Bonham-Carter, *Dartington Hall*, London, Phoenix House

Duberman, M., 1972, *Black Mountain College*, New York, Dutton

Elmhirst, L. K., 1937, *Faith and Works*, published Dartington Hall Ltd., reprinted from *The Countryman*

Elmhirst, L. K., 1961, *Rabindranath Tagore: Pioneer in Education*, London, John Murray

van der Eycken, W. and Turner, B., 1969, *Adventures in Education*, London, Allen Lane the Penguin Press

Fyvel, T. R., 1969, *Intellectuals Today*, London, Chatto and Windus

Gardner, Dorothy, E. M., 1969, *Susan Isaacs*, London, Methuen

Gimson, B., 1952, *Bedales Schools 1893–1951*, published by the Bedales Society

Glennester, H., and Pryke, R., *The Public Schools*, Young Fabian Pamphlet No. 7, Fabian Society

Goffman, E., 1963, *Asylums*, Garden City, N.Y., Anchor.

Goldsen, R. K., Rosenberg, M., Williams, R. M. and Suchman, E. A., 1960, *What College Students Think*, Princeton, N.J., van Nostrand

Graham, P. A., 1967, *Progressive Education,* Columbia, N.Y., Teacher's College Press

Graubard, A., 1972, 'The Free School Movement', *Harvard Educational Review*, Vol. 42, No. 3

Harrison, J. F. C., 1969, *Robert Owen and the Owenites in Britain and America*, London, Routledge and Kegan Paul

Holt, J., 1969, *How Children Fail*, Harmondsworth, Penguin Books Ltd.

Illich, I., 1971, *Deschooling Society*, London, Calder and Boyars

Jencks, C., 1975, *Inequality*, Harmondsworth, Penguin Books Ltd.

Joll, J., 1969, *The Anarchists*, London, Methuen

Jusmani, A. A., 1961, 'The Attitude to the Child in Progressive Educational Theory and Practice in England since 1890', unpublished M.Ed. thesis, University of Leicester

Kalton, G., 1966, *The Public Schools*, London, Longmans

Klein, J., 1965, *Samples from English Cultures*, Vol. 2, London, Routledge and Kegan Paul

Kozol, J., 1972, *Politics, Rage and Motivation in Free Schools*, Harvard Educational Review, Vol. 42, No. 3

Kozol, J., 1968, *Death at an early Age*, Harmondsworth, Penguin Books Ltd.

Lambert, R., 1968, *The Hothouse Society*, London, Wiedenfeld and Nicolson

Lambert, R., 1969, 'What Dartington Will Do', *New Society*, Vol. 13, No. 331

Lambert, R., Bullock, R. and Millham, S., 1970, *Manual to the Sociology of the School*, London, Weidenfeld and Nicolson

Lambert, R., Bullock, R. and Millham, S., 1971a, *Boarding Education*, unpublished typescript (no page numbers) forthcoming in revised form 1975, London, Wiedenfeld and Nicolson

Lambert, R., 1971b, *The Curry Memorial Lecture*, University of Exeter, unpublished typescript

Lane, H., 1928, *Talks to Parents and Teachers*, London, Allen and Unwin

Lewis, R. and Maude, A., 1949, *The English Middle Classes*, London, Phoenix House

McConnell, J. D. R., 1967, *Eton: How it Works*, London, Faber and Faber

MacKenzie, R. F., 1970, *State School*, Harmondsworth, Penguin Books Ltd.

Marris, P. and Rein, M., 1967, *Dilemmas of the Social Reform*, London, Routledge and Kegan Paul

Marsden, D., 1971, *Politicians, Equality, and Comprehensives*, Fabian Tract 411, London, The Fabian Society

Michels, R., 1949, *Political Parties*, Glencoe, N.Y., Free Press

Miles, M. B. (ed.), 1964, *Innovation in Education*, Columbia, N.Y., Teacher's College Press

Millham, S. and Bullock, R., 1973, unpublished typescript on Dartington School

Neill, A. S., 1968, *Summerhill*, Harmondsworth, Penguin Books Ltd.

Newcomb, T. H., Koenig, K. E., Flacks, R. and Warwick, D. P., 1967, *Persistence and Change*, New York, Wiley

Parkin, F., 1968, *Middle Class Radicalism*, Manchester, Manchester University Press

Pekin, L. B., 1934, *Progressive Schools*, London, published by Leonard and Virginia Woolff at the Hogarth Press

Pear, T. H., 1955, *English Social Differences*, London, Allen and Unwin

Phillips, D., 1971, *Knowledge from What?* Chicago, Rand McNally

Punch, M., 1966, 'Three Boarding Schools as Complex Organisations', unpublished M.A. thesis, University of Essex

Punch, M., 1969, 'Progressive Schools Now', *New Society*, Vol. 13, No. 330

Punch, M., 1970a, 'École Paradis: a Short History of Dartington Hall School', unpublished typescript

Punch, M., 1970b, 'W. B. Curry: a Reassessment', *The New Era*, Vol. 51, No. 10

Punch, M., 1970c, 'Homer Lane', *New Society*, Vol. 15, No. 379

Punch, M., 1970d, 'Who is the intellectual when he is at home?', *New Society*, Vol. 16, No. 424

Punch, M. and Swirsky, R., 1947a, 'Freedom for What? The Scotland Road Free School', *The Teacher*, 8 February 1974

Punch, M., 1947b, 'The Sociology of the Anti-Institution', *British Journal of Sociology*, Vol. XXV, No. 3

Punch, M., 1975a, 'Total Institutions: A Conceptual Approach', *Amsterdams Sociologisch Tijdschrift*, Vol. 1, No. 4

Punch, M., 1975b, 'The Elmhirsts and the Early Dartington: A Neglected Experiment', *The New Era*, forthcoming

Roe, A., 1956, *The Psychology of Occupations*, New York, Wiley

Russell, B., 1916, *Principles of Social Reconstructions*, London, Allen and Unwin

Russell, B., 1968, *Autobiography*, Vol. II, 1915–1944, London, Allen and Unwin

Schon, D., 1970, 'The Stable State: Reith Lectures 1970', *The Listener*, Vol. 84, Nos. 2173–8

Selleck, R. J. W., 1968, *The New Education*, London, Pitman

Selleck, R. J. W., 1972, *English Primary Education and the Progressives, 1914–1939*, London, Routledge and Kegan Paul

Sissons, M. and French, P. (eds.), 1964, *The Age of Austerity*, Harmondsworth, Penguin Books Ltd.

Skidelsky, R., 1969, *English Progressive Schools*, Harmondsworth, Penguin Books Ltd.

Sofer, C., 1970, *Men in Mid-Career*, Cambridge, Cambridge University Press

Spencer, G., 1973, 'Methodological Issues in the Study of Bureaucratic Elites: a Case Study of West Point', *Social Problems*, Summer 1973, Vol. 21, No. 1

Stanford, S., 1958, 'Dartington School and Progressive Education', unpublished dissertation for Teacher's Certificate, Homerton College, Cambridge

Stewart, W. A. C., 1968, *The Educational Innovators: 1881–1967*, London, Macmillan

Swirsky, R., 1972, 'Scotland Road Free School', unpublished M.A. thesis, University of Essex

Vernon, P. E., 1962, *Intelligence and Attainment Tests*, London, University of London Press

Wakeford, J., 1969, *The Cloistered Elite*, London, Macmillan

Waller, W., 1965, *The Sociology of Teaching*, New York, Wiley

Weinberg, I., 1967, *The English Public Schools*, New York, Atherton

Wolin, S., 1961, *Politics and Vision*, London, Allen and Unwin

Young, M., 1968, *Innovation and Research in Education*, London, Routledge and Kegan Paul

Young, M., 1973, 'The Little World', unpublished typescript

Young, M. F. D. (ed.), 1971, *Knowledge and Control,* London, Collier-Macmillan

Documents

Badminton School 1858–1958, published by Badminton School

Bedales, Centenary Magazine, 1942, published by the Bedales Society

Bedales School Roll, 1962, published by the Bedales Society

Prospectus 1929 and 1954, Dartington Hall School

Report by HM Inspectors, on Dartington Hall School, 1949

List 70 (1968) List of Independent Schools in England and Wales recognised as efficient, London, HMSO

Department of Education: Statistics 1966–67, London, HMSO

Newsom Report: The Public Schools Commission, London, HMSO 1968

The Place of Boarding in State Education 1965, Report of Conference convened by R. Lambert at Cambridge

The Plowden Report: Children and their Primary Schools, Vol. 1, Report, HMSO 1967

Index

uniform, 9–10, 21, 80–1, 110
United Nations, 71
Urban, Eleanor, 102
Useful Work (at Dartington), 26, 60, 62

vandalism (at Dartington), 54, 60–1
Van der Eycken, W., and Turner, B., 84, 162
Vernon, P. E., 83
volonté générale (and *volonté d'un*), 167

Wakeford, J., 1, 63–4, 115, 158
Waller, W., 60
War (First World), 12, 21, 30, 39, 110
War (Second World), 12, 25–7, 35, 41, 45, 47,
    56–7, 71, 74, 155, 159–60
Waugh, Evelyn, 100
Weinberg, I., 42, 71, 72, 158

Wells, H. G., 20, 22
Wennington School, 11, 90, 100,155, 160
West-Riding of Yorkshire, 161
Williams-Ellis, Amabel, 5, 45
Williams-Ellis, Clough, 29
Winchester, 96
Winnicott, Dr, 47
Wittgenstein, L., ix
Wolin, S., 164
Wootton, Lady Barbara, 20
work (of Old Dartingtonians), 113–25; men,
    118–25; occupations, 113–16; women, 116–18
working class, 30, 38, 81–2, 111, 170

Young, M., vi–x, 24, 35, 155

Zilliacus, L., 101